THIRD WORLD ATTITUDE TOWARDS INTERNATIONAL LAW

THIRD WORLD ATTITUDE TOWARDS INTERNATIONAL LAW

DS Pradhan

MD Publications Pvt Ltd
New Delhi
www.mdppl.com

Published by:

MD Publications Pvt Ltd
"MD House", 11, Darya Ganj,
New Delhi - 110 002
Phone : +91-11-45355555
E-mail : contact@mdppl.com
website : www.mdppl.com

ISBN: 978-81-7533-311-6

Published and Printed by Mr. Pranav Gupta on behalf of **MD Publications Pvt Ltd** at JJ offset Printers, Delhi.

PREFACE

International law is today displacing national law in significance. It is no longer a law which concerns itself with some select issues of war and diplomacy but aspires to control and regulate central aspects of the economic and political life of sovereign States. Indeed, international law is today the chosen instrument of Northern domination. It is the medium through which third world countries are seceding sovereign economic and social space to international institutions such as the IMF, World Bank and WTO. International law thus threatens to reduce the meaning of democracy to electing representatives who, irrespective of their ideological affiliations, are compelled to pursue the same social and economic policies.

International law has emerged from an effort to deal with conflict among states, since rules provide order and help to mitigate destructive conflict. It is developed in a number of ways. First, law often comes out of international agreements and treaties between states. Treaties are the most important source of international law and also serve as the origins of IGOs, which in turn are important sources of law. Second, customary practices that have evolved over time often become codified in law. Third, general legal principles that are common to a significant number of states can become part of the corpus of international law. Finally, law arises from the community of international legal scholars. Particularly on more technical issues, their expertise is often accepted by political leaders.

A gamut of international laws dictate the content of national laws in crucial areas of sovereign decision making such as foreign investment, technology, trade in goods and services, monetary policy, environment, and labor. Thus, for instance, the developed world has insisted in the last two decades on the adoption of legal instruments to free transnational capital of spatial and temporal constraints.

The result is that the process of globalization has had deleterious effect on the welfare of third world peoples. Thus, three billionaires in the North today hold assets more than the combined GNP of all the least developed countries and its 600 million people. In sum, the economic and political independence of the third world is being undermined by policies and laws dictated by the first world and enforced by international institutions it controls. It attempts to look afresh at the history of colonial international law, engage previous trends in third world scholarship in international law, take cognizance of the dramatic changes which have characterized the body of international law in the last few decades from the perspective of third world peoples, record their resistance to unjust and oppressive international laws, and advance new approaches that address their needs and concerns.

I am very grateful to Mr. Pranav Gupta, Director of MD Publications Pvt Ltd, New Delhi, for his kind cooperation and support for this book.

DS Pradhan

CONTENTS

1

International Law and Politics

On June 24, 1976, Air France flight 139 from Tel Aviv to Paris was hijacked by three men and a woman who identified themselves as members of the Popular Front for the Liberation of Palestine, approximately eight minutes after a scheduled stop in Athens, where they had boarded the plane. The jet was then flown to Benghazi, Libya, for refueling. After the release of a pregnant woman at Benghazi, the Airbus continued on to Entebbe airport in Uganda, where it landed at 3:00 A.M. on June 28. Nine hours later, passengers disembarked and were transferred to a seldom-used airport terminal. The hijackers demanded the release of 53 imprisoned "freedom fighters" (forty held in Israel, with the rest scattered among France, Switzerland, Kenya, and West Germany) by the afternoon of July 1 in exchange for the safe return of the 241 passengers and twelve crew members of the hijacked plane.

Otherwise, they threatened to kill all the hostages. On June 30, the hijackers released forty-seven non-Israeli women and children. Shortly before the expiration of the July 1 deadline, Israel agreed to negotiate. The hijackers subsequently released another 101 captives, keeping only Israelis, those believed to be Jewish, and the Airbus crew. The deadline was extended to July 4. At 11:30 P.M. on Saturday, July 3, the Israeli Defense Forces conducted a military raid that rescued the hostages. During the ensuing battle, three captives, one Israeli soldier, at least twenty Ugandan soldiers, and all of the hijackers were killed.

One other hostage, Dora Bloch, who held dual British and Israeli nationality, died in Uganda, though not in the raid. She had been hospitalized in Kampala prior to the time of the raid after she began to choke on a piece of meat that had lodged in her throat while eating. She was left behind, and later killed on Idi Amin's orders. The purpose of Part Two is to develop a set of theoretical propositions concerning the various roles played by international law and organizations in time of crisis from a "functionalist" as opposed to the traditional legal positivist approach to international relations. It focuses upon the Entebbe incident not as an end in itself but as a vehicle for the elaboration of a common analytical framework applicable to the phenomenon of international crisis in general.

This study follows in the path blazed by the International Crises and the Role of Law series published under the auspices of the American Society of International Law. Yet it strives to advance that endeavor one evolutionary stage beyond its genesis. In that series, case studies of various international crises performed the invaluable first task of assembling historical data into a series of descriptive statements concerning the roles of international law and international organizations during these crises.

FOR THE INTERNATIONAL LAWYER

If the reader is an international lawyer, the odds are fairly good that he will start reading Part Two with the following question in the forefront of his mind: Was the Israeli raid at Entebbe a violation of international law? Obsessive preoccupation with the determination of legality or illegality is characteristic of a modern legal positivist approach to international law and international politics. The issue of legality is important, but all too often this becomes the first, last, and only question today's international lawyers ask themselves or are even interested in answers for. Part Two will suggest to the public international lawyer an array of equally important questions that should be of concern to him as well. Part Two will not specifically answer the question of the legality of the Entebbe raid in positivist terms. Yet it will adduce the arguments on both sides of the issue and offer a tentative formulation as to how that question could be answered from a functionalist perspective.

If the reader is an international political scientist, he will not be terribly worried about the legality or illegality of the Entebbe raid. His opening question, rather, will be something along the following lines: Would the government of Israel have refrained from launching the raid at Entebbe if it had determined that such action violated international law? In other words, would any state sacrifice its perceived vital national interests on the altar of international legality? Supposing the negative, is international law really relevant in any meaningful sense to international crises?

International political scientists, and even many public international lawyers, do generally suppose the negative, and in a certain sense they are correct in that conclusion, but not for the reasons generally assumed. During an international crisis, states rarely, if ever, sacrifice their vital national interests for considerations of international law or vice versa because, in situations of apparent conflict between the two, governmental decision makers commence to define or redefine their vital national interests to include considerations of international law; conversely, they define or redefine international law to rake account of their vital national interests. Invariably, decision makers engage in both processes simultaneously. In this fashion, vital national interests are tailored to the demands of international law and vice versa. An initially perceived gap between the two is narrowed from both sides to a point of at least plausible argument concerning its nonexistence.

This process of dialectical interaction between vital national interests and international law during and following a crisis exerts a strong force toward reconciliatory modification upon each. If a similar crisis occurs again in the future, the experience of the first crisis will have already altered the contours of the international system so as to render the second dispute more manageable. Or, a similar crisis might not even erupt again because a body of international law, procedures, or institutions was developed in the aftermath of the first crisis specifically for the purpose of preventing such problems in the future. Likewise, vital national interests will have become altered in the wake of a crisis in order to make recurrence of such a crisis less likely.

In such instances, international law, international organizations, and vital national interests work hand-in-hand to prevent the recurrence of crises and thereby maintain the stability of the international system for all its members, including those unaffected by the first crisis. From the perspective of an international lawyer trained in the "realist" or power politics approach to international relations, these observations are not at all surprising. When analyzed in accordance with the Aristotelian doctrine of the mean, the principles of international law possess an intrinsic core of rationality that creates a workable path between human nature and social convention critical to continued survival.

International law articulates those rules which the actors in the international system have found to be indispensable for international life. And that which is essential to international life becomes enshrined in the rules of international law. States create the rules of international law for the express purpose of serving and advancing their respective national interests. States do not adopt useless, impractical, or dangerous rules to regulate their relations in the first place. Therefore, the requirements of international law should substantially, albeit imperfectly, coincide with the dictates of vital national interests and vice versa. Even in a time of severe international crisis, adherence to the rules of international law usually proves to be in a state's best interest anyway.

Here the writings of the late Professor Lon Fuller of the Harvard Law School become apposite. His work indicates that any system of law is most properly understood as creating a facilitative framework of rules that permits and enhances the quality of interaction among its participants. Law must not simply be interpreted in its Hobbesist legal positivist sense as the making, breaking, and enforcement of rules. Any system of law, even an imperfect one, usually proves to be more beneficial and, therefore, preferable to each participant than the existence of no legal rules at all.

This argument has been developed at length by the Harvard political scientist Thomas Schelling through the application of game theory to conflict situations. The reason why two cars approaching each other on a narrow mountain road obey the rules of the road by each driving on its right-hand side supplies an excellent analogy as to why states will follow international law in time of crisis. This line of argument is not intended to dispose of the international political scientist's question by ignoring it. It is impossible to prove that a government would have taken a hypothetical course of action if it had evaluated the surrounding circumstances and arrived at a conclusion diametrically opposed to the one it did in fact reach:

Would Israel have launched the Entebbe raid if it had determined the raid violated international law, when in fact it determined the exact opposite? An analyst must be content with establishing the reasons why a government did undertake a particular course of conduct, and not allow hypothetical answers to speculative questions to undercut the significance of the lessons taught by historical facts themselves. Part Two will demonstrate that one important reason for the Israeli government's decision to launch the Entebbe operation was its bona fide belief that the raid was consistent with the requirements of international law. Therefore, the political scientist's conjecture that Israel would have launched the raid anyway, even if the government had believed that it was illegal, becomes immaterial to the analysis.

THE NEED FOR A NEW APPROACH

These two archetypal questions of international legal positivism and international political science (was the action legal? what difference does it make?) share in common an either/or view of the universe: either legal or illegal; either vital national interest or international law. Real life and historical fact are rarely so clear-cut, so susceptible to such dogmatic assertions and the automatic derivation of conclusions there from. Part Two eschews the either/or approach for a dialectical interpretation. It focuses upon the dynamic interaction of law and politics during one particular incident of contemporary international affairs charged with the atmosphere of an international crisis.

This dialectical approach to the study of international law and international politics does not detract from the integrity of either. It simply demonstrates that it is a logical and historical fallacy to believe that law and politics are essentially independent of each other. In the realm of international relations, they are so highly interdependent as to be almost indistinguishable. International politics is and becomes international law, while international law is and becomes international politics.

It must be the joint and several tasks of public international lawyers and international political scientists to elucidate the dynamics of interaction between international law and politics in a time of crisis. This chapter will provide both groups with a common framework of analysis that is acceptable to the scientific, philosophical, and methodological foundations of each. It will permit both groups to bring to bear their respective expertise upon these potentially cataclysmic problems of contemporary international affairs.

This chapter will contribute to the development of a more synthesized, multidimensional, and holistic understanding of the nature of international crises and the means by which they can be prevented or controlled. In the process, this functionalist analysis of Entebbe will also demonstrate how and why international law and organizations are critical to conflicts between states over matters of "vital national interest." It will thus refute the conventional political realist hypothesis that both are essentially irrelevant to "high international politics."

THE FIVE FUNCTIONS OF INTERNATIONAL LAW AND ORGANIZATIONS

Part Two falls within the second of the five stages of analysis mentioned above. The purpose of this section, therefore, is the derivation of theoretical propositions concerning the roles of international law and organizations in a particular international crisis. The facts of the Entebbe raid are not recounted (stage one) except to the extent necessary to facilitate the progress of the discussion. The construction of a general model for the role of international law in time of crisis (stage three) is not attempted, since the theoretical propositions to be derived from the Entebbe incident will necessarily be limited to the facts of that case, and similar propositions derived from other case studies have yet to be produced. Nor, consequently, can Part Two formulate predictive hypotheses or prescriptive recommendations (stages four and five) concerning the functions of international law and organizations in future international crises.

This part of the chapter will, however, generate a set of theoretical propositions concerning the roles or functions international law and organizations played or failed to play during the Entebbe crisis. In order to reduce this task to manageable proportions, I shall delineate five functions of international law and organizations in the context of the Entebbe incident and relate the theoretical propositions to them. In sequential order and shorthand form they will be called (1) definition, (2) decision, (3) adjudication, (4) resolution, and (5) redefinition.

To be specific: The first function that international law performed during Entebbe was the definition of the international behavioral standards applicable to the crisis in the perceptions of all the actors involved. Next, international law served as an important element of decision in the Israeli governmental crisis management proceedings. The third function of international law in the Entebbe crisis was adjudication of the outstanding dispute between Israel and

Uganda before the United Nations Security Council. This adjudication prepared the way for the fourth function of international law and organizations in regard to Entebbe – resolution of the crisis by the Security Council.

The fifth and last function consisted of a redefinition of international behavioral standards to beyond those prior exist to the outbreak of the crisis. Entebbe generated the momentum necessary to propel an inchoate international consensus against the taking of hostages into the concrete form of a special U.N. committee for the drafting of an international convention to prevent this phenomenon. Its subsequently adopted United Nations Hostages Convention now codifies the elements of the Entebbe debate consensus and thereby attempts to remedy those problems of international law and international politics exposed by Entebbe.

This list of five functions is not intended to be exhaustive. Yet it should allow the Entebbe crisis to be understood as one paradigmatic manifestation of the dialectical interaction between international law and international politics that begins with the concatenation of a set of preexisting conditions into a chain of events whose effects are still progressing in a cognizable fashion throughout international relations today. A functionalist analysis of international law and politics in time of crisis will reveal the dynamic processes by which the entire international system proceeds to cope with a crisis in order to survive.

The first function that international law performed in the Entebbe crisis was the definition of the situation for all the actors involved. Even before the hijacking of the Air France plane that led to the Entebbe raid, international law had already established standards of behavior that were continually relevant to the facts of the crisis during its various stages of development. These rules of law provided a fountainhead for the generation of conceptions of legality or illegality, right or wrong, just or unjust, through which the actors perceived the unfolding of events. The rules thus shaped the perceptions that conditioned the decision makers' responses to the crisis. There was, at all times, a dynamic interaction between initial conduct, its evaluation in accordance with perceived standards of behavior, and responsive conduct.

Drawing upon the teachings of the behaviouralist school of international political science, a functionalist analysis of international law deemphasizes the traditional positivist concern with whether a particular rule or set of rules was legally binding in a formal sense upon one or more of the parties to the crisis. What becomes critically important instead are the perceptions about rules held by the decision makers themselves? A rule that might not be technically binding may still become relevant to the decision-making process in a variety of ways. For example, neither state X nor state Y might be parties to treaty A, but decision makers in X could nevertheless perceive Y's behavior as deficient in light of the standards enunciated within A.

In a court of law, X would not have the *jus standi* (i.e., "standing") to raise a claim against Y under A per se, although X might argue that A is merely declaratory of customary international law or else has been transformed into customary international law through the accumulation of state practice, the passage of time, the development of an international *opinio juris* (i.e., a belief that it is binding), and a general acceptance of the practice by states. In the realm of governmental decision making, however, and especially during time of international crisis, due to the force of circumstances, crisis management decision makers demonstrate a marked tendency to blur, obscure, or ignore the precise distinctions intrinsic to such formalistic legal technicalities. In their minds principles de *lege ferenda* (i.e., "law coming into being") can readily be treated as *lex lata* (i.e., "fixed law"). From that point these perceptions are quickly translated into political and military action.

HIJACKING

Provisions of the Tokyo Convention on Offenses and Certain Other Acts Committed on Board Aircraft of September

14, 1963, were relevant to the Entebbe hijacking by way of analogy, although not technically binding upon Israel and Uganda in relation to each other at the time, since the former was a party while the latter was not. Article II of the Tokyo Convention obligates the state of landing to take all appropriate measures to restore control of an unlawfully seized aircraft to its commander, to permit the passengers and crew to continue their journey as soon as practicable, and to return the aircraft and cargo to those entitled to possession. It has been argued that irrespective of the Tokyo Convention, these provisions are declaratory of principles of customary international law binding upon parties and non-parties alike. Article 13 of the Tokyo Convention also requires the state of landing to take into custody an alleged hijacker, but the state of landing is not required to choose between prosecution and extradition of the alleged hijacker.

At the time of the Entebbe crisis both Israel and Uganda were parties to the Hague Convention for the Suppression of Unlawful Seizure of Aircraft of December 16, 1970. Article 4 thereof required Uganda to take such measures as were necessary to establish its jurisdiction over the hijackers. Under article 6, Uganda was required to take the hijackers and their accomplices into custody. Article 7 obligated Uganda either to extradite the offenders or to submit their case to its competent authorities for purpose of prosecution.

Though the Hague Convention does not specifically require that the hijackers actually be prosecuted, article 7 required Ugandan authorities to make the decision whether to prosecute as they would for an ordinary offense of a serious nature under domestic law. By the terms of article 9, Uganda had to take all appropriate measures to restore control of the aircraft to its lawful commander, to facilitate the continuation of the journey of the passengers and crew as soon as practicable, and to return without delay the aircraft and cargo to its rightful owners. These were positive norms of international law directly binding upon Uganda which created undisputed obligations in its relations with Israel.

The act of unlawful seizure of aircraft would usually include the act of unlawful interference with an aircraft, as defined by article 1 of the Montreal Convention to Discourage Acts of Violence Against Civil Aviation of September 23, 1971. So, the obligations of that convention were brought into play as well. Article 5 requires a contracting state to establish its jurisdiction over the offense; article 6, to take an offender into custody; article 7, to extradite the offender, or else to submit the case to the state's own competent authorities for prosecution; article 10, to facilitate the continuation of the journey of the passengers and crew as soon as practicable, and without delay to return the aircraft and cargo to those lawfully entitled to possession. Although Israel was a party to the Montreal Convention at the time of the crisis, Uganda was not. Nevertheless, its provisions were relevant to Entebbe by way of analogy. Arguably, these principles were generally declaratory of customary international law on this subject.

PIRACY

The Entebbe situation also presented an analogy to the international crime of piracy as defined by article 15 of the 1958 Geneva Convention on the High Seas. To be sure, this hijacking did not fit within the formal definition of the term "piracy" as set out in the convention, since the action was neither (1) undertaken for private ends, nor (2) directed by one plane against another, and (3) it occurred over Greece and therefore was within the territorial jurisdiction of a state. Yet the analogy was there to be seized upon and used to define the context of the crisis.

HOSTAGE TAKING

Finally, the Entebbe hijacking also bears an analogy to the principle of international law forbidding the taking of civilian hostages during times of armed conflict. Article 34 of the Fourth Geneva Convention of August 12, 1949, explicitly prohibits the taking of civilians as hostages during times of international armed conflict. Article 147 defines this offense to be a "grave breach" of the convention warranting the imposition of severe penal sanctions. Moreover, article 146 of the Fourth Geneva Convention requires a contracting party to search for persons who have committed "grave breaches" and either brings them before its own courts or else hand such persons over for trial to another concerned party.

Article 3, common to all four of the 1949 Geneva Conventions, prohibits the taking of hostages with respect to persons having no active part in hostilities in cases of armed conflict not of an international character. Of course, none of the four Geneva Conventions was directly applicable to the Entebbe hostages' situation because it did not occur during international or civil war. But, if the taking of civilian hostages is prohibited in times of both international and civil war, then a fortiori it is or should be forbidden during peacetime as well. This principle should hold true even during so-called wars of national liberation. Nevertheless, these latter two points had not been codified into positive treaty law by the time of the Entebbe crisis. Entebbe would generate the momentum necessary to close the last loophole on hostage taking in the coverage of international law.

STATE RESPONSIBILITY

Taken together, these sources of international law established basic standards for state behavior and responsibility for incidents of international civil aviation hijacking and transnational hostage taking. A state's failure to live up to the spirit of these sources and to follow, at least in a general fashion, the shared pronouncements contained in them, could only sharpen the perceived incongruity between its action and the fundamental requisites of international deportment. Uganda's outright violation of the terms of the Hague Convention necessarily contributed to the attitude of Israeli governmental decision makers that Uganda's behavior was inexcusable under even the most rudimentary standards of international law and politics. As will be demonstrated herein, these perceptions exerted a profound influence upon the Israeli decision to launch the raid at Entebbe.

THE DEFINITIONAL CONTEXT OF THE ENTEBBE RAID

An entire catalogue of well-known principles, strictures, and doctrines of public international law are directly applicable to the military operation at Entebbe itself, or, indeed, to any contemporary use or threat of force in international relations. Relevant treaty law includes the U.N. Charter's article 2(3) and article 33(1) obligations for the peaceful settlement of disputes; the article 2(4) prohibition on the threat or use of force; and the article 51 right of individual or collective self-defense. Related to the right of self-defense are its two fundamental requirements' for the "proportionality" and the "necessity" of the forceful response to the threat.

Furthermore, as definitively stated by Secretary of State Daniel Webster in the famous case of The Caroline, "anticipatory" self-defense might be justified when the "necessity of that self-defence is instant, overwhelming, and leaving no choice of means, and no moment for deliberation." In addition to treaty provisions, principles of customary international law also operate in this area. They include the doctrines of intervention, protection, and self-help. These three doctrines were, however, unanimously rejected by the International Court of Justice in the seminal Corfu Channel Case (United Kingdom v. Albania) as being totally incompatible with the proper conduct of international relations in the post-World War II era. Even more significantly, the Court repudiated these three doctrines without explicitly relying upon the U.N. Charter because Albania was not yet a party while Great Britain was.

Hence, the Court's holding on this point can be construed to constitute an authoritative declaration of the requirements of customary international law binding all members of the international community irrespective of the Charter. A fortiori, therefore, when both parties to an international crisis are U.N. members, such as Israel and Uganda at Entebbe, articles 2(3), 2,(4), and 33 absolutely prohibit any threat or use of force that is not specifically justified by the article 51 right of individual or collective self-defense.

Nevertheless, the facts of the Corfu Channel Case, unlike those of Entebbe, did not involve an imminent threat to human life. A dissenting opinion by Judge Azavedo and an individual opinion by Judge Alvarez recognized the right of a state to intervene and use force in another state in the event of an "emergency" or in "exceptional circumstances," respectively. The Entebbe hostage-taking crisis might very well have fit within these putative exceptions to the universal prohibition against the use of force across state lines.

Finally, three seminal General Assembly resolutions have a distinct bearing on this issue: the Declaration on the Inadmissibility of Intervention in the Domestic Affairs of States and the Protection of Their Independence and Sovereignty, the Declaration on Principles of International Law Concerning Friendly Relations and Cooperation among States in Accordance with the Charter of the United Nations, and the Definition of Aggression.

Considered together, these three resolutions can be interpreted to stand for the general proposition that, in the emphatic opinion of the members of the U.N. General Assembly, nonconsensual military intervention by one state into the territorial domain of another state is prohibited for any reason whatsoever. Hence the Israeli raid at Entebbe could quite possibly be classified as a "breach of the peace" or an "act of aggression" within the meaning and purpose of U.N. Charter article 39 interpreted by reference to these resolutions.

THE NEED FOR A FUNCTIONALIST ANALYSIS OF THESE RULES

The purpose of this chapter is not to analyze the problems inherent within these principles (e.g., what precisely does the article 51 language "armed attack" require?); their interrelationships with each other (e.g., do intervention, protection, and self-help survive under the regime of Charter article 51?); and then to apply them as defined, explicated, or clarified to the facts of the Entebbe crisis, thereby rendering a decision as to the legality or illegality of the raid. That task has already been quite competently discharged in numerous articles on the Entebbe raid, so it would be superfluous to replicate that line of analysis here.

This route towards examination of the Entebbe crisis is characteristic of a legal positivist approach to the subject of international law in time of crisis. Whatever its value for other problems of international relations, a legal positivist approach to a particular international crisis or to the phenomenon of international crisis in general amounts to an essentially sterile exercise which is not very productive for the improvement of crisis management procedures or for the promotion of international law and organizations. After all, there are only so many ways in which the concepts enumerated above can be juggled, and when they all come down at the end of an article, their configuration often represents, or at least neatly coincides with, the instinctive, preconceived value judgments of the writer/juggler concerning the "right" or "wrong" of the parties to the crisis.

In this fashion international legal positivism and, unfortunately by way of association, public international law as well, are almost ineluctably transformed into vehicles for the expression of personal opinion or, worse yet, disfigured into tools for political purposes: i.e., the legitimization of conduct by one party to an international dispute with the simultaneous castigation of its adversary. Because of international legal positivism's obsessive concentration with rendering adjudications of right or wrong, it possesses an inherent propensity for such instrumental use within the utilitarian calculus of international affairs.

When viewed from a positivist perspective, international law quite readily and almost ineluctably serves as a primary source for the manufacture of *ad hoc* or *ex post facto* justifications for governmental decisions taken on the basis of non legal factors such as national interest, power politics, and economic gain. This positivist tendency toward self-serving use of international legal principles lies at the heart of the international political science critique of international law as basically irrelevant to both international crises and the major problems of contemporary international politics. International political scientists unquestioningly accept a legal positivist approach to international law as the paradigmatic methodology of international legal studies.

They seem unconsciously to equate public international law with international legal positivism. In their minds, this positivist methodology becomes indistinguishable from the substantive significance of international law itself. Failure on their part to perceive the fundamental distinction between the substance and the methodology is understandable, however, since international legal positivism is in fact the predominant mode of thinking about international law within the discipline of international legal studies. International political scientists are therefore oftentimes just as positivistic as some public international lawyers in their comprehension of the international legal order. Nevertheless, the former should not be faulted too seriously for taking the latter at their collective word that the methodology of international legal positivism is *pari materia* with international legal studies.

By accepting the primacy of a legal positivist approach to international law, international political scientists and, a fortiori, many public international lawyers are inevitably led to the conclusion that international law is essentially irrelevant to international crisis. Here both groups of academics commit the same analytical mistake for identical reasons: Just because international legal positivism might be irrelevant to international crisis, it does not logically follow that international law and organizations are irrelevant as well. The peculiarities and shortcomings of this particular methodology must not be vicariously attributed to the principles, institutions, and procedures of public international law itself.

Instead of rejecting the relevance of international law and organizations to international crises, what should be done is to denigrate the utility of an international legal positivist approach to the study of international crises and to replace it with a functionalist approach. For when analyzed from a functionalist perspective, international law and organizations become not simply relevant but in fact critical to the development of an international crisis. This functionalist approach to the problem will establish both why and how international law was relevant during the Entebbe crisis. Such information is far more useful to understanding future international crises and the means whereby they can be prevented and controlled than an international legal positivist's simplistic determination of right or wrong.

2

The Old and the New

It is a commonplace, by now, to say that we live in a revolutionary age. In a sense, of course, the whole of recorded history has been a process of revolution or at least of change, for in no one era has mankind stood completely still. Even the mediaeval "Dark Ages" contained within them the seeds of the Renaissance and Reformation. What characterizes the present era, however, and differentiates it sharply from earlier periods of historical development, is the very range and intensity of the changes, and the fact that they are occurring on so many fronts. One has, in this regard, to accept the fact that we are dealing with a world revolution that is really a series of continuing revolutions, finding outlets in numbers of different, if complementary, ways.

The first great revolution of our time, completing a process begun with the outbreak of World War I in 1914 and the subsequent downfall of the old dynasties and empires of Central and Eastern Europe, is what Marxist legal scholars like to identify as the "downfall of imperialism." This began, of course, with the October Revolution of 1917 and the overthrow of the old czarist régime in Russia, and was followed up, after the Central Powers' military defeat in 1918, with the abdications of the Sultan of Turkey, the Emperor of Austria-Hungary, and the German Kaiser.

More important than the essentially symbolic replacement of a sultan or emperor by a republican president, were the political changes affected by World War I in the name of nationalism, independence, and liberalism. In deference to Woodrow Wilson's Fourteen Points, the economically viable and politically stable (if unimaginative) dual monarchy of the Habsburgs was replaced by a group of weak and struggling, mutually intransigent "succession states" whose political difficulties were often gravely complicated by racial and religious minority problems and by territorial boundaries that often sacrificed ethno-cultural justice to supposed geopolitical "natural frontiers."

We will return later to the political legacies of the Carthaginian peace imposed on Europe by the victors in a war that was supposed, in one of Woodrow Wilson's inspired phrases, "to end all wars." Suffice it to say, at this point, that Woodrow Wilson's proclaimed ideal of national self-determination reached its ultimate consummation after World War II with the emergence of movements for decolonization, independence, and self-government on a well-nigh universal scale.

In some cases self-government was established gracefully by an act of wise statesmanship with an eye to the future, as with the granting of independence to the Indian subcontinent in 1946 by British Prime Minister Attlee's Labour Government. In other cases it was conceded reluctantly and only after an extended test of arms, as with the French recognition of Indo-China under the Geneva Accords of 1954 in the wake of the Dienbienphu military disaster, or the equally belated French acknowledgment of Algerian independence, or the Portuguese government's protracted military resistance to the "national liberation movements" in its ancient colonies in Africa (but not in India, where the Indian government successfully reclaimed the so-called Portuguese enclaves by a unilateral coup de main).

However achieved, decolonization has been the most striking historical development of the decades following World War II. The resulting flood of "new" countries from Africa, Asia, and the Caribbean has not merely transformed organizations like the United Nations, which rested on an original, if short-lived, "victors' consensus" from World War

II; it has created a vast new arena for the competition and interaction of different social and economic systems. It has also brought, in its wake, a whole new range of post-decolonization problems.

With the liquidation of Portugal's colonial empire by the end of the 1970s, the achievement of independence for Angola and Mozambique by force of arms, and the transformation of the white-minority-governed, breakaway British colony of Rhodesia into black-majority-governed, sovereign Zimbabwe in the spring of 1980, classical colonialism interpreted in United Nations' parlance and in actual political practice as "salt-water imperialism" and the governance of an Asian or African territory by a "parent" European régime has finally come to an end. Southern Africa (the white-minority-governed Republic of South Africa) perhaps stands as the lone exception.

Does this mean that national self-determination, with which decolonization was always twinned during the 1950s, 1960s, and 1970s as an imperative principle of international law, has also been achieved and that nothing remains to be done under its aegis? The question is important not merely for the ethno-cultural minority or regionally-based separatist movements that one finds in so many parts of the non-colonial world today – in Great Britain, France, Belgium, Switzerland, Italy, Spain, and Yugoslavia, for example but also within the former colonial territories themselves. In the case of the non-colonial countries already referred to, national unity and national sovereignty have been invoked by central governments that have, at the same time, tried to respond to the centrifugal forces within their states by emphasizing constitutional-governmental pluralism and the devolution of key community decision-making power on a federal or generally regional basis.

Within the former colonial territories, and in spite of the frequent arbitrariness of political frontiers inherited from the "parent" power, claims by ethnic minorities for national self-determination (or for their union in an ethnically more homogeneous and rational unit with similar ethnic minorities outside the state) have been resisted, by armed force where necessary, in the name of national sovereignty and the integrity of the post-independence territorial frontiers. The principle of legitimacy - a conservative principle at all times - has been invoked to sanctify the political settlement and frontiers inherited from the original colonial powers, lest deference to the more radical, natural-law-based claims to national self-determination destabilize the political situation in post- decolonization Asia and Africa and lead to interminable territorial wars among the "succession" states, on the pattern of post-Westphalia Europe of the seventeenth and eighteenth centuries.

The second great revolution of our time is an ideological one. It began, by most accounts, with the Russian Revolution of 1917 and reached a climax with the cold war conflict of the late 1940s and the 1950s. After 1959 it seemed to take a new turn, with the developing Russian-Chinese schism. World War I, again in conventional Marxist terms, represented the "last working out of the bourgeois-capitalist system" - supposedly its dying gasp. Of course, the Western-based liberal capitalist system survived that conflict, though it underwent profound internal modification as a result of the world economic depression of the late 1920s and early 1930s, and the progressive acceptance - in all major Western democratic societies and eventually by all major political parties - of collectivist, "welfare state" ideals of human dignity and social betterment, and of the community planning techniques that those ideals implied.

When the Iron Curtain finally descended across Central Europe in the late 1940s - thus concretizing, as an effective political reality, the *de facto* settlements resulting from the German military defeat of 1945 and the Russian military occupation of the Balkans, Eastern Europe, and East Germany (including East Berlin) - and the two rival military blocs faced each other across the ideological frontier, they were each rather different from the theoreticians' abstract models of the 1917 vintage.

The West, if it ever had been bourgeois-capitalist in the full Marxist sense, had long since evolved into the accepted patterns of the contemporary, social democratic, planned state. The Soviet Union, for its own part, had moved from its original post-1917 idealistic revolutionary fervour, through the modified capitalistic, NEP revival of the early and middle 1920s, on through Stalin's early era of bureaucratic consolidation, the first of the Five Year Plans, the Stalinist Terror of the middle and late 1930s and the great intra-Party purges of the treason trials, and finally to the undisguised authoritarianism of the dictator's last, paranoiac years, which ended with his death in 1953.

We shall have more to say, at a later stage, about the concept of bipolarity and about the twin military bloc system - represented in Europe by the rival, though militarily complementary, NATO and Warsaw Pact systems - that provided the political balance of power or (in a nuclear age) balance of terror on which world peace rested, however delicately and precariously, from the break-up of the victorious World War II Alliance, very shortly after World War II, until the achievement of the Kennedy-Khrushchev détente with the peaceful resolution of the Cuban missile crisis in October 1962. Suffice it to say, for the moment, that bipolarity and the twin military bloc system, projected on a world scale, meant not only a consolidation of political authority within each bloc (including the completion of Soviet political-military hegemony in Eastern Europe by the end of the 1940s), but also a naked struggle for the extension of power beyond the post-1945, tacitly accepted spheres of control and influence.

This meant not only incessant probing in borderline areas between the two blocs, where the lines of demarcation had not been clearly drawn (as in Berlin), not only mischief making in "buffer state" areas where internal weakness and uncertainty of purpose seemed to invite a "fishing expedition" (as in Korea), but also continuing propaganda, infiltration, and internal subversion in so-called uncommitted countries in Asia, Africa, and Latin America. As the "winds of change" brought either decolonization or widespread social unrest, these continents tended to become further battlegrounds for the two opposing blocs - battlegrounds where, if direct military action was excluded by tacit agreement, every form of political-psychological pressure, propaganda, and economic blandishment was positively included.

This was the competition of the ideologies, designed to demonstrate beyond doubt which system could most quickly and effectively advance a developing or "new" country through the early stages of political nationhood and economic growth to full social and economic well-being. At this point, we approach the third great revolution of our time. The revolution in economic science and technique has radically transformed the contemporary world community. In one manifestation, the economic revolution may be viewed as an aspect of the decolonization and liberation of former colonial countries that were tied too narrowly, and certainly too exclusively, to the economic fortunes of the parent country.

But beyond this, the economic revolution contended that if the lessons of Keynesian economics and of development economics in general are properly applied, a "new" Afro-Asian country need not be condemned by any inexorable laws of economic development to repeat the slow, laboured history of Western states from feudal times before attaining the level of these advanced industrial civilizations. The revolution in economic thought preached that, given the proper initial development aid in terms of both material resources and skilled technical advice, it is possible to progress quickly through the various stages of economic growth and, in some cases, to skip certain stages altogether.

The revolution in economic thought left open the question of which path to the advanced industrial society is the most effective in terms of getting there most quickly and also, perhaps (though this is a highly sophisticated type of inquiry, more likely to be applied in older or declining societies than in the more impatient "new" countries) in terms of minimizing the harm inflicted upon major community values such as free speech, respect for minority rights, and the like. In a sense the answer to this question, involving in part the decision about where to strike the balance between the interests in rapid economic growth and other community values, will determine which of the current three main roads to national development and community well-being - Western liberal capitalist, post-Stalin Soviet Communist, or Chinese Communist - one will opt for.

Nor has the revolution in economic thought, so far, been able to show what to do in a world community where - given that the lessons of progression through the various stages of economic growth have been satisfactorily mastered - the gap in basic standards of living between the present, advanced industrial societies (both Western capitalist and European communist) and the presently developing countries (Asian, African, Caribbean, and Latin American) is continually widening because of the former's more quickly accelerating rate of economic growth.

In some respects this ever-widening "margin of misery," cutting across conventional East-West, communist-capitalist alignments and in effect establishing a new North-South alignment in which the economically prosperous confront the economically underprivileged, non-white, vast majority of the world's population, is likely to be the politically most explosive element in the world community for the last part of the century. The very real frustration of third world political leaders is manifested in their concerted attempt - particularly in the specialized arena of the United Nations General Assembly, where the sheer weight of the "new" countries' voting power has effectively displaced the big power hegemony of yesteryear - to establish a more equitable and inclusive new international economic order by the legislative fiat of General Assembly resolutions.

Two resolutions were adopted, without vote, by the General Assembly at its sixth special session on 1 May 1974: the Declaration on the Establishment of a New International Economic Order, and the related Programme of Action on the Establishment of a New International Economic Order. The further Charter of Economic Rights and Duties of States were adopted by the General Assembly at its twenty-ninth regular session on 12 December 1974 (this time by a recorded vote of 120 to 6, with 10 abstentions).

Taken together these clearly constitute a code of imperative principles of the "new" international law - here, the new international economic law. But the gap between abstract law-in-books and community "living law" (or law-in-action) is nowhere more apparent than in this area. For it is clear that, under the present international economic system, the active cooperation and assistance of the first and second world ("have") countries, both liberal capitalist and communist will be needed to translate these postulated ideals of the third world ("have not") countries into concrete, operational terms in the world community today.

Unless there is some change in the basic, intellectual attitudes of first and second world countries, substantive changes in the world economic order must be accompanied or even preceded by substantive changes in power alignments in the world public order system itself. In this regard, Mohammed Bedjaoui, one of the most distinguished members of the "new wave" of third world jurists, seems right to insist on linking the quest for a new international economic order with the more general obligation of our times to devise a "new" or "renewed" international law.

The last main revolution in the present era of continuing world revolution is the revolution in science and technology. In its most dramatic form, this is represented by the advent of the nuclear age and the development of large-scale nuclear weapon technology, which has transformed conventional warfare and introduced an uneasy, big-power nuclear "balance of terror" on which world peace now rests. The spread of nuclear science and technology has, however, introduced the dangers of wide-spread proliferation of nuclear weapons and nuclear irresponsibility on the part of a host of medium-sized or smaller countries, in place of the nuclear détente (or tacit understandings as to non-user of nuclear weapons) arrived at by the responsible" nuclear powers - especially the two bloc leaders the Soviet Union and the United States.

This development, and the progressive weakening of internal control within each of the two main political-military blocs as Soviet-Western détente has been extended and the danger of a direct confrontation between the two bloc leaders largely disposed of, have introduced a new element of instability into international relations that creates an urgent need for new and more comprehensive rules and patterns of world public order. Beyond this, of course, the onset of the space age, with the massive scientific advances of the post-World War II years, has opened up exciting new challenges that seem to demand scientific collaboration in joint programmes transcending ideological frontiers rather than the isolation that has seen the best scientific manpower in each ideological system forced to work in the watertight compartments established by political boundaries.

The space age, even more than the nuclear age, seems to offer the dramatic possibility of an international law of positive cooperation in place of the old international law of conflict. Impressive cooperation in space research and exploration was achieved between the Soviet Union and the United States in the latter years of the Johnson administration and, especially during the Nixon administration after the detailed Moscow Summit Accords of May 1972.

This was highlighted, in the space area, by the Soviet-US Agreement concerning Cooperation in the Exploration and Use of Outer Space for Peaceful Purposes of 24 May 1972, which was both a logical successor to and a building upon the general idea of the peaceful uses of outer space embodied in the jointly (Soviet and US) sponsored, general Treaty on Principles Governing the Activities of States in the Exploration and Use of Outer Space, Including the Moon and other Celestial Bodies, of 27 January 1967. Unfortunately, the momentum of Soviet-US space cooperation was lost in the late 1970s, as one of the casualties of the revived Soviet-US tensions that marked the end of the Carter administration's four-year term.

In the related area of international communications - and specifically international telecommunications by satellites and satellite television broadcasting - the opportunity for fruitful Soviet-US collaboration was passed by in the mid-1960s when the relevant international organizational infrastructure was being established, probably because of the implications for cold war ideological competition and the continuing propaganda war between the two blocs. Instead, two separate and rival inter- national organizations were established - the US-dominated INTELSAT and the Soviet bloc INTERSPUTNIK.

As a result, the establishment of minimum international ground rules to control programme content that approaches the level of propaganda deliberately beamed to rival bloc countries, and to prevent accidental spillover of one country's programmes into another country's receivers without its prior permission, has been left to general accords devised on the basis of difficult, ad hoc bilateral negotiation between the two rival blocs. This is a pity. As an entirely new area of activity, without the historical backlog of cold war hostilities, international communications - like general space research and exploration - had seemed to offer the prospect of developing its own autonomous corpus of legal principles and its own distinctive international administrative organization in direct response to its special technological imperatives.

We have spoken to date of the revolution in the world community - in the society in which international law or any framework and basic patterns of world public order must operate. And the question must now be asked, has there been a corresponding revolution in international law and juridical concepts of world public order? For we teach, in our national law schools, of the necessary relation or symbiosis between law and society - between positive law rules and written prescriptions, and the community in which those same rules are to operate. For without a certain minimum correspondence between the positive law and basic societal facts, the positive law is doomed to remain law-in-books - mere hortatory propositions that will never become community "living law."

There was a time - particularly between the two world wars - when national political leaders indulged light-heartedly and incontinently in the poetry of international law-making, and regarded their work as complete when they had elaborated an ideal code at an appropriately high level of generality and abstraction. The 1928 Kellogg-Briand Pact to "outlaw war" is a perfect example of just such a casual act of international legislation by simple fiat, without much concern for the tiresome, underlying causal factors of international tension whose removal or alleviation could alone give meaning to the law makers' high-level declaration and help make it genuine international law-in-action.

For in its own historical context of continental Europe and the West between the two world wars, the Kellogg-Briand Pact skated easily over the underlying causes of international tensions at that time. The essentially one-sided Peace Treaty of Versailles of 1919 had placed all political and moral responsibility for the First World War - a classic example of a war of colliding imperial systems - on the defeated Central Powers. It had also imposed the full burdens of ignominious foreign military occupation, forced territorial transfers, and crippling economic reparation on those who had so narrowly lost the War. The Carthaginian Peace of 1919 inevitably contained within itself the seeds of its own decay (as even the victors lost faith in its inherent rectitude and political common sense), and the seeds of its eventual challenge (again by traditional means - recourse to armed force).

Today we are much more pragmatic and empirical in our approach to international problem solving and less inclined to believe that absolutist solutions involving the destruction of a defeated enemy or the elimination of an ideological opponent can produce lasting solutions. The aftermath of World War II, when the leaders of the victorious coalition competed with each other in political and economic offers to the defeated enemies, Germany and Japan, on whom they had imposed full guilt for the War and also unconditional surrender only several years before, should induce a new element of modesty as well as freedom from hypocrisy and the temptation to preach one's own highly subjective, too often completely self-serving, version of morality, in the practical conduct of foreign policy.

We teach, in any case, that exercises in abstract, high-level postulation of a priori principles, without first studying the underlying problems to which such principles are supposed to relate and indeed to provide a solution, are exercises in political and legal irresponsibility. They are the more reckless and uncaring because their political authors too often know in advance that the high hopes they engender are likely to end in cruel deception. If we look at the corpus of "classical" or traditional international law today, we find that, on its surface and as practiced by its main interpreters and appliers - honoratiores or "dignitaries" of the law, as the great German sociologist Max Weber called them - it displays little that might be called revolutionary. This takes us back to the origins of classical international law itself and the concept of the international society whose needs and aspirations it was supposed to represent.

It is not so very long since the international society of effective participants in international relations among states (what we today, in the spirit of universalism, call the world community) was considered limited to the "civilized nations," these being the Western European or European-derived, essentially Christian societies that had been founded on the rise of commerce. The fiction was that these countries found their legal personality in their juridical sovereigns and that international law was the expression of their collective conscience.

Deference to international law and acceptance of its binding force was effectuated through the principle of comity, and the notion of the ethical obligation of each head of state, as a Christian monarch, to give effect to agreements or to commonly observe customary rules of conduct. By the beginning of the nineteenth century, the membership of the world community had been expanded, by common consent, to take in a non-Christian society, Turkey. And in the latter half of the nineteenth century, coinciding with the new era of modernization and Westernization inaugurated by Emperor Meiji after 1867, the bounds of the world community were stretched to encompass Japan.

All others - nation-states, private associations, or individuals - while capable of being objects of international law and bound by its obligations, were not subjects of international law, who were entitled to claim the benefit of rights deriving from it. The character and content of classical international law right down to the present day, reflects the ideological narrowness and cultural homogeneity of the original "family compact." For classical international law is not merely rooted in Western legal writings, court decisions, and state practice; its substantive content tends to reflect the interests being pressed by the politically dominant Western societies during the heyday of their commercial and industrial expansion abroad.

Some of these rules, it must be said, may claim a more general acceptance today based on an asserted reasonableness and common sense that transcends their particular conditions of origin. This was thought to be the case with the classical law of the sea which, as first developed by the early seventeenth- century Dutch writer Hugo Grotius, recognized the common interests in free commercial navigation unrestricted by too many or overly pressing claims of national sovereignty. National sovereignty was essentially limited, at least until the recent Geneva Conferences on the law of the sea, to a three-mile territorial sea. This concept prevailed over the early Portuguese and Spanish claims to national paramountcy even on the high seas.

Yet after remaining largely unchallenged for three hundred years, the classical international rules making up the law of the sea began to crumble before the drive of so many states for national appropriation of the wealth of the sea, the continental shelf, and even the deep ocean floor. The pressure for change came from the third world states (logically, and perhaps with a certain moral claim of right) but also from first and second world countries. President Truman's 1945 proclamation of the United States' sovereignty over the continental shelf adjacent to the American coast - a unilateral act directed immediately towards national appropriation of offshore oil deposits - opened the floodgates to other countries.

As the French jurist René-Jean Dupuy concluded, the law of the sea, which according to classical doctrine had essentially been a law of movement, became transformed into a law of appropriation, with the accent shifting from a personal law to a territorial law characterized by a new parochialism in place of the old universalism. In fact, the law of the sea has become an integral part of the law on the new international economic order - one important means of redressing the current imbalance between third world countries and privileged, post-industrial societies.

The three-mile territorial sea disappeared before these concerted national demands. Only the great military-naval powers (the Soviet Union and the United States), or countries like Japan without either a perceptible continental shelf or fishing resources close to their coasts, or the unfortunate landlocked states, were interested in resisting pressures to change the old rules. It is, of course, among the ironies of our time that not all third world countries, because of the accidents of geography, were capable of effectively sharing in that part of the new international economic order now annexed to a redefined, updated law of the sea, and that some of the wealthiest post-industrial societies - the United States and Canada, for example - are among its principal economic beneficiaries.

That part of the law of war known as *temperamenta belli* and devoted to mitigation of the barbarities and cruelties of warfare was also a concept first sponsored by Grotius, in reaction to the senseless outrages and gratuitous violence of the Thirty Years War. It might seem to correspond so obviously to general world community interest today as to need no justification. And yet the development of new modes of armed conflict - the "wars of national liberation" mounted by irregular, "rebel" or guerrilla forces against the parent

European colonial power or, as in Vietnam, against the US Army and its "client" government - has called the traditional rules into question where they limit their protection to regular members of the regular armed forces of a recognized government engaging in declared war.

For that matter, it is asserted, the rebel or guerrilla forces may not merely claim the full privileges of the law of war for their actions against the colonial power; there may even be an affirmative duty cast upon other states to help such rebel forces in their armed struggle for decolonization and independence. The narrowness of the original ideological basis of international law is evident. It is the legacy of the historical accident that the original honoratiores who largely created its main substantive rules and principles were Western European and Christian. As the respected Instituto Interamericano de Estudios Juridicos Internationales declared, in a group study prepared in 1964:

The continuing political and territorial expansion that the European powers so often achieved through military means brought with it and left in its wake a large number of myths. Perhaps the most significant of these was the concept of the inherent universality and perennial nature of international law - a concept that was linked with the old and undefined concepts of natural law. A derivative belief was that a priori juridical standards, which could be demonstrated and justified by pure reason and which politically antedated European territorial expansion governed juridical relations among states.... The immanence of a state order was assumed and propositions which historically seemed very closely correlated to the political self-interest of the European powers were accepted as juridical norms.

By their talents and vigour the European peoples extended their influence throughout the world; and Westernization almost came to be considered as an essential requisite to the achievement of progress. Meanwhile the myth of the immanence and immutability of international law remained unchanged. Even those authors who made studies of the history of international relations before the political predominance of the West tended to acknowledge Western Christian standards as the apex of the development of international juridical norms.

The two world wars of this century dispelled these assumptions. The framework of the world changed, and for the modern state the classical international machinery was no longer sufficient.... Wars were no longer investments in blood and steel made by states to round out their borders or to acquire markets. They were sudden blazes of destruction and hatred which swept away the juridical order - improperly observed, but at least existent - that limited conflicts. Colonial expansion, which no longer had the characteristics of Victoria's days, is another example. Freedom of trade, the protection of nationals abroad, and the propagation of Christianity ceased to be justifications.

Christianity was no longer regarded as the only true religion, and all peoples were thought to have the right to live out their destiny without undergoing Westernization. The dissatisfaction that so much of the non-Western membership of the contemporary world community now feels with the historically-received, "classical" international law that must be applied to present-day problems is indicated in varied representative reactions.

Among jurists, the late and gifted Professor Eugene Korovin - the doyen of Soviet international lawyers for many years - called in 1961 for the replacement of what he identified as the "routine system" of international law by a new programme that would express the "epoch of struggle between two opposing social systems; the epoch of Socialist revolutions; the collapse of imperialism; the abolition of the colonial system; the transition on to the Socialist road of more and more peoples; and the victory of Socialism and Communism on a world scale."

The representative of one of the "developing" African countries, at the special United Nations Conference on International Law held at Mexico City in the fall of 1964, bitterly attacked the Statute of the World Court for its identification (in Article 38 (1) (c)) of "the general principles of law recognized by civilized nations" - as one of the sources of law that the court is to apply in deciding cases coming before it. This provision, the African representative said, was hardly likely to dispel the "new" countries' general lack of confidence in the World Court.

In the World Court itself, widened intellectual-legal horizons corresponding to marked extensions in membership in the official world community following the influx of Afro-Asian countries to the United Nations from the mid-1950s onwards, and reflecting, for the first time, an effective Afro-Asian voice in the special political constituency (the UN General Assembly and the UN Security Council) charged with the election of judges to the court, show up in the occasional judicial special opinion. Thus Judge Ammoun, in his specially concurring opinion in North Sea Continental Shelf in 1969, also took aim at the concept of "the general principles of law recognized by civilized nations" enshrined in Article 38 (1) (c) of the Court Statute:

The discrimination between civilized nations and uncivilized nations, which was unknown to the founding fathers of international law, the protagonists of a universal law of nations, Vittoria, Suarez, Gentilis, Pufendorf, Vattel, is the legacy of the period, now passed away, of colonialism, and of the time long-past when a limited number of Powers established the rules, of custom or of treaty-law, of a European law applied in relation to the whole community of nations. Maintained and sometimes reinforced at the time of the great historical settlements - Vienna 1815. Berlin 1885, Versailles 1920, Lausanne 1923.

Yalta 1945 - European international law had been defended by jurists of indisputable authority in the majority of branches of international law.... However great and powerful the thinking of these renowned jurists may be, their concept of a family of European and North Atlantic nations is nonetheless beginning to be blurred by the reality of the universal community, in the thinking of the internationalists of a new age such as S. Krylov, M. Katz. W. Jenks and M. Lachs. What is more, the Universalist jurists of Europe had been preceded by those of Asia and the Middle East: Sui Tchoan-Pao, Bandyo- Padhyoy, Rechid....

The criterion of the distinction between civilized nations and those which are allegedly not so has thus been a political criterion - power politics - and anything but an ethical or legal one. The system which it represents has not been without influence on the persistent aloofness of certain new States from the International Court of Justice. Judge Ammoun returned to this theme in another specially concurring opinion, rendered as part of the World Court's advisory opinion in Western Sahara in 1975, when he rejected the European and Western concept of territory as terra nullius and therefore legally open to annexation and colonization by imperial powers.

The standard applied by the European powers was highly subjective and always self-serving - "the materialistic concept of terra nullius, which led to this dismemberment of Africa following the Berlin Conference of 1885," in Judge Ammoun's own words. An African jurist, Judge Forster, in his specially concurring opinion in the same Western Sahara advisory opinion, echoed Judge Ammoun. Judge Forster found that the court's official opinion of court in that case, being rooted in essentially European and Western legal ways of thought, "minimiz[ed] the exceptional importance of the geographical, social and temporal contexts of the problem.... It is Africa of former times which is in question, as to which it cannot arbitrarily be required that its institutions should be... a carbon copy of European institutions."

All this indicates, of course, that there is a fairly widespread crisis of confidence in international law today. For many peoples, particularly in the "new" countries, the corpus of classical, historically-derived international law provides no affirmative base for satisfying their claims for economic advancement and social betterment. In many respects, it seems to represent a positive barrier to those claims. And organizations like the World Court and the United Nations policy-making organs - which, for most of their history, have seemed to many peoples, particularly in the "new" countries, to be essentially Western- composed or Western-dominated - have too often seemed to be more preoccupied with the petit-point of international law than its imaginative reshaping to meet radically new conditions in international society.

The prime task of the international lawyer today becomes, therefore, one of building a new system of world public order with an ideological base broad enough to derive support from, and to encompass, all the main competing, social and economic systems of the present day; and of developing, in the international arena, that necessary symbiosis between positive law and social change that we regard as axiomatic for our own internal law system. In a word, any viable system of world public order or international law must capture the dynamic of the world revolution of our time. How this can best be attempted in a world of ideological conflict will be the subject of the succeeding discussion.

3

Third World and Contemporary International Law Values

The values of international law at any time in its historical development are reflected in the authoritative decisions made in all main arenas and through all main processes of world community law making. In the contemporary era, the values are to be found in the resolutions of the General Assembly; decisions of the Security Council and of the principal United Nations specialized agencies; the judgments and advisory opinions of the International Court of Justice; the self-legislation involved in international treaty making (multilateral, but also limited, bilateral treaties), and in state acts (including unilateral declarations of state intention) and sometimes the decision to refrain from state action, which may operate by way of estoppel.

The American jurist of the first half of the present century, Roscoe Pound, who conceived of law as a process of reconciliation of competing community interests (public, social, individual), saw the need for identifying key ordering principles of law if the process of balancing interests in resolution of conflicts was to be rendered rational and placed on a predictable, objectively verifiable basis. Such ordering principles of law, in Pound's view, would be extrapolated from the authoritative decisions of a given society by a process of induction, and then rationalization and generalization, from the mass of competing interests present in the particular societal problem situations being decided in the society and from the particular community choices made among those competing interests in the final resolution of conflicts.

The ordering principles of law that were thus induced were named by Pound as the jural postulates of a civilization area and civilization period. Pound's approach to identification and choice of the jural postulates was thus thoroughly empirical and as a result necessarily relativist, reflecting the values officially applied in a given society, through its official law-making arenas and processes, at a given time, but not more than that; and certainly not new or inchoate values still in process of emergence and acquiring public recognition and acceptance through the ordinary community dialectical processes.

The jural postulates, once identified, would perform a clarifying and ordering function in the general community law-making processes, unifying otherwise disparate details; and for a stable society, with a certain cultural homogeneity and an already existing consensus on political, social, and economic basic questions, this might well be the prime objective in legal development. For non-homogeneous, non stable societies that were still in full evolution in their attitudes to fundamental issues of political, social, and economic choice, however, the jural postulates, insofar as they would reflect the value choices of official decision makers taken at a particular point in time only, would be likely to operate conservatively, as a brake on societal development or an instrument for maintaining the status quo.

The way out of this dilemma clearly lay in developmental theories of law and society, involving, in the end, historical determinism and conceptions of the long-range trends and direction of society. The German liberal democratic legal theorist of the Wilhelminian era, J. Kohler, made his own essay at solving the dilemma through the neo-Hegelian notion of the unfolding of civilization in law, with the official decision maker's legal mandate and role thereby becoming one of actively assisting and furthering this process of historical development.

This still left the question, present not less with historically deterministic theories of law than with simple legal relativism, of what to do in the case of a "retrogressive" civilization, and how indeed to recognize it as such at the moment of decision. Should the official decision maker be emancipated in such cases from his legal mandate and duty to apply the jural postulates of the civilization, and, if so, on what basis should he finally decide? The question became especially acute in Kohler's own national society, Germany, a generation or more after he developed his theories. For some jurists the ideal personal solution of the dilemma of value choice would be one of escape into von Ihering's "heaven of juristic concepts" (Begriffs-Himmel) and of the deliberate immunization of oneself from problems of value choice and value application in law.

For others with more civil courage, however, the moral dilemma of legal value choice was to prove not so difficult to resolve in actual, concrete cases, the answer being provided by a recognition of the existence of some at least minimum principles of humanity and decency basic to any civilized legal system. If then, in extreme or pathological situations the problem of ultimate value choice is likely to be more notional than real, there will still remain the issue of how to identify and select among competing values in a society that is plural in ethnic-cultural terms; that is clearly in transition as to its basic social and economic organization; and that has not yet achieved a full ideological synthesis of opposing views as to the movement of history and as to its own long-range direction and objectives. There are many such societies, of course, at the municipal, national level; but it is to the contemporary world community that we must now address ourselves in particular.

VALUES AND VALUE CHOICE

The contemporary world community, viewed as a particular civilization area at a particular moment in history or civilization era, manifests a number of main dilemmas as to identification and choice of jural postulates or goal values.

VALUE IDENTIFICATION

The contemporary issue here is what are or should be the main ordering principles or goal values of an ideologically and ethnic-culturally plural world community, not merely in transition in its basic social and economic organization but with different regions or groupings of states at markedly different levels of social and economic development and coexisting of necessity together. Modern constitution-making ventures for municipal, national societies usually attempt to resolve the problem of the goal values of society by postulating them in the constitutional charter itself as an authoritative guide to official decision makers at all levels and, more generally, as an attempt to inform and educate the public about the main aspirations of the society.

The drafters of the Spanish Republican Constitution of 1931 established a constitutional innovation, since borrowed in the Irish Republican Constitution of 1937 and the post-decolonization Indian Republican Constitution of 1950, of listing directive principles of state (or social) policy - concerning the main issues of community choice in cultural, social, and economic matters-in a special chapter included in the constitutional charter itself. Other, contemporary constitution makers may seek to achieve the same result by incorporating such social and economic postulates into a constitutional bill of rights, particularly where such a bill of rights seeks to go beyond the somewhat skeletal Anglo-Saxon Common Law, essentially laissez-faire, constitutional model that is normally limited to the "open society" style of political and civil rights, and to enter directly upon the key issues of social and economic choice of today.

Most of the constitutional charters adopted, or proposed after World War II illustrate this new trend in constitutional drafting; it is most pronounced in the case of non-Western societies, but some of the better "renewed" Western constitutional charters of recent years show the same positive openings to social and economic issues. Still other constitution makers may use the preamble to the constitutional charter for the enunciation of high-level philosophical principles as to law and society; such charters acquire, in consequence, a hortatory, pedagogical quality, and will need institutional and processual follow-up if the necessarily abstract general norms of the preamble are effectively to be translated into constitutional law-in-action in the future. But at least the official state intents as to the goals and directions of the society for the future are conveniently collected in the one place and presented clearly and unequivocally.

The United Nations Charter, as the basic constitutional instrument of international society, must constitute the principal legal source of the jural postulates or legal goal values of its own particular civilization area and civilization era, the contemporary world community. It is, in comparative constitutional terms, a modern document, enacted as recently as 1945. But, as noted in other areas of international law, time has a habit of galloping today, and so the Charter's postulates, such as they are, may need supplementing and updating and, in some cases, renewal or redefinition. In the actual drafting of the Charter there were, as we have noted, historical differences among its founding fathers as to just what the Charter was intended to do and as to just what its legal characterization should be a limited treaty between sovereign states, on the more restrictive, Soviet approach, or something more, as many Western countries seemed to imply.

In the result, and in what concerns postulation of goal values or philosophical objectives, the Charter comes closer to the rather skeletal Anglo-Saxon Common Law constitutional charter model than to the philosophically much richer and more detailed paradigms developed in continental European civil law constitutionalism (both Western and Eastern Europe) and in related non-European systems of the postwar period. The Charter is very strong and usually very explicit in its enunciation of institutions and procedures and decision-making processes, but correspondingly much lighter in its approach to definition of goal values, ordering principles, and even legal standards; and there is no attempt to organize these and collect them in a disciplined fashion in any one place- for example, in a special charter-based chapter or bill of rights.

While the Charter preamble is richly poetic in language, it tends to be abstract and general and unconcrete in dealing with the purposes of the Charter and of the new international order that it set up. There are references in the preamble to the "scourge of war"; "fundamental human rights"; "the dignity and worth of the human person"; "the equal rights of men and women and of nations large and small"; "justice and respect for the obligations arising from treaties and other sources of international law"; to promoting "social progress and better standards of life in larger freedom" and to promoting also the "economic and social advancement of all peoples."

The immediately ensuing Chapter I ("Purposes and Principles") (Articles 1 and 2) attempts to offer somewhat more low-level and concrete secondary legal principles in application of the preambular high-level formulations; and these do indeed establish an emphasis, befitting a world public order system established at the end of a great military conflict, upon peace keeping, on peaceful settlement of disputes, and on refraining from the "threat or use of force against the territorial integrity or political independence of any state" (Article 2 [4]). Chapter I of the Charter also postulates the "sovereign equality" of all members of the United Nations (Article 2 [1]); though, as with the original definition of constitutional "equal protection" under the United States Constitution's post-Civil War Fourteenth Amendment, it is, in terms, a formal, juridical equality only.

There is explicit mention of the principle of "equal rights and self- determination of peoples" (Article 1 [2]), and the affirmation of the need for "international cooperation in solving international problems of an economic, social, cultural, or humanitarian character, and in promoting and encouraging respect for human rights and for fundamental freedoms for all without distinction as to race, sex, language, or religion" (Article 1 [3]). Beyond the preamble and Chapter I ("Purposes and Principles"), there are, scattered through the detailed machinery sections of the Charter, the type of "standards" provisions to be found in every national legal system, that call out for evaluation in any given case and development on a case-by-case basis; for example, the reference in Chapter II ("Membership") (Articles 3-6), to the fact of membership being open to "peace-loving states, which accept the obligations contained in the present Charter and, in the judgement of the Organization, are able and willing to carry out these obligations."

References, such as that already referred to above, to the mandate of the General Assembly under Article 13 (1)(a) to promote and encourage the "progressive development of international law and its codification" may, in strictly juridical terms, authorize an activist approach to international law making for the future, if the decision makers concerned have the civil courage and the necessary political consensus behind them to want to attempt that.

In sum, except for peace and peace keeping, self-determination, and equality of states, the Charter itself does not provide too much help as to the jural postulates or goal values to guide the updating and future development of international organization and international law generally. Fortunately, however, like the earlier Anglo-Saxon common law laissez- faire constitutional models which appear to have influenced its drafting, the Charter is relatively open-ended and neutral in philosophical terms, once one goes beyond the several ordering principles already referred to.

There is therefore absolutely nothing to prevent the Charter-in the fashion of other living constitutional instruments before it-from being built upon and added to by other, subsequent constitutional acts or customary law "glosses" not in conflict with its original text. This process of creative novation, on an incremental, sometimes case-by-case basis over the years since 1945, through developing United Nations practice as expressed in the formal legislation of declarations based on General Assembly resolutions or similar fundamental acts, judicial decisions, executive- administrative acts, and the like, has been the lifeblood of international organization in the postwar era.

Rendered necessary, in terms of the instruments and processes of constitutional change, through the complicated machinery for formal amendment of the Charter established under Chapter XVIII ("Amendments") (Articles 108-109), which establishes virtually insurmountable barriers to direct change to the Charter except on trivial issues not touching on the Big Powers' prerogatives, this system of indirect change presents all the advantages of continuing, organic development on a pragmatic, empirical, step-by-step basis. There has indeed been a dialectical development of United Nations law and practice since 1945, with historical unfolding from year to year in accordance with the continually evolving consensus within the General Assembly over that time period.

Teleological or purposive interpretation, in accord with that continuing consensus, has guided the historical evolution and adaptation of the Charter and charter law, as it has done with all viable national constitutional systems. The important point is that whatever the Charter may lack in terms of postulated a priori constitutional ordering principles or values, on a thoroughly empirical approach there has been little difficulty in identifying the key jural postulates or goal values of contemporary United Nations law-in-action, and little difficulty in maintaining the necessary political consensus and support for their practical implementation-in supplement to the very few such postulates that are indeed formally identified, a priori, in the preamble and the opening two sections of the Charter. Current dilemmas as to the goal values of contemporary international law tend to concern questions other than their identification as such, and relate rather to their factual application in concrete cases or their ranking inter se when they happen to conflict in action.

VALUE RANKING

The problem here is that most legal problem situations are polycentric and will involve two or more goal values present in one fact complex. Sometimes those goal values will be in direct competition, leading to quite different end results, depending on which one is invoked by the rival parties and by the authoritative decision makers concerned. To take an example, in the original charter formulation the peace imperative, involving among other things the legal interdiction of the threat or use of force, is clear, just as is the principle of self-determination of peoples.

Is a subject people entitled to have recourse to the use of force, with or without the direct military aid of its ideological allies or associates outside the country, when the dominant (imperial or colonial, and in any case foreign) power imposes clogs upon the orderly, constitutional realization of the political self-determination principle? The resolution of the value dilemma in this context would require, in the abstract, the establishment of some sort of hierarchy or ranking of values, establishing authoritatively and on an a priori basis, in advance of all actual problem situations, which of the competing values is the most important and deserving of preference by decision makers.

In the concrete, and as a matter of United Nations developing historical practice (in the absence of any advance, a priori, authoritative ranking of values), there have not been too many problems. The developing juridical conscience of the world community, as expressed through General Assembly resolutions and other official acts, has supplied reasonably clear guidelines for harmonizing and rendering compatible the invocation and application of the values in concrete cases.

VALUE CONCRETIZATION

The jural postulates or goal values, to the extent that they are indicated in the preamble and the opening sections of the Charter and also in legal-doctrinal writings, are formulated only at a very high level of generality and abstraction. To be made operational, they need to be rendered into much more low-level and concrete secondary or even tertiary principles capable of immediate application to actual problem situations.

Once one moves from the abstract and general primary principles to the more specific and practical secondary or tertiary principles, one finds that the tidy intersystemic consensus as to the goal values of United Nations and contemporary international law begins to become strained.

For not merely do the various political-ideological systems have frequently differing conceptions of the meaning or connotation of those goal values, but they may also disagree as to their factual application in concrete cases or even as to whether they apply at all in the specific fact contexts. Thus it is clear, for example, in the area of human rights, to which, as an abstract principle or goal value, all major political ideological systems have pledged their allegiance, that for reasons of particular historical background and development and also the basic socioeconomic infrastructure, the three main blocs or groupings of states within the United Nations-Western, Socialist, and Third World - differ as to the range and extent of the concept itself.

Such interbloc, intersystemic ideological differences influence the purported application of the concept of human rights so as to include the "new" social and economic rights as well as the "old" or "classical" political and civil rights, and also the degree of practical deference to be accorded to each; and the relevance of the "new" concept of collective or group rights in contradistinction to the "old" personal or individual rights. It is an area in which the charge of Eurocentrism and of a morally self-righteous and self-serving ignoring of the socioeconomic infrastructure underlying all legal right-duty relationships is most often raised against the Western-bloc countries.

The historical contradictions here between the rival political-ideological systems have not yet been fully and finally resolved within the United Nations' own internal dialectical processes. But significant advances have been made, and the lines of possible eventual reconciliation or synthesis of the distinctive attitudes and approaches of the rival systems are appearing. One needs to make an ally of time for purposes of an eventual resolution of the problem.

Other problems will arise, however, in the factual application to specific problem situations of goal values already agreed upon, at the level of the abstract and general primary principles, by all main legal systems. Everyone accepts - in public, at least - the principle of the self-determination of peoples but there may be disagreement in terms of its more concrete and immediate application. For example, is the principle of self-determination of peoples limited only to classical colonial situations involving a European "parent," imperial country holding subject the indigenous native population of an overseas colony-a legal category now approaching the point of being exhausted as a result of the General Assembly's successful political drives in the 1950s, 1960s, and 1970s to liberate the remaining remnants of the old European colonial empires of yesteryear?

Or does the principle apply also to new, post-decolonization, or even non-colonial, situations? There are also problems of factual characterization when, in a non-colonial situation raising self-determination claims, a "parent" European imperial country may insist that the matter is, in terms of Article 2 (7) of the Charter, one "essentially within the domestic jurisdiction" of itself, and hence, by definition, not raising international law self-determination issues and therefore not licit in legal terms. Once again, United Nations practice over the years reveals that questions such as these, while raising political difficulties, are not legally intractable; and the evolving juridical consensus within the United Nations has come through, in time, to provide an agreed interpretation and solution that have been perforce accepted by, if not altogether satisfying, all main blocs-Western, Socialist, and Third World.

SELF-DETERMINATION OF PEOPLES, THE DECOLONIZATION IMPERATIVE

On all the empirical evidence of United Nations practice, we would have to consider self-determination of peoples-in its narrower original historical, pre-Charter formulation as political self-determination-as the motor principle in the progressive development and unfolding of United Nations and general international law since 1945. More than any other legal principle, political self-determination has been the catalyst for United Nations legal activism, stimulating fundamental change to the basic fabric of the world community - a veritable political and social revolution, effectuated peacefully in disciplined and systematic fashion, in the interstices of legal reform measures, here a series of General Assembly resolutions and executive-administrative and judicial acts building upon the original Charter-based principle.

The Charter enunciation finds its most concrete and explicit formulation in problem-oriented secondary principles in the Declaration on the Granting of Independence to Colonial Countries and Peoples, adopted by General Assembly Resolution 1514 (XV) of December 14, 1960. The vote on the General Assembly resolution was an overwhelming 89-0, but there were nine abstentions (Australia, Belgium, Dominican Republic, France, Portugal, Spain, Union of South Africa, United Kingdom, United States), the abstaining states (which had not cared to vote no!) being for the most part the still remaining European imperial powers that had not yet liberated their colonial territories overseas.

If it was the declaration of 1960 that so largely erected self- determination, decolonization, and independence into imperative principles of international law, or *jus cogens*, the drive for political self-determination was given practical realization, in a highly pragmatic fashion, in a host of executive-administrative and judicial actions in other United Nations arenas. Small independent African states like Ethiopia (which had briefly and fleetingly been twice exposed to Italian "colonization") and Liberia (a free settlement in Africa made in the nineteenth century by the erstwhile victims of the European slave trade and their descendants, newly liberated in the United States) began a veritable guerrilla war of litigation before the International Court of Justice, designed to liberate southern Africa from the white minority rule of the Union of South Africa, itself a latter-day survival of Dutch, and then British, imperial colonial development.

The immediate object before the International Court was the termination of the old League of Nations mandate over South West Africa (Namibia), the former German colony, which the victors of Versailles had conferred upon the Union of South Africa in their peace treaty of 1919 dictated to defeated imperial Germany, and which the Union of South Africa had then proceeded to assimilate to full legal ownership and control. After a series of procedural, adjectival law-based rebuffs for the moving Third World countries, the International Court of Justice, following on fierce General Assembly criticisms of the substantive consequences of its earlier decisions, finally in 1971 declared the Union of South Africa's mandate to be legally terminated.

The prologue to the court's effective volte-face, in its 1971 advisory opinion was effectively coordinated political action within the General Assembly and Security Council, producing the formal request to the court for ruling on the issue of the continued validity, then, of the original mandate, given the evolution of international law in the intervening half-century and the preeminent role accorded in contemporary international law to political self-determination. The actual legal follow-up to the court's 1971 ruling ran into a number of political roadblocks in the General Assembly and elsewhere, but the end of the road seemed clear and inescapable: final decolonization, independence, and self-government for Namibia and, after that, full majority government for South Africa, as the legal culmination of the drive for political self-determination for southern Africa initiated with the General Assembly's first inquiries, at the opening of the 1950s, into the "racial situation" in South Africa.

Discussion of the Namibia question directs attention to the fact that it required a certain intellectual-legal jump for authoritative international decision makers to accept applicability of the Declaration on the Granting of Independence to Colonial Countries and Peoples not merely to "colonies" as conventionally understood to be the overseas territories, inhabited by indigenous non-European peoples, of the European imperial powers, but to what was in abstract, formal legal terms not a "colony" as such but a League of Nations mandate. But once the International Court of Justice had summoned up the civil courage and intellectual-legal imagination to break through the artificial procedural, adjectival law barriers that it had itself created in its earlier rulings on South West Africa, that substantive law jump proved not too difficult or intellectually demanding to make.

More serious questions today have to do with whether the legal imperative of political self-determination denotes not merely what we might now almost call "classical" first phase decolonization situations- those involving liberation of aboriginal (non-European) peoples from their original European imperial masters-but also second phase decolonization situations, where no substantial aboriginal population is involved in the European colonial territory, and, much more important, non-colonial situations where no European colonial power is any longer involved and what we are dealing with is a contest for political power within one state between two or more "succession" (post-imperial) indigenous, aboriginal peoples, without the complication of a significant expatriate European presence.

The first of these problems is clearly the easier one to answer, for there are so few of them remaining. They are the accidental remnants of European colonial empires-isolated lumps of rock or uninhabited islands seized, by force majeure where necessary, to guard the long sea routes to some distant inhabited colonial territory, now lost, or to serve as a refueling station or a botanical or scientific observation post. Granted ordinary common sense, an imperial power that had already lost the inhabited colonial territories that these scattered colonial outposts once served as naval stations would have made its own cost-benefit analysis in reasonably timely fashion and proceeded to liquidate its remaining colonial investment as expeditiously and painlessly as possible.

That erstwhile imperial powers do not always do so can be attributed, no doubt, to a number of factors: simple oversight or absent-mindedness; the hope, against all hope and rational scientific verification, that there may be oil or something else of value in those bleak remaining outposts and the desire for a quick (if temporary) economic gain at the expense of some political embarrassment. Over and beyond all these, however, there seems to be a special nostalgia or madness that besets former imperial powers looking back in anger from an often economically dismal present to the conceived romantic splendors of the imperial past. It seems to be psychologically very, very difficult for ancient imperial proconsuls and their attendant lawyers and scribes to give up, so strong is the bureaucratic momentum today of old imperial ideas.

The Canadian government discovered, to its surprise and its own ill-concealed irritation, in the period 1980-1982 that diehard back-bench members of the British Parliament still insisted that (somehow or other in legal terms) those back-benchers remained "legal guardians" of the Canadian Constitution, invested with "legal trustee" powers to supervise the practical functioning of the Canadian federal system. The Canadian government insisted successfully that since Canada had obtained her full juridical independence from the United Kingdom a full half-century before, such British Parliament back-benchers' legal pretensions were, in fact, legal nonsense and legally unacceptable-a Canadian government legal position in which British Prime Minister Thatcher acquiesced.

But if members of the British Parliament could as late as 1982 tilt at legal windmills in support of a fanciful claim still to exercise some form of legal hegemony over independent Canada- long since, in effect, decolonized on an amicable, fully consensual basis in the so-called Statute of Westminster of 1931-how much more difficult would they find it to acquiesce sensibly and gracefully in the liquidation in the same year, 1982, of the largely abandoned naval refueling base in the far South Atlantic originally taken, a century and a half before, by force majeure from the Argentinians,-the Falklands (Malvinas). Seventeen years of British-Argentinian bilateral negotiations had apparently seen the British government ready on two occasions to withdraw from the Falklands

(Malvinas), but the matter was never considered of high priority and was allowed to drift, the British-Canadian bilateral negotiations of 1980-1982 over final "patriation" of the Canadian Constitution having further delayed action on the file in the British Foreign Office.

We shall refer in another context to the rash action of the Argentinian government in resorting to direct military action before bilateral diplomatic negotiations had been broken off or political-diplomatic possibilities within the United Nations had been fully explored and exhausted. Suffice it to say here that the Falklands (Malvinas) do not fall into the "classical" decolonization category, there being no indigenous, aboriginal people already in place on the islands, before whose claims the European imperial power must yield.

Argentina's legal claims rested, in fact, on other still quite substantial legal grounds: an original Spanish imperial territorial title maintained by Argentina under the rules of state succession and through the special Latin American regional international law doctrine of uti possidetis; an original Argentinian effective occupation of the islands that had been terminated only illegally and by force majeure by the British imperial power; and, finally, "new" international law doctrines of geographical contiguity as the basis of legal title, in the absence of other countervailing claims of a recognized legal character. Cumulatively, the Argentinian claims were sufficient and impressive.

By contrast, the British claims rested on no more than an original, patently illegal act of seizure of the islands, followed by long-term occupation. The latter-day claim, advanced in 1982 after the opening of military hostilities between the United Kingdom and Argentina, that the British subjects settled on the islands by Great Britain, and their descendants - in fact, a scant 1,800 people today - had a legal right of national self-determination, to be exercised by remaining as a British imperial colony, hardly deserved to be taken seriously in the context of United Nations history and practice over the years since 1945. *De minimis non curat lex*, as a legal maxim, applies as much to national self-determination as to other areas of law.

The United Nations had, on a legally principled basis, refused to countenance political partition of Cyprus into two independent units so as to give separate political self-determination to 120,000 Turks and to 480,000 Greeks, as a solution for that island's problems, even though the two national communities concerned occupied essentially distinct and different geographical regions; and the United Nations was hardly likely to concede to the 1,800 on the Falklands (Malvinas), as a basis for rejecting Argentina's legal claims, what it had declined to concede to very much larger population units elsewhere.

The British argument as to the privileges and interests of the 1,800 British-descended inhabitants of the Falklands (Malvinas) would seem better realized legally in a claim for some degree of regional autonomy and local self-government within the framework of an eventual political settlement returning the islands to Argentina, and for some degree of financial subsidy or compensation to those inhabitants desiring to emigrate from the islands after such eventual political settlement. These were policies, after all, which the United Kingdom had been advancing in the approach to political settlement of her own long-standing Ulster problem - the British-held territorial enclave remaining in the northeast corner of the Republic of Ireland after its political independence and separation from the United Kingdom.

Within that British enclave the British government had so far resisted, on a de minimis basis, the arguments of the Roman Catholic minority (forming nearly half the population), who wanted to join with the predominantly Roman Catholic Republic of Ireland. Discussion of the Falklands (Malvinas) problem directs attention to the fact that, with the major exception of South Africa and the exception also of the remaining vestigial remnants of the old British colonial empire (Gibraltar, Hong Kong, and the so-called New Territories), the book has been virtually closed on decolonization questions proper.

A glance at the agenda of the General Assembly's Fourth Committee, which is specially charged with decolonization questions, in search of other items, reveals largely picayune questions, apart from some strictly post-decolonization, "succession state" problems arising after the departure of the European imperial power concerned. Of these only the Western Sahara problem, involving final determination of the identity of the successor state or states to imperial Spain, now departed, appears of major importance or as having in it the seeds of future international, intraregional conflict.

So much so, indeed, that the Fourth Committee was able to complete its agenda and terminate its work for the thirty-seventh session of the General Assembly on November 19, 1982, a full month before the other specialized committees. (One should add, perhaps, that the Antarctica question is potentially important, insofar as the 1959 Antarctic Treaty dedicating the region to scientific research and cooperation simply froze existing territorial claims, such as they were, without purporting to confirm or deny them. Insofar as the original territorial claimants, signatories to the 1959 treaty, were in very large part former imperial powers or their dependents, who had taken part in the original imperial "rush for spoils" in colonial territories overseas, there seems no reason for extending special credence or legal deference to their territorial claims, in terms of contemporary international law in its postcolonial evolution and development.)

The real and burning issues as to political self-determination today are likely to be, then, post-decolonization and even non-colonial in character. Almost all the "succession states" to the old European colonial empires in Africa and even Asia have been multinational states in ethnic- cultural and linguistic terms, whose ethnic composition and political frontiers were so often arbitrarily or casually determined, either by imperial fiat or by intra-European international agreement like the Congress of Berlin of 1885. European statesmen then drew up territorial borders for regions hardly known to the Europeans concerned, often cutting up existing tribal communities, and in any case defining static geographical boundaries for what were in some cases purely nomadic communities that did not recognize such territorially based fixed divisions.

The "division of the spoils" in Africa was, as recognized in the International Court of Justice's 1975 advisory opinion in Western Sahara, not merely European in its political motivations but Eurocentrist in its conceptualizations and legal configurations; and this is what was passed on to the post-decolonization "succession states." Does political self-determination apply as an imperative principle of law today, to rectify the frequently arbitrary, capricious, and irrational territorial dispositions made by the European imperial powers among themselves in that purely European "rush for the spoils"? In terms of United Nations received opinion and practice, the answer today is No!; or, at least, Not Yet! It is pointed out that the "made-in-Europe" territorial dispositions concerned were for the most part made three-quarters of a century, or even much more, before the decolonization of the 1950s and 1960s; and that, for better or worse, the historical accident of particular European colonization had given a degree of second (European) language and also legal and administrative cohesiveness and unity that supplied an element of integration and common collective purpose that was sorely needed to overcome the invariable post-decolonization economic difficulties.

Attempting to turn the clock back in history and to redress today, on a purportedly ethnic-cultural or tribal basis, the received imperial colonial frontiers would create much confusion and impede realization of the post-decolonization planning imperatives. History, here imperial-colonial history, creates its own political and social facts of life, and it may sometimes be easier to start with those facts and try to correct them in the future on a consensual basis, through the ordinary constitutional process in the postcolonial societies concerned. Beyond that, however, lies the far more important principle of stability and continuity-legitimacy, if you wish-in the vastly troubled post-decolonization "succession state."

A distinguished Arab diplomat whose own state, by a happy accident of history, has no very significant ethnic-cultural or national minority problems commented, in relation to the Ethiopian-Somali border conflicts and to Somalian irridentist claims against the Ogaden region, that the new Third World "succession states" that had succeeded in the postwar era to the old European colonial empires in Africa and Asia had too many problems of their own and could hardly afford the luxury of a European-style, post-Treaty of Westphalia of 1648 century or two of territorial wars between rival states to "rectify" frontiers problems. For these purposes, even at the price of some "regional" hardships or injustices, political stability in the face of grave external and internal challenges, economic and other, dictated that the principle of state sovereignty (including sanctity of existing frontiers, such as they might be) should prevail over the principle of political self- determination.

It is an axiological or interests-balancing approach well understood and accepted as such within the United Nations family, and it is recognized de facto in the settled United Nations practice as to post-decolonization territorial and frontiers questions of "succession states." In another, different if parallel situation, the then chancellor of the Federal Republic of West Germany, Willy Brandt, accepted the political facts of the war's-end territorial settlements imposed by the Yalta and Potsdam Conferences in Central and Eastern Europe, and the two-Germanies solution, as the price to be paid for East-West, interbloc peace and security in Europe. This was, in essence, the political and legal trade-off involved in the so-called Ostpolitik series of bilateral treaties effected between the Federal Republic of Germany and its neighbors in Eastern Europe at the end of the 1960s and in the early 1970s, which both legitimated the de facto political-military divisions of 1945 and also promised cooperation in political and economic relations across the existing ideological Iron Curtain.

In purely non-colonial situations, existing unitary states like France and the United Kingdom which have been rediscovering particularist ethnically-culturally or linguistically based minorities that were thought to have been long ago assimilated or absorbed, are now experimenting with regional autonomy and territorial decentralization of decision-making power. Constitutional-institutional pluralism is, of course, another and perfectly acceptable approach to political self-determination within an existing state that does not choose to bifurcate or otherwise to fragment itself. Perhaps the post-decolonization "succession states," insisting on state sovereignty and security of existing frontiers as the lesser of two legal evils today, could experiment with federalism and pluralism as a means of allowing political self-determination within the state, until such time as they might feel confident enough to allow a completely free choice of other options involving territorial redistribution or reallocation across existing state frontiers.

Problems like the Western Sahara, since the removal of the imperial Spanish element, seem more readily assimilable to "classical" decolonization exercises, and therefore more open to application of classical modes of exercise of the right of self-determination - for example, popular consultation by way of referendum or similar tried and tested popular consultation. The Palestine issue, including both the West Bank and the Occupied Territories, is far more complex because of the superpower interest and involvement on both sides, and should be examined in that context; though it can be said here that it is also strictly a post- decolonization affair, the original act of decolonization having occurred with the termination-in part by force majeure and the pressure of direct action from an original Israeli national self-determination movement-of the British League of Nations-derived mandate in 1948, and the division of the mandated territory and creation, *inter alia*, of the new "succession state" of Israel.

NEW INTERNATIONAL ECONOMIC ORDER

Economic sovereignty or economic self-determination may in contemporary international law terms, be viewed as simply one part of the larger concept of self-determination of peoples, which, in its early nineteenth-century origins in Western laissez-faire liberal thinking on international law and relations, was concentrated on its political outlet and expression only.

Economic affairs, according to laissez-faire scholars, were beyond the domain of the state and organized political society as a whole. Contemporary scientific thinking on international law and relations, both Soviet and Western, would acknowledge, with varying degrees of emphasis and enthusiasm, a necessary and inevitable interrelation between political ideas and economic ideas.

It is not simply the Marxian notion of law as being a mere superstructure of rules and principles erected on an underlying base of the social and economic organization of society. In Western legal thinking at the apogée of laissez-faire influence, at the close of the nineteenth century and early in the twentieth century, a conservative "old Court" majority on the United States Supreme Court could indeed rule, over the strong dissents of Justices Holmes and Brandeis, that legislation on minimum wage and maximum hours of work deprived a worker of his "liberty of contract" and should therefore be struck down as unconstitutional.

However, in more contemporary eras, Western courts and Western political decision makers have been legally sophisticated enough to distinguish between liberty of contract in the abstract and liberty of contract in the concrete, and to recognize the state's right to intervene by legislation to correct economic imbalances in society and to equalize economic opportunities. The increasing political impact of social democratic ideas in Western society in modern times has brought recognition of the close ties between political and economic facts, and the acknowledgment that economic development is a prerequisite to full political expression.

Nevertheless, economic sovereignty or economic self-determination as an imperative principle of contemporary international law, as a matter of history, developed separately and independently of the United Nations Charter and of United Nations practice generally. Woodrow Wilson's Fourteen Points, which provide an intellectual bridge between the nineteenth-century Western liberal postulate of national self-determination and the Charter principles, were silent, to the point of being politically naive or anachronistic, about the basic economic facts of life in international relations.

The historical application of Wilsonian idealism in political self-determination in Central Europe broke up the one stable economic and trading unit then existing and created in its place a myriad of small "succession states" that were quite incapable of existing as viable economic units in their own right. In part because of the inherited intellectual tradition of exclusively political emphasis in the principle of self-determination-in part, no doubt, also because of the prime emphasis on the political-military element in the peace settlement imposed by the ideologically disparate members of the World War II victors' alliance (lest attention to social and economic issues should threaten their already, by war's end, fragile victors' consensus)-the United Nations Charter, as drafted in 1945, largely skirts or avoids economic issues.

The emergence of those economic issues thereafter is part of the historical, dialectical process of development of United Nations law through subsequent legislative acts of the General Assembly and specialized agencies and committees, and through developing custom and practice by way of "conventional" glosses on the Charter. The new economic orientation and objective of the principle of self-determination - a development that is fully compatible with the original Charter preambular formulation-is achieved by a process of development separate from and parallel to the recognition and expansion of political self-determination in United Nations law.

The starting point may be taken as General Assembly Resolution 626 (VII) of December 21, 1952, which recognizes the right of peoples freely to use and exploit their natural wealth and resources, as inherent in their sovereignty; and this principle emerged within the United Nations in direct political response to the Anglo-Iranian oil crisis of 1951, when Iran's premier, Muhammad Mossadegh, nationalized the foreign (British)-owned assets of a British-based multinational oil company then exercising an economic monopoly stranglehold on the production, exporting, and pricing of

Iran's oil resources. This emerging new principle of economic self-determination was continued and extended through General Assembly Resolution 1515 (XV) of December 15, 1960, on the sovereign right of states to dispose of their wealth and natural resources, and General Assembly Resolution 1803 (XVII) of December 14, 1962, on permanent sovereignty over natural resources.

These two major legislative acts, enacted by General Assembly resolution, were the products of the special Commission on Permanent Sovereignty over Natural Resources, itself established by the United Nations General Assembly Resolution 1314 (XIII) of December 12, 1958, and of the continuing debates in the United Nations Economic and Social Council. The rapidly evolving consensus within the Economic and Social Council and in the General Assembly concerning the economic base of international law and relations and international development logically and inevitably led to the three great economic law-making ventures of the early 1970s, which formulated by General Assembly resolutions the Declaration and the Programme of Action for a New International Economic Order, and the Charter of Economic Rights and Duties of States.

The New International Economic Order (NIEO) becomes a political and legal term of art, denoting the drive within the United Nations itself-the leitmotiv of General Assembly international law making for the balance of the 1970s and the early 1980s -to redress the North-South political imbalance in the contemporary world community by economic means, through United Nations "affirmative action" (or "reverse discrimination," to use some current, Western common law, constitutional terminology) on behalf of economically depressed Third World countries.

The trilogy of law-making acts on the New International Economic Order was the product of a working coalition of forces within the General Assembly among a number of groups, some informal and loosely organized and some well-disciplined and cohesive, and in any case overlapping in their membership. Coalition building, which is best achieved through membership and participation in as many as possible of the General Assembly's plurality of alliances and associations, with their assorted political-ideological, cultural-linguistic, economic and trading, regional and geographical criteria, was the key, then as now, to successful law-making ventures within the United Nations.

The de facto alliance on behalf of the New International Economic Order involved the so-called Non-Aligned Countries, originally developed as an Afro-Asian neutralist group trying to establish political disengagement from the two rival political-military blocs, Soviet and Western, of the Cold War era; and the so- called Group of Seventy-Seven, which developed later, had a strong Latin American component, and was concerned primarily with economic questions, especially the renegotiation of original economic ties and contracts with Western industrial countries concerning development and exploitation of primary products and raw materials.

With the expansion of membership in the Group of Seventy-Seven to well over a hundred (the original name was, however, retained), there came an extension of the influence of the Arab-Asian central core of the Non-Aligned Countries' group, as a result of the substantial overlapping of ranks between the two groups. When there are added to these two groups the OPEC countries, Communist China, and the Soviet Union and Soviet bloc, a very powerful and cohesive voting alliance emerges with members who in certain cases are associated with more than one of the different components of the alliance.

On the other hand, the major Western countries, not having membership in any of these various "regional" groupings making up the NIEO alliance, were left isolated, as reluctant participants in a law-making process that they seemed incapable of either defeating or influencing constructively. The declaration and the program of action were adopted, without vote, at the General Assembly's sixth special session in May 1974. The Charter of Economic Rights and Duties of States was adopted by the General Assembly at its twenty-ninth regular annual session in January 1975, by a vote of 120-6, with 10 abstentions. The six negative votes were all cast by Western-bloc countries: Belgium, Denmark, the Federal Republic of Germany, Luxembourg, the United Kingdom, the United States. The ten abstentions were by Western countries, plus two Western-associated countries, Israel and Japan.

The decisions on the three NIEO acts clearly represented a major political defeat for the Western bloc, though part of the Western voting embarrassment can be attributed to confusion over the "consensus rule" as applied at the sixth special session of the General Assembly in May 1974. The Third World countries were certainly annoyed at the decision of major Western countries to accompany their silent acquiescence, in the consensus adoption and enactment of the declaration and the program of action, by the filing of express "reservations" to those documents.

And so the Third World countries were not disposed to compromise in regard to the subsequent Charter of Economic Rights and Duties of States, and their resulting intransigence over that text meant the loss of the votes of the main (Western) countries whose support and cooperation would be sorely needed in the practical implementation of the programmatic approach to a new economic base for international relations. It would hardly be possible to adopt a new economic framework as a basis for a world public order and render it operational as international law-in-action, by legislative fiat alone.

The Charter of Economic Rights and Duties of States, as the product of a coalition of forces within the General Assembly, bears the evidence in a number of places of drafting compromises or exchanges that militate against its overall conception and styling. On the one hand, it follows what may be called the cornucopia approach to legal drafting: when in doubt, put everything in and leave it to subsequent historians to work out why. It also embraces what historically is known as the Weimar Constitution drafting principle: if faced with latent or even patent contradictions in demands pressed in the drafting stage, include them all and hope that the passage of time will resolve the antinomy by disposing of one or the other alternative. Thus the Charter proclaims state sovereignty in unrestrained form in its opening articles:

a. Article 1. Every State has the sovereign and inalienable right to choose its economic system as well as its political, social and cultural systems in accordance with the will of its people, without outside interference, coercion or threat in any form whatsoever.

b. Article 2. (1) Every State has and shall freely exercise full permanent sovereignty, including possession, use and disposal, over all its wealth, natural resources and economic activities. (2) Each State has the right:
    - To regulate and exercise authority over foreign investment within its national jurisdiction in accordance with its laws and regulations and in conformity with its national objectives and priorities....
    - To regulate and supervise the activities of transnational corporations within its national jurisdiction and take measures to ensure that such activities comply with its laws, rules and regulations and conform with its economic and social policies....
    - To nationalize, expropriate or transfer ownership of foreign property, in which case appropriate compensation should be paid by the State adopting such measures, taking into account its relevant laws and regulations and all circumstances that the State considers pertinent....

But the Charter also goes on to apply stern injunctions against any one state's attempt to influence or coerce another state through economic measures.

a. Article 16. (2) No State has the right to promote or encourage investments that may constitute an obstacle to the liberation of a territory occupied by force....

b. Article 18.... In the conduct of international economic relations the developed countries should endeavour to avoid measures having a negative effect on the development of the national economies of the developing countries, as promoted by generalized tariff preferences and other generally agreed differential measures in their favour....

c. Article 32. No State may use or encourage the use of economic, political or any other type of measures to coerce another State in order to obtain from it the subordination of the exercise of its sovereign rights.

Some parts of the Charter are essentially rhetorical proclamations, as with the pronouncement on the elimination of apartheid (Article 16 [1]). Other parts of the Charter are the new "socialist" international law of the late 1950s and the early 1960s, with a postulated duty of the advanced industrial states to make restitution and compensation to other states (Article 16 [1]). There are also specific articles on the Law of the Sea (Article 29) and on international environmental policy (Article 30). The range is very wide, and so the coverage tends to be somewhat diffuse, leaving the impression that the new Charter may be largely hortatory and perhaps intended as such. How, then, is it to be rendered operational, and thus influential or controlling in economic relations between the developed and developing countries, for the future? The problem, as stated, is polycentric, and so must be the answer.

One aspect of making the New International Economic Order operational, as proclaimed in the new Charter, lies in its moral example in providing clear signals to the governments of the main capital-exporting countries, which those governments will then communicate to their own major national corporations (and also multinational corporations effectively controlled by them) as economic guidelines to investment in natural resources discovery and exploitation in Third World countries.

The effect of publication of such economic rules of reason in international law documents like the new Charter may be to discourage or drive away national corporations or multinationals from foreign investments in certain cases, and in that sense might be viewed as counterproductive in terms of the long-term aspirations of the *ad hoc* voting coalitions that produced the enactments in the General Assembly in the first place. On the other hand, more pragmatic business leaders in postindustrial societies may well discover, on examination, that they can adjust quite easily and live with the stipulations in the new Charter, which amount in the end to rules of prudence or economic good citizenship for investors and traders operating in international arenas. This in fact, it may be suggested, is proving- with the aid of calmer counsel from the main Western foreign and trade ministries concerned-to be the case.

A second aspect of the campaign to make the programmatic New International Economic Order genuinely operational lies in the forms of economic direct action that had been initiated even before the NIEO's formal enactment in General Assembly resolutions in 1974. This involves cartel-like action by Third World countries that may happen to control large percentages of the world's assets, in particular, scarce natural resources. The pressures successfully applied by the OPEC cartel after October 1973, for massive increases in world market prices of crude oil, demonstrated the first real solidarity among Third World countries in the use of their control of raw materials as an economic weapon.

They may also have given developing countries a real sense of political power in the world community for the first time. Yet, paradoxically, the oil price increases also exaggerated differences between Third World countries because of those countries' extremely divergent growth rates. No such moves could occur without innocent victims, and the victims-those most affected by the oil price increases - were very poor already. The Western industrial countries might have provided some help, for instance through the oil facility of the IMF, but they clearly preferred to favor their own group within the OECD. The OPEC countries did come to the aid of the poorer countries, but they applied their own system of preferred grading, according to special cultural links, and Arab and Muslim countries seemed to come out ahead in this.

What the OPEC cartel-style action has served to indicate, however, is the practical limits to such collective economic pressure-group activity. Operating for the best part of a decade throughout the 1970s, under the most favorable circumstances, with the seemingly most indispensable of all natural resources, oil, the OPEC countries were eventually beset by drastically falling prices, themselves the product of the drives (which their own cartel-like activities had stimulated) for development of alternative energy sources (including nuclear energy and the revival of the use of technologically outmoded energy sources like coal), for discovery of new oil supplies not controlled by OPEC countries, and for reductions in unnecessary national consumption of energy.

So effective were these responses to the OPEC actions that member countries of OPEC began themselves, covertly or otherwise, to violate OPEC directives as to production quotas and pricing, accelerating the decline in oil prices themselves. If such problems could arise with a world oil cartel, how much more difficult would it be to organize and maintain similar collective Third World economic pressure-group activity on other less essential or less scarce natural resources-mineral or commodity foodstuffs? The conclusion is, and must be, that such primary products cartels, if organized, can be at best only a limited, ancillary or subsidiary weapon for attaining a New International Economic Order.

A politically more promising approach, long-range, might be the extension of the same generic methods successfully employed in achieving the legislative acts on the NIEO in the General Assembly to other United Nations specialized committees or commissions or conferences endowed with a special economic mandate or opportunity. Such an occasion was provided, throughout the decade of the 1970s until the formal signature of its resulting final act or treaty, in December 1982 by the so-called Third United Nations Conference on the Law of the Sea.

This started out as what seemed to be a normal legal codification exercise, but one deliberately kept away from the International Law Commission and even the General Assembly's specialist Sixth (Legal) Committee out of fear that those forums would be dominated by the lawyers of the Big Powers and produce only a conservative restatement of the "old" or classical international Law of the Sea with its presumed inbuilt bias in favor of the Western states that had been politically dominant in the classical Law of the Sea's origins and development.

The Third United Nations Conference on the Law of the Sea, however, soon showed itself to be an important arena for developing and extending the New International Economic Order in application to marine and submarine resources, both fishing and mineral. While more traditional legal issues still received attention, the biggest battles throughout the decade of detailed political and legal negotiations concerned such economic resources and their disposition and control and profit for the future. What was striking, in fact, was the number and range of states ready to abandon over three centuries of *mare liberum* doctrine in favor of a new species of *mare clausum,* in which more and more areas of the sea, its fishing and marine life stocks, and its submarine mineral resources were blocked off and appropriated by individual states.

Only certain types of states continued to maintain the classical international law concept of the sea: the two superpowers, with large military submarine fleets and interests in maintaining a right of over flight for their military aircraft over as much of the sea as possible; states with large merchant marine fleets and therefore a clear and immediate economic interest in preserving existing rights of passage at sea; and states with either no coastal fishing resources of their own or no continental shelf and hence no offshore mineral and related resources to exploit.

The traditional three-mile territorial sea of "classical" international law gave way to a "patrimonial sea" that often extended as far as two hundred miles out from the low-water line along the coast and was recognized and enforced by means of interlocking, usually bilateral accords concluded between states sharing the same special economic interests. Even more dramatic in their impact were the claims advanced for control over the continental shelf, the seabed, and the ocean floor and their resources. Here a clear conflict emerged. The advanced industrial states alone had the scientific- technological capacity to exploit the oil, mineral, and other resources involved and therefore favored a laissez-faire approach, which in theory meant that these resources would be open to all states, but which in practice meant that they would be reserved for the advanced postindustrial states themselves.

On the other hand, the industrially underdeveloped countries, and also the landlocked or coastal states with no continental shelf and thus no offshore mineral resources of their own to exploit, favored "internationalizing," in a special ad hoc UN control authority, the ownership of the resources concerned, the direction and planning of their mining, and the sharing of financial profits on some generally equitable basis. These rival claims were in a certain real sense unbridgeable, except by the sort of exercises in reciprocal give-and-take to which the two superpowers had become accustomed in working out détente. Here, however, the two superpowers were not the two opposing key players, for their interests were often complementary, and the number of players was very much greater.

This and the fact that the differences were much more North-South than East-West in the conventional post-Cold War sense, explained the delay throughout the 1970s in reaching substantial consensus on the content of a new Law of the Sea. The final United Nations Convention of the Law of the Sea, which emerged from the more than a decade of work of the Third United Nations Conference on the Law of the Sea, was signed in Jamaica in December 1982. It extended classical international law's territorial sea to twelve marine miles; established an exclusive economic zone for every coastal state, extending two hundred miles beyond its shores, in which it would have exclusive rights to fish and other marine life; and declared the exclusive right of the coastal state to exploit the oil, gas, and other resources in its continental shelf up to 350 miles from its coast.

The most crucial and politically divisive sections, however, concerned seabed and ocean floor mining beyond these limits. The mineral resources concerned were, in effect, declared-in the words originally employed by Malta's Ambassador Pardo in the General Assembly a number of years before, when the campaign for the new treaty was started-to be "the common heritage of mankind," with a special international seabed authority to administer them, to allocate licenses to mine and to establish mining quotas, and ultimately to determine allocation of profits, and with a special international tribunal to resolve disputes arising under the new convention.

Although 119 states signed the treaty on December 10, 1982, the first day it was open for signature, the United States was conspicuous by its non-signature. In fact, twenty-two countries attended the signing ceremony but did not sign the treaty - among these, as already indicated, the United States, and also the United Kingdom, the Federal Republic of Germany, Italy, Belgium, Japan, the Republic of Korea, and Israel. Twenty-four other countries, which had been invited to attend, did not. As the United Nations legal counsel, Erik Suy, pointed out, however, the 119 signatures constituted a record, in United Nations terms, for the first day that a treaty had been open for signature.

What would the non-signatories do? There were some suggestions that the United States and its predominantly Western or Western-associated cohorts would sign their own "mini-treaty" (in opposition to the official, "maxi-treaty" signed by the 119 states in Jamaica on December 10, 1982), purporting to allow them to carve up the seabed and its mineral resources among themselves; that the United States and others might choose to apply the Jamaica treaty selectively, treating only those parts that suited their own special interests (right of innocent passage through the territorial sea and free passage for military and nonmilitary ships and planes beyond) as normative in legal terms, but choosing to ignore altogether those treaty rules (particularly those as to seabed mining) that they disliked.

The latter approach would have some doctrinal-legal base, of course, insofar as large parts of the Jamaica treaty purported merely to restate classical, customary rules of international law, and these would, of course, be binding in the absence of the treaty and binding on non-signatories too. But such a selective approach was scornfully rejected by signatories to the Jamaica treaty; in the words of a Soviet minister, Mr. Guzhenko, the United States could not pick from a basket of fruits only what it liked.

As for the suggestion that the United States and its Western cohorts would sign their own "mini- treaty" as a purported legal base and authority for acting in defiance of the Jamaica treaty, the president of the conference, Ambassador Tommy Koh of Singapore, indicated politely but firmly that any such action would be promptly challenged before the International Court of Justice. What was striking at the Jamaica signing ceremonies in December 1982 was the new attitude of quiet confidence on the part of the Third World leaders. The realization that they might have committed a major political blunder and isolated themselves by not rallying to the 119 state signatories on the opening day seems to have come belatedly to some of the Western nonsignatories; some indicated discreetly that since the treaty would remain open for signing for two years, there would be time for possible changes or revisions in the convention text before they would need to make a final decision.

A mere codification exercise was transformed over a decade of diplomatic negotiations, into something more-a case study in the elaboration and application, in one major area of world community activity, of the new economic development law. Moreover, the Third United Nations Conference on the Law of the Sea's international law-making process was complemented and extended by another important legal venture. This was supplementing the essentially high-level abstract, general, primary principles of international law as to the New International Economic Order, contained in the General Assembly declaration, program of action, and Charter of 1974-1975, by some more concrete and immediate and secondary or tertiary legal rules and norms.

A project to "operationalize" the international law of the New International Economic Order was launched by several successive General Assembly resolutions. Resolution 166, adopted at the thirty-fifth annual session in the autumn of 1980, requested the United Nations Institute for Training and Research (UNITAR), to "prepare a list of the existing and evolving principles and norms of international law" in this area; to "prepare an analytical study, on the basis of the list referred to"; and to complete it in time for the next, thirty-sixth annual session in the fall of 1981.

The study was continued from the 1981 session by Resolution 107, with a direction to complete the work in time for debate at the thirty-seventh annual session in the autumn of 1982. In fact, UNITAR could make only a partial fulfillment of that mandate by the indicated deadline, the failure being readily attributable to lack of a permanent, qualified research staff and the necessity, in consequence, of organizing work on an ad hoc basis. The preliminary UNITAR report, subtitled "Analytical Papers and Analysis of Texts of Relevant Instruments," limited itself to four postulated principles of international law concerning the NIEO:

- Preferential treatment for developing countries;
- Stabilization of export earnings of developing countries;
- Permanent sovereignty over natural resources;
- Right of every state to benefit from science and technology.

It was indicated that the remaining principles of the NIEO, still to be researched, would be the following:

- Entitlement of developing countries to development assistance;
- Participatory equality of developing countries in international economic relations;
- Common heritage of mankind.

Although the UNITAR research project had extensive recourse to such source materials as resolutions of the General Assembly, bilateral and multilateral agreements, international tribunal decisions, and international arbitral awards, from which to induce its legal rules and norms concerning the NIEO, it was criticized in the debate in the General Assembly's Sixth Committee for a certain apparent superficiality and selectiveness or partiality in its approach to its work. These more obvious deficiencies might be remedied by reaching out to other, more empirically based sources for the follow-up report -for example, as UNITAR itself indicated national court decisions and teachings of the most highly qualified publicists of the various nations, agreements between states and transnational corporations, and national legislation.

A list of "eminent persons representative of all geographical regions," stated to have been consulted by UNITAR in its work, revealed itself on examination to be somewhat heavily Eurocentric in character (particularly weighted toward United States professors), though perhaps this had been done deliberately by UNITAR in order to forestall any criticisms of Third World bias by overcompensating with a patent Eurocentric (here, American) emphasis in the formation of the expert advisory panel. However, there was nothing to suggest that these and other intellectual problems with the research project's planning and development could not be corrected in the future. For the ordinary United Nations historical-dialectical process of elaboration and concretization of principles, through the give-and-take of debate and discussion and compromise in the Sixth Committee and the General Assembly, would undoubtedly follow in the usual way.

4

Debt and Underdevelopment

The 1980s are often referred to (by, among others, the World Bank) as the 'lost decade' for the development of the Third World. The harsh reality behind this euphemism is that for hundreds of millions of the poorest people in the world life is getting steadily worse. James P. Grant, executive director of the United Nations Children's Fund (UNICEF), reports that 'For almost nine hundred million people, approximately one sixth of mankind, the march of human progress has now become a retreat. In many nations, development is being thrown into reverse.'

UNICEF further reports that since the early 1980s Latin America has experienced at least a 10 per cent drop in living standards, and Africa more than a 20 per cent drop. Since these figures are averages the poorer sections of the populations in those continents have inevitably suffered an even greater deterioration in the quality of their lives. In its World Development Report 1990 the World Bank confirms this appalling picture, acknowledging as 'a disaster' that 'The living standards of millions in Latin America are now lower than in the early 1970s. In most of Sub-Saharan Africa living standards have fallen to levels last seen in the 1960s.'

Why are conditions of life in many parts of the Third World getting worse? There are many causes. But fundamentally these causes flow from the weak and disadvantaged position of Third World countries in the world economic and political system. I will argue that in particular the Third World debt crisis plays a major role in obstructing the development of Third World countries by draining them of vital resources and finance. The debt crisis ensures that the poorest people in the world are subsidizing the incomparably richer institutions, such as banks, companies and governments, of the western world.

This chapter has three main purposes. In the first section I give a brief account of how the scale of Third World debt became so huge so rapidly. In the second section I indicate some of the consequences of this debt for the governments and, more importantly, the peoples of the debtor countries. In the third section I consider what should be done about the debt and by whom. I argue that Third World countries would be justified in ceasing the servicing of their debts to the west, but that the best solution to the Third World debt crisis would be for western institutions such as governments and banks to embark upon the wholesale and unconditional cancellation of these debts. While it is recognized that the issues are complex, adequate grounds are given for believing this conclusion to be compelling.

THE GROWTH OF THIRD WORLD DEBT

In 1990 the World Bank estimated that the total accumulated debt of the developing countries was $1,341 billion. The magnitude of this sum is not easy to comprehend. Suppose that it were spread evenly throughout the underdeveloped world. Each person in the Third World would then owe several hundred dollars, which is more than the average wealth production per person in a whole year in many Third World countries. But of course the debt is not evenly spread throughout the underdeveloped world. The burdens it imposes fall particularly heavily upon some countries (especially, but not exclusively, in Africa and Latin America) and upon some people in those countries, as will become clear later.

The total debt of developing countries to western

institutions-such as commercial banks, governments, the International Monetary Fund (IMF) and the World Bank - has grown rapidly. In 1960 it stood at around $18 bn. It more than quadrupled to $75 bn in 1970. The rate of growth accelerated dramatically in the next decade, so that by 1980 the debt had reached $639 bn, more than eight times the 1970 figure. By 1990 this had more than doubled again to $1,341 bn. Thus in three decade's developing country debt had grown to a staggering seventy-four times its size in 1960!

One way of assessing the seriousness of a Third World country's debt is to compare it to the country's annual Gross National Product (GNP). Very many Third World countries, especially in Latin America and Africa, owe more than their annual total production of wealth. For example, in 1989 Argentina, Bolivia, Nigeria and Zambia all owed more than their GNP for that year. Some countries owed more than twice their annual GNP, e.g. Congo, Mauritania and Somalia. And a small number of countries owed even higher multiples of their annual wealth, e.g. Mozambique (nearly five times GNP), Nicaragua (more than six times GNP) and Guyana (more than seven times GNP).

A number of factors have combined to generate the growth of these staggering levels of debt. In the space available I can briefly outline only some of the more important ones. First, there has been a long-term, serious decline in the prices which the export commodities of the Third World can obtain on the world market. Consequently, it has become increasingly difficult for the underdeveloped countries to obtain resources by trade. Commodity prices at the end of 1986 were the lowest in real terms for fifty years. The World Bank estimated in 1988 that by the end of the century prices would rise only modestly. According to the Financial Times, if this estimate is correct then commodity prices will have halved in real terms during the period 1950-2000.

For Africa, the decline in commodity prices has been even sharper. In 1988 the World Bank also calculated that 'a typical basket of African exports now buys a third fewer imports than

10 years ago; if oil exports are excluded, the loss in purchasing power climbs to 50 per cent'. Furthermore, earnings from oil exports also shrank during the 1980s as world oil prices fell. In 1990 the oil exports of Nigeria (Africa's principal oil producer) were worth less than half of what they had been in 1980.

Second, the growing trade protectionism in the advanced capitalist world makes it harder for Third World countries to gain access to markets for their exports. Protectionism is on the increase as governments impose yet more tariffs, quotas, and the like, on the exports of other countries. This hits the Third World particularly hard. The way the system operates greatly hinders Third World countries from earning finance through processing their own natural resources, as Ben Jackson explains:

> The further Third World countries go up the scale of processing, the greater the efforts of rich countries to keep their products out.... Rich countries know they're on to a good thing, and allowing poor countries to do their own processing would threaten their ability to reap most of the profits. The greatest trade barriers put up by rich countries tend to be concentrated on the basic industries which Third World countries can most easily set up to process their natural resources.... Eighty per cent of poor countries' manufactured exports to the European Community are in sectors facing protectionist barriers (and 56 per cent in the United States).

Susan George, drawing upon a 1987 General Agreement on Tariffs and Trade (GATT) report, indicates that a decreasing percentage of the advanced world's imports are coming from the Third World. The result is that 'While less developed countries held 28 per cent of world trade in 1980, by 1986 their share had dropped to 19 per cent.' Once again, Africa is especially hard hit. While comprising approximately 12 per cent of the world's population, its share of world trade had declined to 2.5 per cent by 1990.

The combined effect of the two factors discussed so far has been to diminish the value of Third World exports and to obstruct Third World efforts to maintain export revenues by increasing the volume of exported goods. But simultaneously, the Third World has faced two further pressures. The growth of industrialization and urbanization in many underdeveloped countries, together with improvements in mass communications, has contributed to raising the expectations and aspirations of the poor for a better quality of life. Third World governments have thus come under increasing pressures to satisfy the rising demands of their peoples. Inevitably this has tended to increase the flow of imported goods from the developed world.

Furthermore, the cost to the Third World of imported manufactured goods has steadily increased. For example, when the Organization of Petroleum Exporting Countries (OPEC) substantially raised the price of oil in 1973, and again in 1979, these increases were passed on by companies in the developed world in the form of higher prices of manufactured goods. (Also the oil price rises themselves added to the import bills of those Third World countries - the vast majority - which are oil importers.) An additional factor increasing import costs has been pressure from the IMF upon Third World governments to devalue their currencies. (The effect of such devaluation is to make exports cheaper, but to make imports more expensive.) Often the IMF has insisted upon this (together with other measures which are discussed in the next section) as a condition of providing any financial resources to a Third World country.

Thus the Third World was caught between declining export revenues and increasing import costs. This created a need for finance which western banks became eager to meet. From the early 1970s onwards western banks began substantially to increase their loans to the Third World, especially Latin America. In the belief that 'Countries simply could not go bankrupt' and that a Third World nation could be relied upon to continue servicing its debts, the banks regarded the Third World loan business as highly profitable. Consequently, 'No one wanted to be left out.

Immense effort went into selling loans to the Third World.' Until the late 1970s interest rates were relatively low, and this increased the attractiveness to Third World countries of bank loans. But mostly these loans were commercial arrangements at variable rates of interest. When interest rates rose, as they did from 1977-1981, and (following a brief period of declining rates in the mid-1980s) again in the late 1980s, further debts were piled up for those Third World countries which owed a high proportion of their debts to the banks. Two preliminary conclusions are supported by the evidence and analysis which I have so far presented.

First, the Third World as a whole, and Latin America and Africa in particular, occupies a position of structural weakness in the world economic and political system, in which it is especially vulnerable to the policies of the institutions of the advanced capitalist world regarding such matters as trade and interest rates. Second, the institutions of the advanced capitalist world have reaped many benefits from the weak position of Third World countries. Declining Third World commodity prices, growing trade protectionism to control imports from the Third World, increased prices of manufactured goods exported to the Third World and the development of a profitable Third World loans business have all helped to support the institutions and economies of the advanced capitalist world at the very same time as piling up the financial burden on the Third World.

A final factor in increasing debt which must be considered is the role of Third World governments and political leaders. Undoubtedly they have often contributed to the social and economic crises in their countries. The plight of the peoples over whom they rule has all too often been worsened by errors of political and economic judgement and by outright greed and corruption. But the errors, or crimes, of such governments and leaders are not the primary and fundamental causes of the crises in their Third World countries. This is not, of course, to whitewash the rule of such figures as Somoza, Marcos and Pinochet.

By becoming the willing junior partners to the financial and political leaders of the advanced capitalist world they benefited from the disadvantaged position of their countries in the world economic and political system. But they were not responsible for that weak structural position in the first place. The main cause of the general plight of the Third World, and the debt crisis in particular, is the seriously disadvantaged position of the under-developed countries in the world economic and political system, and the domination of that system by the banks, companies and governments of the advanced capitalist countries in their own interests.

CONSEQUENCES OF THE DEBT FOR THE THIRD WORLD

The consequences of the debt for the countries and peoples of the Third World are devastating. First, a huge amount of resources has to be committed to servicing the debt. For example, according to the World Bank, in the seven years from 1983 to 1989 the developing countries spent in excess of $908 bn just on servicing their debts. Yet in that same period the total debt grew from $893 bn to $1,261 bn.

One reason for the continued growth of the debt despite the colossal level of debt servicing is that many Third World countries were forced to borrow more money, not only for the reasons explained in the previous section, but also in order to be able to continue to service their existing debts. Western banks had been happy to oblige with further loans as long as continued debt servicing remained secure and the loan business remained profitable. Until 1982, when the Mexican government declared a unilateral moratorium on its debt servicing, the Third World loan business was extremely profitable for the banks.

But from 1983 onwards, the commercial banks have grown increasingly reluctant to lend further amounts, as they have become aware of both the problems of Third World countries in maintaining their debt servicing and the popular pressures in the Third World to scale down or even halt such transfers of financial resources to the west. The reduction in the flow of commercial bank lending to the Third World since 1982 had the effect that in 1983 the net transfer of resources in relation to the debt between the developed capitalist countries and the Third World went into reverse. Every year since 1983 the Third World has suffered a huge net financial loss to the institutions of the western world through the mechanisms of debt servicing. The following World Bank figures represent net transfers from developing countries to the developed world solely in relation to debt:

1983 $2.8 bn
1984 $21.7 bn
1985 $36.7 bn
1986 $38.3 bn
1987 $41.3 bn
1988 $42.1 bn
1989 $39.8 bn
1990$27.5bn (projection)

Thus, in relation to their debts the developing countries from 1983 to 1989 transferred to the advanced capitalist world a net total of $223 bn. This is a gigantic transfer of resources from the Third World to the institutions of the developed world. It fully justifies Susan George's judgement that 'Third World debt...is a mechanism by which the poor in the poor countries can be forced to finance the rich in the rich countries.' The above figures indicate that the problem of the debt-related net loss of Third World resources to the west increased each year from 1983 to 1988. Does the slight reduction for 1989, and the more substantial reduction projected for 1990, suggest that the position of the Third World is now beginning to improve? Unfortunately not. It mainly reflects the rapid growth in arrears on debt servicing payments. Total arrears have grown from $27 bn in 1985 to $79 bn in 1989, and are projected to increase still further.

The World Bank points out that for Third World countries there is 'financing implicitly provided by the accumulation of arrears', but despite this reports that it has not led to any increase in investment or growth in those countries which have accumulated arrears. Yet this is hardly surprising. For many countries falling into arrears on their debt servicing, there is not a conscious choice to reallocate those resources elsewhere in the economy, but rather an inability to continue to transfer that level of resources to their creditors.

As it became more difficult, from 1983 onwards, for Third World governments to arrange further loans, they faced the question of how else they could gain the foreign currency needed to maintain debt servicing. Although some expansion of exports took place, for reasons explained in the previous section there were limitations to the progress which was possible. Only two main methods remained. First, the government could commit an increasing proportion of its export earnings to debt servicing. Second, large cuts in imports could be imposed. Many indebted countries now spend a very large proportion of their export earnings on debt servicing. Hard-won foreign currency, which could be spent on development, is instead being sent back to the west. Many Latin American countries spend between a quarter and a half of their export earnings in this way.

For some African countries the problem is as bad or worse. Ghana spends a half of its export earnings on debt servicing, and Algeria more than two-thirds. Only the accumulation of substantial arrears has saved many other African countries from a similar position. Melvyn Westlake has calculated that ten African countries would have to spend four-fifths of their export earnings on debt servicing if they were to meet all of their scheduled payments.

Many Third World countries have also resorted in the 1980s to substantial reductions in imports to save money for debt servicing. For Latin America and the Caribbean as a whole the level of imports in 1980 was regained only in 1989. Some countries in the region (e.g. Brazil, the Third World's biggest debtor) did not even manage this. In sub-Saharan Africa the situation was much worse. In the region as a whole imports in 1989 had still not regained their 1980 level, and for Nigeria, the largest debtor in this group, 1989 imports had collapsed to just over a third of those in 1980.

These two methods of accumulating foreign currency for debt servicing have very similar effects. The expenditure of a large proportion of export earnings on debt servicing rather than imports is entirely unproductive in terms of the development of a Third World country. A good deal of the finance which the country has earned through trading its products is thereby not available to benefit the people of that country but is transferred straight back to the developed world. Similarly, substantial cuts in imports reduce the quality of life of most of the people in a Third World country by depriving them of goods not available from domestic production, e.g. many manufactured products. Additionally, such cuts also hinder the economic and social progress of the country by making it harder to obtain the materials necessary for industrial, agricultural and infrastructural development.

Many Third World governments in difficulties with their debts have sought help from the IMF. In return for its financial assistance the IMF insists upon the government adopting such policies as currency devaluation (discussed earlier), cuts in government spending, privatization of state enterprises, abolition of price controls and the reduction of inflation through cutting domestic consumption (by, for example, increasing taxes and interest rates). A package of such policies, tailored for an individual country, is referred to as an 'adjustment programme'.

The adoption of such a programme by a Third World government at the behest of the IMF not only brings some IMF financial assistance; perhaps more importantly, other institutions such as governments, commercial banks and the World Bank take this as a symbol of the government's financial responsibility, and it can therefore lead to further loans from these sources. However, 'adjustment programme' is another euphemism; in reality it means austerity and privation for the people of a Third World country. This is not a controversial claim. It is acknowledged by no less a person than the managing director of the IMF, Michel Camdessus, when he describes IMF programmes as 'very tough [and] harsh'.

The effects of such programmes are to hold down the standard of living of the country's people through, for example, lower real wages, cuts in government spending on health, education and social programmes, and cuts in subsidies on basic foodstuffs. The results for large sections of the population are rising levels of unemployment, hunger, malnutrition, illness and illiteracy. But as Ben Jackson explains, the burden of all this falls particularly heavily upon women:

[T]he victims of debt are the poor. And within their ranks, women and children suffer most. Women have to cope and devise survival strategies when the country's debt-stricken economy means that household incomes fall and prices rise. Already, women are overstretched by their dual role. They are producers of both goods and services-as farmers, market traders, industrial workers. On top of this they do most of the unpaid household work, like gathering fuel and water (often from far away), caring for children, nursing the sick and managing the household. As debt and austerity programmes bite deeper, the economic pressure on women increases.... Yet at the same time they are expected to fill the gap as carers after health and social service cuts.

The effects of adjustment programmes are examined in detail by UNICEF in The State of the World's Children 1989. The evidence and arguments produced by UNICEF fully confirm Jackson's analysis, as well as highlighting the tragic effects upon Third World children:

As the social effects of adjustment processes become more obvious, it can also be seen that the heaviest burden is falling on the shoulders of those who are least able to sustain it. It is the poor and the vulnerable who are suffering the most.... With some honourable exceptions, the services which have been most radically pruned are health services, free primary education, and food and fuel subsidies-the services on which the poor are most dependent and which they have least opportunity to replace by any other, private, means.... [I]n the 37 poorest nations of the world, spending per head on education has fallen by nearly 50% and on health care by nearly 25% in the last 10 years.... UNICEF's staff knows from first-hand experience that in most countries the real cost of such cuts is being paid, disproportionately, by the poor and by their children.

To conclude this section, the consequences of the debt crisis for the Third World may be briefly summarised as follows. It is not the minority rich elite which bear the burden of debt, but rather the poor majority. It is they who are driven deeper into poverty, hunger and illness. The effects of the debt are particularly severe for Third World women, whose oppression and exploitation are thereby intensified. Finally, the debt crisis bears down especially heavily upon the most vulnerable human beings in the entire world, namely the children of the Third World poor.

PROPOSED SOLUTIONS TO THE DEBT CRISIS

Many ideas and proposals have been put forward as to how the problem of Third World debt should be solved. In this section I will outline and briefly assess eight such proposals. First is the view that Third World countries should continue to service all of their debts, on the grounds that these are contractual obligations which were freely entered into by the governments of such countries. This view was official western policy until 1988. But as arrears of debt servicing payments accumulated, and as economic and social conditions deteriorated in Latin America and Africa, western banks and governments abandoned this policy as no longer feasible.

Before moving on to examine the policy which the west has since adopted it is worth pointing out the chief weakness in this first view. Given the position of structural inequality which Third World countries occupy within the world economic and political system, and their extreme vulnerability to economic and political forces entirely beyond their control, it is quite implausible to claim that most Third World debt was freely entered into. As I explained in the first section of this chapter the debt grew in response to the increasing disadvantages faced by the Third World. The model of two parties on a more or less equal footing freely entering into a mutually binding contract is quite simply inappropriate here.

Since 1988 the new western policy-has been to favour limited debt relief. This was heralded by the Toronto initiative on African debt (1988) and followed by the Brady plan. This second view marks a small step forward in recognizing that even with huge sacrifices many parts of the Third World cannot even meet interest payments on debts, let alone begin to repay the debt itself. In so far as the principle of debt cancellation has been conceded this is to be welcomed.

But great care has been taken in the formulation and implementation of these plans to set stringent limits to the debts to be cancelled. Consequently, only a small fraction of Third World debts has so far been cancelled. In its 1990 survey of the world economy the Financial Times commented that with regard to the Toronto plan on African debt 'the benefits are so small', and as for the Brady plan 'the financial benefits have fallen short of expectations'. This assessment is confirmed by the World Bank's report that the estimated increase in the developing countries' total debt from 1989 to 1990 is 'projected to exceed debt reductions under the Brady Initiative and other programs of debt relief and reduction'. The current plans for debt 'forgiveness' are so modest that far from reducing total Third World debt they are allowing it to increase still further.

The third proposal requiring discussion is that of 'debt-for-equity swaps'. The essential feature of this scheme is that a country pays off part of its debt by transferring the ownership of a share of one or more of its industries to institutions in the advanced capitalist world. Institutions which are owed money by a Third World country, such as commercial banks, or transnational corporations to whom the banks have sold some of the debts they are owed, then acquire property (equity) in the industries of that country. This method of paying debts became increasingly used in the late 1980s, with $9 bn of debt being swapped in 1988.

However, this is a recipe for the loss of Third World financial resources by different means. It is a method by which western institutions can acquire a growing stake in the industries and economies of the Third World (and yet more 'leverage' over how those economies operate). A proportion of the profits made in such Third World industries are then returned to those western institutions according to the size of the stake which they have acquired. Even the World Bank has been moved to sound a muted warning that Third World countries are creating a future problem of growing profit remittances to the developed world. Susan George quite rightly characterizes this method as 'neo-colonialist'.

Instead of running Third World countries by direct political rule, as in colonialism, the interests of governments in the advanced capitalist countries can now be pursued instead by the economic power wielded over the economies of those countries. The fourth proposal for solving problems of debt is 'debt-for-nature swaps'. With this method an organization with a concern for environmental conservation (e.g. the World Wildlife Fund) relieves a Third World government of part of its debt in exchange for that government agreeing to carry out certain conservation projects. For example, in 1987 the Bolivian government was relieved of $650,000 of its debt in return for agreeing to finance and organize the Beni Biosphere Reserve.

One criticism of such swaps is that they ignore, or even violate, the rights of the inhabitants of the area to be conserved. Ailton Krenak, president of the Forest Peoples' Alliance in Latin America, made such a criticism of the Beni Biosphere Reserve agreement, claiming that it had involved 'the most brazen disregard for the rights of the indigenous inhabitants'. He argued that 'Debt for nature swaps put the environmentalist organizations in the position of negotiating with our governments for the future of our homelands.' If, in this particular case, these criticisms are well founded, it does not follow that debt for nature swaps must necessarily ride roughshod over the interests of local peoples. The Co-ordinating Body for the Indigenous

Peoples of the Amazon Basin has put forward debt swap proposals which incorporate recognition of the rights of the indigenous peoples in the Amazon region to maintain their traditional ways of life and manage their own land and resources. (Whether such proposals are agreed by the governments in the region is, however, another matter.)

A more fundamental weakness of the 'debt-for-nature swaps' method is that it has relieved only a minute amount of Third World debt and is projected to save only comparably tiny sums in the future. Therefore, as Ben Jackson argues, there is a serious danger that such projects distract attention away from the prime issue in the debt crisis, namely the urgent need to tackle the problems posed to Third World countries by the massive scale of debt servicing they are expected to carry out. The fifth proposal which I want to consider is that put forward by Susan George in A Fate Worse than Debt. She calls this 'creative reimbursement' or 'debt, development and democracy'. The essential features of her proposal are that Third World countries should pay their debts, but in local currencies rather than those of the creditor nations, and also through 'reimbursement in kind' by which she means the conservation of their natural resources and cultural heritages for the benefit of all humanity.

George recognizes that if western institutions were ever to accept these terms they would be making huge concessions to the Third World. She proposes that in return for these concessions the west should require Third World countries to establish democratic governments, and to achieve greater social equality by implementing a process of development especially aimed at the poorest layers of society. This is a disappointingly weak conclusion for George to come to after the power and incisiveness of her analysis of the debt crisis throughout the rest of the book. Indeed, it is open to a number of serious objections. First, the debt still has to be paid, albeit in a different form.

Therefore, the burden of debt will continue to weigh (if slightly less heavily) upon the peoples of the Third World.

Second, the west retains a coercive relationship to Third World countries by demanding political and social changes from them in return for the concessions made in the forms which repayments may take. As against this, I want to argue that the west has no moral authority to impose this coercion upon the Third World. Very often Third World resources (e.g. tropical rainforests) have been squandered and exploited precisely because of the demands of the developed world (e.g. for debt repayments). Furthermore, the west has supported (and often installed) countless Third World dictators when it has suited the interests of western governments. Iraqi President Saddam Hussein, for example, was backed and armed by the west throughout his eight-year war against Iran.

And when Third World countries have democratically elected governments which are not acceptable to the west (e.g. the Allende government in Chile, the Sandinista government in Nicaragua) leading western governments, such as the United States, have actively sought their downfall, often by illegal means. The idea that the leading governments of the developed western world would have the necessary moral authority to coerce the Third World into the debt, development and democracy strategy is nothing short of preposterous.

George recognizes that in order to achieve her proposed solution considerable public pressure upon western governments would need to be mobilized and 'greater unity among the debtors themselves, would be required. However, I will argue that public pressure in the west, and greater co-operation in the Third World, would be more fruitfully directed at achieving the cancellation of Third World debts rather than their transmutation into a more diplomatic form. Sixth is the idea that individual Third World countries should simply renounce their debts and refuse to pay any further debt servicing. Although understandably attractive to Third World governments in desperate straits this would be a very risky strategy for an individual debtor country to embark upon. Enormous pressures would be imposed by western institutions to bring such a government back into line.

However, the ability of the governments of the advanced capitalist countries to ensure continued debt servicing would be considerably reduced if a number of major debtors were collectively to agree to halt their debt servicing. As we saw earlier, this is already happening in a partial and unplanned way, as the inability to pay leads to accumulating debt servicing arrears. But it has yet to be transformed into a collective, deliberate plan on the part of several major Third World debtors to repudiate their debts (the seventh proposal). The evidence and arguments presented in this chapter strongly support the view that Third World governments would be justified in adopting such a plan.

Their debts add considerably to the structurally disadvantaged position they already occupy in the world economic and political system. They lead to increasing privation and exploitation of Third World peoples, and hinder the economic and social development of Third World countries. Nevertheless, there would still be risks for those Third World governments participating in a collective refusal to repay debts. While the advanced capitalist world would probably not be able to force them back into compliance it could still inflict damaging retaliatory blows on their societies (for example by depriving them of western exports such as medicines and food).

Therefore, a far preferable solution to the Third World debt crisis, if it were possible to achieve it, would be for the governments of the advanced capitalist world to embark upon wholesale and unconditional debt cancellation. That they have a moral obligation to do so follows from the arguments. The debt crisis causes untold suffering in Third World countries, and also obstructs their future development.

The obligation to cancel debts flows from the most minimal requirements of international justice, namely that the poorest and most oppressed people in the world ought not to have their predicament made even worse by institutions with far greater financial resources and political backing. My argument therefore does not depend upon the probability or otherwise that following western debt cancellation Third World governments would redirect financial resources currently spent on debt servicing into the economic and social development of their people. (Some would and others wouldn't.)

The argument turns rather upon the obligation to relieve Third World debtor countries of an unjust burden which currently obstructs their development. While not a sufficient condition for real progress on Third World development, the cancellation of debt is certainly a necessary one. It should be noted that in addition to the plans for limited debt relief discussed earlier, western governments do cancel more substantial debts when in individual cases it suits their purposes.

The United States government cancelled $7 bn of Egyptian debt in return for the Egyptian government's support in the 1991 Gulf War. A further substantial debt write-off came when a group of western governments (the 'Paris Club') cancelled up to $16 bn of Poland's debt in order to assist Poland's transition to a market economy. Debt cancellation can also be offered to a Third World government to pressure it into a course of action in the interests of a western government. For example, in September 1991 the United States government sought to 'persuade' the government of the Philippines to retain a US military base by extending the treaty which expired in that month.

If forthcoming, Philippine agreement 'directly opens the way for funds from the US Treasury that can be used for debt relief. The US will also be influential in securing funding from the International Monetary Fund, World Bank, and the Japanese government.' (However, the Philippine senate decided to resist this pressure and rejected the US proposals.) These types of debt cancellation which are tied to the interests of western governments have little or nothing to do with the real needs of Third World peoples and the pursuit of international justice. Rather, such cancellations pursue the continuing domination of the world economic and political system by the governments of the advanced capitalist countries.

Given the historical record of these governments only the unconditional cancellation of Third World debts, for which

I have argued in this chapter, could begin to free Third World nations from western-imposed obstacles to their economic and social development. One objection often made to proposals for wholesale cancellation of Third World debts is that this would be a traumatic shock to the economies of the advanced capitalist countries. Two points may be made in reply. First, the economies of the advanced capitalist countries are far better placed than those of the Third World to absorb the burden of Third World debt.

The annual production of wealth in the whole of the Third World is less than two-thirds of that in the USA alone! The member states of the Organization for Economic Co-operation and Development (OECD, a grouping of the most advanced capitalist countries) have a combined annual production of wealth which is more than four times greater than that of the Third World. Total Third World debt is approximately 8 per cent of this annual OECD wealth. These startling disparities between the financial resources of the developed and the underdeveloped countries show quite clearly that while total debt is a huge amount relative to Third World resources, it is a very much smaller proportion of the wealth of the advanced capitalist world.

Second, even if it were true that debt cancellation would disrupt the economies of the advanced capitalist countries, this would not show that the Third World should continue to service its debts. Rather it would be yet a further indication of the injustice of a world economic system whose richest members depended on net financial transfers from its poorest ones in order to support their economies. A further objection to wholesale debt cancellation is made by Georges Enderle, one of the very few philosophers to have discussed the ethics of Third World debt. Enderle accepts that 'From the perspective of the industrial countries, a total cancellation could be realized without creating big problems.' Nevertheless he argues that such total cancellation is not ethically justifiable: 'debt cancellation would violate the principle of commutative justice in so far as those debtor governments or population groups who have profited from credit-taking would not have to pay back the debt burden'.

Enderle's argument is flawed in two fundamental ways. First, it is misleading to talk in general terms of debtor governments or populations having benefited from credit-taking. As was explained earlier in this chapter, much Third World debt was incurred simply in order for Third World countries to cope for a little longer with their increasingly disadvantaged position in the world economic system. In retrospect it may have been a short-sighted policy, in that it landed Third World governments with a huge debt servicing burden. However, many Third World governments had little choice but to build up these debts. They were certainly encouraged to do so by the governments of the advanced capitalist countries, who 'bear a heavy responsibility' for the debt crisis.

It is also misleading for Enderle to suggest that debt cancellation would mean that the Third World 'would not have to pay back the debt burden'. Rather, the cancellation of Third World debt would bring to an end a process of repayment which has gone on for more than thirty years. As this chapter has explained, the governments and peoples of the Third World have already repaid vast amounts of finance to the developed world, and are continuing to transfer to the west huge net flows of precious resources each year.

The argument developed so far, that western institutions ought unconditionally to cancel Third World debts, has a practical significance. Given the record of western governments and other institutions it is virtually inconceivable that they would embark upon wholesale, unconditional debt cancellation out of the goodness of their hearts. Enormous pressures would need to be brought to bear upon them to achieve such action. A number of campaigns exist which seek to build up such pressures, and the arguments presented in this chapter can help to strengthen the case which such campaigns advocate.

However, a very large difficulty remains. While the western unconditional cancellation of debt is (I have argued) the preferable solution to the Third World debt crisis, it is scarcely imminent. Realistically, it may take a long time before western governments and banks are pressured into such cancellations on a scale large enough to bring real benefits to the peoples of Third World debtor nations. But the burdens imposed upon the Third World by the debt crisis are far too severe for Third World countries simply to wait for public pressure to bring a change of policy in the west. Granted, then, the unavailability (for the present) of the preferred solution, what can the governments and peoples of the debtor nations do?

In response to this problem, and to conclude this chapter, I will briefly consider the views advanced by Sue Branford and Bernardo Kucinski in the final chapter of The Debt Squads: The US, the Banks and Latin America. They argue that 'Far from having a moral obligation to the creditors to go on paying the debt, the governments of Latin America have a moral obligation to their people to stop paying the debt.' How this obligation should be carried out is, they suggest, a matter on which 'governments must be pragmatic', since the best tactics to adopt in dealing with the west will depend upon the specific circumstances of each debtor country.

In developing their argument Branford and Kucinski draw upon the work of Anatole Kaletsky, who has made one of the most detailed studies to date of Third World government default as a possible response to growing indebtedness. It is impossible to present the details of Kaletsky's analysis here. Briefly, he argues that debtor nations have more options available to them than either continued debt servicing or outright repudiation of their debts. Kaletsky coined the concept of 'conciliatory default' in accordance with which a debtor government would not seek to provoke the west by an explicit repudiation of its debts, but rather would default on some of its debts, particularly those to commercial banks, while adopting a non-provocative and conciliatory manner to other western institutions, especially the governments concerned. By such a method a Third World debtor could avoid uniting its creditors against it:

One of the misconceptions which arise from failing to distinguish between conciliatory default and provocative repudiation is the belief that all the foreign economic interests in a debtor country will unite in boycotting it if it defaults. In reality, they may have no incentive to do so; for a default on medium-term bank debts which was carefully planned and presented in a conciliatory manner could leave unscathed the interests of foreign traders, multinational direct investors, and providers of trade finance.

Kaletsky further argues that the western governments concerned would be unlikely to resort to damaging retaliation in the event of a conciliatory default. He gives a number of reasons for thinking that such retaliation to a conciliatory default would not be in the interests of governments in the advanced capitalist world, e.g. the possibility that western retaliation could provoke an outright repudiation by a Third World government of all of its debts.

Branford and Kucinski argue that Kaletsky's analysis is particularly suited to the predicament of Latin American debtor governments since the majority of their debts are owed to the commercial banks. Therefore, they suggest, a Latin American government could default on its bank debts while maintaining a conciliatory attitude to the western government(s) concerned, and ensuring that the default is 'presented regretfully as a painful necessity, not as a political challenge to the world's financial system'. As long as wholesale, unconditional debt cancellation is not forthcoming from the advanced capitalist governments the method of 'conciliatory default' is perhaps the best option available to those Latin American governments seeking substantial reductions in the burdens which debt imposes on their peoples.

Damaging consequences from retaliatory action by western governments could almost certainly be avoided by skilful deployment of this approach. Is the method of conciliatory default relevant to solving the debt crisis in African countries, where the majority of debt is not to the commercial banks but to western governments and also to international institutions such as the IMF and the World Bank? There may be rather less scope here for defaulting on some debts while maintaining relations with other creditors.

The rapid accumulation of debt servicing arrears in Africa is, in a way, conciliatory default; the debtor nations do not repudiate their debts, they simply cannot afford to pay them. But as noted earlier the scale of arrears so far has been insufficient to ease the burdens imposed by the debt to any substantial extent. Perhaps ways could be devised of applying the method of conciliatory default to the specific circumstances of the African debtor nations, and perhaps these would include the further accumulation of arrears. However, to provide sufficient resources both to benefit the peoples of these countries and to begin to develop their devastated societies will require reductions in debt servicing on a far greater scale than have so far been achieved.

Finally, however successful conciliatory default might be at lessening the burden of debt on Third World countries, as a solution to the Third World debt crisis it is still second best. It reduces rather than ends the servicing of debts. Therefore, it may slow down but it cannot halt the loss of precious resources and hard-won finance which the Third World desperately needs to retain for the benefit of its peoples and the development of their societies. My conclusion is that the unconditional cancellation of Third World debt by the institutions of the advanced capitalist countries must remain the best solution. The initiative for achieving this solution lies with the peoples of the advanced capitalist countries. Through campaigns and struggles in solidarity with the peoples of the Third World, western governments and other institutions must be made to bring the Third World debt crisis to an end with a programme of wholesale and unconditional debt cancellation.

5

Global Justice and the Third World

Approximately 10,000 people starve every day. There was a severe drought last year in Africa and about 20 million people, spread through eighteen countries, face severe shortages of food: shortages that will in some instances bring on starvation and in others, for very many people, will bring about debilitating malnutrition - a malnutrition that sometimes will permanently and seriously damage them. The Brandt Report of 1980 estimates that 800 million people cannot afford an adequate diet.

This means that millions are constantly hungry, that millions suffer from deficiency diseases and from infections that they could resist with a more adequate diet. Approximately 15 million children die each year from the combined effects of malnutrition and infection. In some areas of the world half the children born will die before their fifth birthday. Life for not a few of us in the industrially developed world is indeed, in various ways, grim. But our level of deprivation hardly begins to approximate to the level of poverty and utter misery that nearly 40 per cent of the people in the Third World face.

As Robert McNamara, who is surely no spokesman for the left, put it, there are these masses of 'severely deprived human beings struggling to survive in a set of squalid and degraded circumstances almost beyond the power of sophisticated imaginations and privileged circumstances to conceive'. Human misery is very much concentrated in the southern hemisphere (hereafter 'the South') and by any reasonable standard of justice there is a global imbalance of the benefits and burdens of life - the resources available to people - that calls for an extensive redistribution of resources from the industrial countries of the northern hemisphere ('the North') to the South.

This, of course, assumes that there is something properly called global justice and this, in certain quarters, will be resisted as a mirage or as being an incoherent conception. We can properly speak of justice within a society with a common labour market, but we cannot speak of justice for the world community as a whole. We cannot say, some claim, of the world community as a whole that it is just or unjust. Justice is only possible; the claim goes, where there are common bonds of reciprocity. There are no such bonds between a Taude of Highland New Guinea and a farmer in Manitoba. In general there are no such bonds between people at great distances from each other and with no cultural ties, so, given what justice is, we cannot correctly speak of global justice.

The call for a massive redistribution of resources also assumes, what neo-Malthusians will not grant, namely that we can carry this out without still greater harm resulting. Part of the demand for the redistribution of resources is in the redistribution of food and in the resources (including the technology and the technological know-how) to realize agricultural potential. Neo-Malthusians believe that this redistribution, at least for the worst-off parts of the Third World, is suicidal. It is a moral truism, but for all of that true, that it would be better, if no greater harm would follow from our achieving it, if we had a world in which no one starved and no one suffered from malnutrition.

But, some neo-Malthusians argue, greater harm would in fact follow if starvation were prevented in the really desperate parts of the world, for with the world's extensive population-explosion resulting from improved medicine and the like, the earth, if population growth is not severely checked, will exceed its carrying capacity. An analogy is made with a lifeboat. Suppose the sea is full of desperate swimmers and the only available lifeboat can only take on a certain number. It has, after all, a very definite carrying capacity. If too many are taken on the lifeboat it will swamp and everyone will drown. So the thing is not to go beyond the maximum carrying capacity of the lifeboat.

We are, neo-Malthusians claim, in a similar position vis-à-vis the earth. It is like a lifeboat and if the population goes out of control and gets too large in relation to the carrying capacity of the earth there will be mass starvation and an unsettlement bringing on a suffering vastly exceeding the already terrible suffering that is upon us. Sometimes our choices are between evils and, where this is so, the rational and morally appropriate choice is to choose the lesser evil. It may be true that we may never do evil that good may come, but faced with the choice between two certain evils we should choose the lesser evil.

Better four dead than twenty. But, some neo-Malthusians claim, vis-à-vis famine relief, this is just the terrible situation we are in. Parts of the earth have already, they claim, exceeded their carrying capacity. The population there is too great for the region to yield enough food for its expanding population. Yet it is in the poorer parts of the world that the population continues to swell and, it is terrible but still necessary to recognize, it is the above horrendous situation that we are facing in many parts of the world. Neo-Malthusians maintain that if we do not check this population explosion in a rather drastic way the whole earth will in time be in the desperate position of the Sahel.

Redistributive reform is soft-hearted and soft-headed, encouraging the poor to increase their numbers and with that to increase the sum total of misery in the world. I shall talk about neo-Malthusianism first and then, after I have considered the International Food Order, turn to a consideration of whether we have a coherent conception of global justice. Neo-Malthusianism, I shall argue, is a pseudo-realism making dramatics out of a severe and tragic morality of triage when the facts in the case will not rationally warrant such dramatics-will not warrant in these circumstances a morality of triage. In the first place, while lifeboats have a determinate carrying capacity, we have no clear conception of what this means with respect to the earth.

What population density makes for commodious living is very subjective indeed; technological innovations continually improve crop yield and could do so even more adequately if more scientific effort were set in that direction. Second, for the foreseeable future we have plenty of available fertile land and the agricultural potential adequately to feed a very much larger world population than we actually have. Less than half of the available fertile land of the world is being used for any type of food production. In Africa, for example, as everyone knows, there are severe famine conditions and radical underdevelopment, but African agriculture has been declining for the last twenty years.

Farmers are paid as little as possible; masses of people have gone into the large urban centres where industrialization is going on. Domestic food production is falling while a lot of food is imported at prices that a very large number of people in the Third World cannot afford to pay. Yet Africa has half the unused farm land in the world. If it were only utilized, Africa could readily feed itself and be a large exporter of food. The principal problem is not overpopulation or even drought but man-made problems, problems on which I will elaborate in a moment when I discuss the Postwar International Food Order.

Third, the land that is used is very frequently used in incredibly inefficient ways. The *latifundia* system in Latin America is a case in point. In Latin America as a whole, and by conservative estimates, landless families form 40 per cent of all farm families. One per cent of all farm families control, again by conservative estimates, 50 per cent of all farm land.

This landed elite has incredible power in Latin America and they use this power to keep the peasantry poor, disorganized and dependent. The *latifundia* system is an autocratic system, but - and this is what is most relevant for our purposes - it is also a very inefficient system of agricultural production.

The landowner, not infrequently through his farm manager, has firm control over the running of the farm and over the destinies of his farm labourers. The *latifundios* are very large estates and the land on them is under worked. Much of it is used for pasture. Only 4 per cent of all the land in large estates is actually in crops. There is more fallow land, that is land not even used for pasture but held idle, than there is land in crops. If the *latifundia* land were redistributed to peasants and they were allowed to work it intensively and particularly if they formed into peasant co-operatives, the food production would be increased enormously. Again, it isn't the lack of land or the size of the population that is the problem but the way the land is used.

Fourth, there is the problem of cash crops: crops such as peanuts, strawberries, bananas, mangoes, artichokes, and the like. Key farm land, once used by local residents for subsistence farming, is now used for these cash crops, driving subsistence farmers off the best land into increasingly marginal land and, in many instances, forcing them to purchase food at very high prices, prices they often cannot afford to pay. The result has been increasing malnutrition and starvation and impoverishment. Previously in New Guinea most of the tribal peoples had a reasonably adequate diet. Now, with the incursion of the multinationals and the introduction of cash crops, severe malnutrition is rife.

The good land is used for cash crops and the farming for local consumption is on the marginal land. Mexican peasants, to take another example, did reasonably well on a staple diet of corn and beans. With the advent of multinational food producers, they became a rural, but typically underemployed, proletariat, in one not atypical instance, planting, harvesting and processing in freezing plants strawberries for export and importing food to replace the staple food they had previously grown themselves. The catch was that the food they purchased was typically less nutritious and was at prices they could hardly afford. Again, in those Mexican communities' malnutrition is rife but the principal cause here, just as in New Guinea, is in the socio-economic system and not in droughts or population explosion.

In fine, against neo-Malthusians, it is not the case that the basic cause of famine is the failure of the food supply relative to the population. Rather the basic cause of famine is poverty and certain economic policies. People who are not poor are not hungry. We look at North-South imbalance and it is plain as anything can be that this is the result of the workings of the world economic system and a clear indicator of that is the food economy. A stark difference between North and South is in the vast malnutrition and starvation which are principally a phenomenon of the South. But these famine conditions result from the working of the economic system in allocating the ability of people to acquire goods. As Amartya Sen has shown for the great Bengal famine of 1943-4, a famine in which around 3 million people died, it was not the result of any crop failure or population explosion.

In 1942 there had been an extraordinary harvest but the 1943 crop was only somewhat lower and was in fact higher than the crop of 1941 which was not a famine year. Sen's figures show that the 1943 crop was only 10 per cent less than the average of the five preceding years. Yet 1943 was a famine year of gigantic proportions. Why? The answer lies in people's economic position. People have entitlements to a range of goods that they can acquire. Whether they have such entitlements, whether they can command the goods they need, depends on the workings of the economic system.

Given-to take a current (1983) example - the minimum wage in Brazil (something for which approximately a third of the workforce labours), if that situation persists, many workers will not have the entitlement to the food they need to survive. In fact, right now a day's wage enables them only to command a kilo of beans. They can, that is, only purchase a kilo of beans for a day's work at the minimum wage. So people in such circumstances, understandably, reasonably and indeed rightly, take considerable risks to loot supermarkets and the like. People starve when their entitlements are not sufficiently large to buy the food necessary to keep them alive.

That, to return to Sen's example of the great famine in Bengal, is precisely what happened in Bengal in 1943-4 and is happening again in Brazil and, with greater severity, in a not inconsiderable number of other places. The food available to people is a matter of income distribution and that, in the capitalist system, is fundamentally rooted in their ability to provide services that people in the economy are willing to pay for. In poorer countries for many people about two-thirds of their total income goes for expenditures on food. Where there is some rapid industrialization newly employed workers are likely, with increased entitlements, to spend more on food.

This, under a capitalist system, will force food prices up and it is very likely as a result that the entitlements of very poor agricultural-labourers who own no land and have only their labour power to sell-will fall, until, even with a constant supply of food in their environment, they will no longer be able to purchase food to meet their minimum needs. Where people are on the margin of sustainable life, a famine may be created by such an increase of demand with little or no decline in the food supply.

What we need to recognize is that hunger, malnutrition and famine are fundamentally questions of distribution of income and the entitlements to food. And here, of course, we have plainly questions of justice and, I shall argue below, questions of global justice. But in trying to achieve a moral assessment of what should be done in the face of such extensive starvation and malnutrition, neo-Malthusian accounts are very wide of the mark, principally because of their failure to understand what causes and sustains such misery.

In order to make more perspicuous my discussion of global justice and to make even clearer why we should not regard the starvation and malnutrition facing the South as a matter of actual food shortages caused by or at least exacerbated by population explosion, I want to do a bit of political sociology and describe - an interpretative description if you like-the rise and fall of the Postwar International Food Order. Since the early 1970s the perception of scarcity and disaster because of that scarcity has been a popular refrain of much of our discussion of the world food economy. But this, as I in effect indicated in the previous section, is more ideology than fact. To understand what is going on, we need to come to understand the political economy of food as it was developed after the Second World War in the capitalist world.

The capitalist world, after the last Great War, went from the gold standard to the dollar standard with the United States clearly becoming the preponderant world power. In the 1950s and 1960s, the American state, reflecting plainly the interests of its capitalists, developed a policy of food aid to Third World countries. These were countries which were often trying rapidly to industrialize. This food aid, at one and the same time, provided a lot of cheap food for their new and very inexpensive industrial labour force and a respite for the American farmers with their, relative to the market, overproduction. (We must remember that since the Roosevelt years the farmers had come to be a powerful lobby.)

But it should also be noted that this food aid programme helped turn self-sufficient agrarian countries into economically dependent countries dependent on food aid. It led to a commodification of food and to placing structurally these Third World countries in the commodity exchange system of the capitalist order. The easiest way to see how the postwar food order developed and declined is to chart the fate of wheat in the world economy. In the 1950s and 1960s the surplus in wheat in the United States was sustained both for domestic political reasons and to pull the newly emerging Third World countries firmly into the capitalist orbit. It was an astute way to help make the world safe for the flourishing of capitalism.

Cheap food exported and subsidized from America encouraged in Third World countries the growth, in the process of industrialization, of urban populations. It encouraged, that is, the formation of a proletariat and a lumpenproletariat from a previously peasant population - a proletariat and a lumpenproletariat dependent on cheap food sold to them principally as a commodity. A previously self-sufficient agriculture in Third World countries radically declined and ceased to be self-sufficient. Much of the rural population, in a state of impoverishment, as a huge reserve industrial army, was in effect driven into the cities and in tandem with that, as rural production declined; rural life became ever more impoverished.

Though there were in the 1950s and 1960s great hardships for both the new urban workers and the peasants in the countryside, none the less the system based on the export of cheap food from America worked in some reasonable fashion until the early 1970s. Then it began to come apart. This International Food Order 'encouraged a massive increase in the numbers of people in all countries separated from direct ties to agriculture'. In such a situation an increase in grain prices will trigger an increase in scarcity, though the scarcity is not rooted in what 'can technically be produced but in what people with constant or declining real monetary incomes can buy'.

What we had facing us in the 1960s was an 'extraordinary growth of urban populations - an aspect of proletarianization - and agricultural underdevelopment'. The capitalist rationale for this activity was plain; food aid was intended to assist capitalist development in the Third World while appeasing the farm lobby in America. The thing was to integrate these Third World societies into the capitalist economic system: a system which was becoming a world system. Cheap foreign wheat facilitated this by facilitating the growth of urban populations, but it also contributed to underemployment and poverty in the countryside in these very same countries. But in the 1970s the International Food Order began to break down. Grain surpluses dwindled, prices rose, food aid was cut back.

The food aid programme gradually ceased to have a capitalist rationale. What had happened was that the food aid programme had in the course of time made commercial markets work. By virtue of its very success, food aid became increasingly superfluous from a capitalist perspective. Some of the urban workers could now afford to buy food under market conditions, though many in the urban centres (those marginally employed or unemployed) had the need for the food but in a market system no longer had the entitlement. Similar things obtained for rural farm labourers rotting in the countryside where agricultural production had been cut back.

The difficulty for Third World countries in continuing to get cheap food was exacerbated by the huge Russian-American grain deals of 1972 and 1973. Consumerism and a meat diet American-style became a goal in the Soviet Union and in Eastern Europe. And even though détente is now a thing of the past, or at least temporarily shelved, the grain sales to the Soviet Union still go on. But food aid to the Third World has almost vanished, the western agricultural sector continues to decline, farmers become fewer, now pitted against consumers, and food prices continue to rise so that the many poor in Third World countries lose their entitlements.

Capitalism, of course, needs a workforce that can reproduce it but with newly developed industrial enterprises in the Third World a little starvation and malnutrition will not hurt, will not affect the efficiency of capitalist production, as long as they have, as they indeed have, a huge labour pool to draw upon. Individual workers can starve as long as there are plenty of replacements. Things like this happened with the industrialization of the western world under capitalism in the nineteenth century. It is now being repeated in the Third World in the twentieth century.

GLOBAL JUSTICE AND THE THIRD WORLD

With this sketch of political sociology before us, we can now return to the topic of global justice. There are some who would maintain that talk of justice can only coherently be applied within particular societies or at best between societies similarly situated and in a condition of mutual co-operation.

I want to show why this doctrine is false and why it is quite morally imperative for us to speak of global justice and injustice and to characterize these notions in a perspicuous fashion. Those who would argue against extending justice arguments into a North-South context, and into the international arena generally, will argue that when we talk about what is to be done here we need to recognize that we are beyond the circumstances of justice.

For considerations of justice coherently to arise there must, between the people involved, (a) be a rough equality in the powers and capacities of persons, (b) be a situation where people do co-operate but largely on the basis of reciprocal advantage and (c) be a situation where all parties are in a condition of moderate scarcity. It is, many have argued, only in such circumstances that issues of justice are at home. Only in such circumstances, the claim goes, can we appeal to principles of justice to adjudicate conflicting claims on moderately scarce goods.

For principles of justice to function, there must be enough reciprocity around for people to find some balance of reciprocal advantage. If they cannot find that, they have no basis for regulating their conduct in accordance with the principles of justice. However, if these really are the circumstances of justice, it looks at least as if we can have no global justice, for the richest nations do not seem to be related to the poorest ones in such a way that the rich nations secure a reciprocal advantage if justice is done. It very likely makes more sense for them to go on cruelly exploiting the poor nations as they have done in the past.

There is, in short, in most circumstances at least, little in it for them if they would do what, in circumstances of greater equality, we would uncontroversially say is the just thing to do. The mistake here, I believe, is in sticking with the existence of a skein of actual co-operative reciprocity as essential for the circumstances of justice. The world is certainly not a co-operative scheme. We do not have in place internationally schemes for mutual support. It is even rather far-fetched, given the class nature of our own societies, to regard discrete societies as co-operative partnerships, but certainly the world is not. We do not have in place there the co-operative reciprocal interdependency which, some say, is essential for justice.

However, this condition for the very possibility of justice is too strong. That this is so can be seen from the following considerations. There is a worldwide network of international trade; poor countries stand to rich countries in complex relations of interdependence, indeed in an interdependency relation that places poor countries in a position of dependence. The rich nations, functioning as instruments for gigantic capitalist enterprises, have dominated and exploited underdeveloped countries using their resources and markets on unfair terms. Between North and South - between rich and poor nations - there are conflicts of interest and competing claims under conditions not so far from moderate scarcity such that conditions giving scope for arguments of justice obtain.

In intra-state situations we do not need conditions of actual reciprocity of mutual advantage for issues of justice to be in place. The Australian Aborigine population could be too small, too weak and too marginal to mainstream life in Australia for the non-Aboriginal population to gain any advantage from not seizing their lands and driving them from them without any compensation. But such an action would not only be plainly wrong; it would be grossly unjust. Yet it is quite possible that the non-Aboriginal population would stand to gain rather than lose from such an action. Still, that would not make such an action one whit the less unjust.

What we need to invoke instead is a moral reciprocity not resting on actual schemes of co-operation for mutual advantage but instead on a broadly Kantian conception of moral equality in which justice requires that we all treat each other as equals, namely, we are to treat all people as persons and in doing so treat them as we would reasonably wish to be treated ourselves. In other words, we must, in reasoning justly, be willing to universalize and to engage in role reversal. It does not take much moral imagination for us, if we are relatively privileged members of the so-called First World, to realize that we would not wish to live the marginal existence of many people in the Third World.

We would, that is, not wish to starve or have our children starve or to be in one way or another crippled by malnutrition or live, where this could be avoided, without anything like an adequate education or without adequate housing and the like. We would not accept role reversal here. If our feet, that is, were in their shoes, we would not take as morally tolerable, where such conditions could be avoided and such conditions of life for ourselves. But there is no relevant difference here between us and them. If, in such circumstances, we would not will it for ourselves, we cannot will it for them either.

In the light of our conception of the moral equality of people, we could not accept such inequalities as just. Yet it is just such inequalities that the International Food Order, a deliberate policy objective of the United States, acting for the capitalist order, has brought about in the postwar years. Even given Nozickian notions of justice in rectification, it would be correct to say that many people in Third World countries are not being treated justly. However, the injustice of such an order is even more evident if we develop a conception of justice as fair reciprocity.

People, through conquest, domination and exploitation, have been made worse off than they were before these relations were brought into place. They have been driven into bargains they would not have made if they had not been driven to the wall. They are plainly being coerced and they are surely not being treated as moral equals. If we start with an idea of moral reciprocity in which all human beings are treated as equals, we cannot accept the relations that stand between North and South as something that has even the simulacrum of justice. But any tolerably adequate understanding of what morality requires of us will not allow us to accept anything less than a commitment to relations of moral equality.

Starting from there we can see that global justice is a plain extension of domestic justice when we remember that in the international arena as well as in the domestic arena we stand (a) in conditions of interdependence, (b) in conditions of moderate scarcity (if we pool our resources) and (c) in conditions where our interests sometimes conflict. Moreover, by any plausible principles of global justice we might enunciate, the relations between North and South are so unjust that extensive redistributions of resources are in order. Whatever critical standards we use to regulate conflicting claims over scarce goods, we cannot, if we have any tolerably good knowledge of the facts in the case and a sense of fairness, but think the present relations are unjust and require rectification.

There is not even in the various states of the North a fair access to basic natural and cultural resources, but viewed globally to speak of anything like a fair access to basic natural and cultural resources, where people are being treated as equals, can be nothing but a cruel and rather stupid joke. If we start from a premise of moral equality as the vast majority of social theorists and moral philosophers right across the political spectrum do, from Robert Nozick to G.A. Cohen, we will believe that the interest of everyone matters and matters equally. There is no not believing in that if we believe in moral equality.

For liberal egalitarians, such as Ronald Dworkin, this will involve a commitment to attain, not equality of condition but equality of resources, while for a radical egalitarian it will involve, as well, under conditions of productive abundance, a commitment to try to move as close as we reasonably can to an equality of condition. While rejecting all such egalitarian readings of moral equality, Nozick, with most other philosophers and economists on the right, thinks of moral equality as consisting most essentially in protecting individual rights to non-interference.

Individuals in a just social order must be protected in their rights peacefully to pursue their own interests without interference from government, church or anyone else. Even if the kind of redistribution from North to South I am advocating did not bring about financial hara-kiri for people in the North, it would still involve an interference with their right peacefully to pursue their own interests where they are not harming anyone. Thus such redistribution would still be wrong.

There are at least two responses that should be made here. The first is to assert that such capitalist behaviour has in fact harmed people. Sometimes this has been intentional, often not. But in any event, harm has been done. This is a factual issue, but if the factual descriptions I have given are near to the mark, and particularly if I have accurately described the workings of the International Food Order, the capitalist order centred in the west has indeed harmed, and continues to harm, very deeply many people in the Third World. But in our historical circumstances this is unnecessary for we could have an economic system whose underlying rationale was production to meet human needs and which was controlled democratically.

Moreover, we now have the technical capacity to develop our productive powers so that the needs of people could be met. But the capitalist order has been massively supported in a very large part of the North and a not inconsiderable number of people in the North have been the beneficiaries of a socio-economic order that did so exploit. (Of course, there are others in the North who are just victims of that order.) This being so, even Nozickian notions of justice in rectification would require redistribution between North and South. However, a second response seems to me more fundamental, less puritanical and less concerned with blaming people. To see best what is at issue we should precede rather indirectly. We not only have rights to non-interference, we also have rights to fair co-operation and these rights can conflict.

A very important liberty is the liberty to be able to guide one's own life in accordance with one's own unmystified preferences. Central to liberty is the capacity and opportunity to make rational choices and to be able to act on those rational choices. This is much broader than to construe liberty as simply the absence of restrictions or interference, though it certainly includes that. What is vital to see here is that liberty will not be adequately protected if we limit our rights to the protection of rights to non-interference.

We must also give central weight to the rights of fair cooperation. If the right of all to effective participation in government and, more generally, to effective direction of their lives is to be attained, there must be in place in our social organizations a respect for the right of everyone to fair cooperation. It is, of course, evident that respect for this right is not very widespread in the world. It will not only not be in place where there is subordination and domination; it will also not be effective where there is widespread starvation, malnutrition, exploitation and ignorance. What is unavoidable is that in class-based societies rights to fair co-operation and rights to non-interference will conflict.

To move towards correcting the imbalances between North and South, we will have to move to a collective ownership and control of the means of production, for otherwise economic power becomes concentrated in the hands of a few and they will dominate and exploit others. But moving to collective ownership will in turn have the effect of overriding the rights to non-interference of Horatio Alger types who, capitalistically inclined, seek to acquire productive property through hard work and honest bargains. (It is hardly accurate or fair to say that there are no capitalists like that, particularly small capitalists.) In following their entirely peaceful interests - they have no wish to dominate or impoverish anyone - they wish to invest, buy and sell, and own productive property.

If we are to protect their rights to non-interference, these activities can hardly be stopped, but if they are allowed to go on, the institutional stage is set, whatever the particular agent's own inclinations may be, for the undermining of rights to fair co-operation. So we have a fundamental clash of rights: rights of non-subordination with rights to non-interference. To overcome the great disparities between North and South, even to put an end to the conditions of immiseration in the South - starvation, malnutrition, lack of work, extreme poverty - there would have to be significant and varied redistribution from

North to South. In doing this we would have to give rather more weight to the rights of fair co-operation than to rights of non - interference. But - and here is what is alleged to be the catch-there is no significant consensus concerning which rights are to be overriding when they conflict.

There would be a consensus if we came to command a clear view of these rights and their relations, along with some other powerful moral considerations, and came, as well, to command a clear view of the relevant social realities. Surely people have a right to pursue their interests without interference. But there are interests and interests. (Indeed, rights are most paradigmatically linked to our vital interests.) There is, among these interests, our interest in maintaining our bodily and moral integrity.

To require, for example, that a person (say, a quite ordinary person), quite against her wishes, donate a kidney to keep someone alive whose value to the society is extensive is, that fact notwithstanding, still an intolerable intrusion on that involuntary donor's bodily integrity; to require a person to give up her religion or political convictions to enhance social harmony or even peace is another intolerable intrusion in that person's life - it simple runs roughshod over her civil liberties. But the interference with the peaceful pursuit of a person's interests that would go with a collective ownership of the means of production would not touch such vital interests. Rather what would be touched is her freedom to buy and sell, to invest and to bequeath productive property.

But these interests are not nearly as vital as the above type of interests which genuinely are vital for our personal integrity. When the price for overriding those less vital interests is, as it is in the North-South situation, the overcoming of starvation, malnutrition, domination, subordination, great poverty and ignorance (certainly vital interests for any person), there is no serious doubt about in which direction the trade-offs should go. That there is not a massive consensus about this results, I believe, not from deeply embedded moral differences between people but from disputes or at least from different beliefs about what is in fact the case and about what in fact can come to be the case. Ideological mystification leads us to believe that there is nothing significant that could be done about these matters or nothing that could be done short of impoverishing us all or undermining our civil liberties. But that is just ideological mystification.

REDISTRIBUTION VERSUS CAPITALISM

So we know that from the moral point of view, justice, or at least humanity, requires an extensive redistribution between North and South. We also know, if we have anything of a sense of realpolitik, that nothing like this is going to happen within the present socio-economic order. We can, as I have tried to indicate, know something of what morality requires here, but what is far more important to know, and much less obvious, is what are the mechanisms by which this conception of moral requiredness can become a reality in the lives of people so that our societies can be turned around. You may think that what I am about to say is too *parti pris* or perhaps you will even believe it to be vulgar, but it seems to me to be plainly true all that notwithstanding. And, even if it is vulgar, it is better to say something which if true is importantly true than to be evasive out of a sense of nicety or out of fear of saying something obvious.

What I think is plainly true is this: our capitalist masters, in principal control of the consciousness industry, have a plain interest in maintaining something not very different from the present North-South state of affairs. To stabilize things they might, in certain circumstances, where they envisage a threat, favour some minor redistribution of wealth, but it would be very much against their interests, and that of a tiny stratum beholden to them, to make any extensive redistributions - redistributions that would touch their secure power base. Capitalism requires, and indeed can accept, at most a somewhat improved and more efficient version of the present and that, in turn, requires great injustice and inhumanity. It could only marginally improve our lot.

A necessary but not a sufficient condition for attaining the end of such global injustice and inhumanity is the shedding of capitalism. As long, that is, as we live in a capitalist system, we are going to have such injustices. At most we might lessen their severity a bit. If we are morally serious and not ideologically blinkered, we will realize that it is our central social task to get rid of capitalism. But concretely how this is to be done, given capitalist dominance in western industrial societies, is anything but obvious. (This is exacerbated by the technological sophistication of these societies - by their awesome means of surveillance and control.)

However, that the way or the ways are not obvious does not mean, if our efforts are over the long haul, that it cannot be done or that we should settle, as many do, for some reformist tinkering inside bourgeois parameters. We are not going to get justice or even a reign of common humanity that way. Recognizing that there are no quick fixes, we need to continue to struggle, without hiding from ourselves the sobering and indeed depressing recognition that things are probably going to get much worse before they get better.

6

Active International Cooperation

The doctrine of "peaceful coexistence" was the leitmotiv of Soviet foreign policy after the de-Stalinization campaign officially began in 1956, when Premier Khrushchev's accession to political leadership in the Soviet Union. In his address to the 22nd Congress of the Communist Party on 17 October 1961, Premier Khrushchev assured his audience of top-level Soviet decision makers that the principles of peaceful coexistence which he attributed to Lenin, had "always been the central feature of Soviet foreign policy." Premier Khrushchev coupled his remarks on peaceful coexistence with a call for more extensive business relations with all countries, including Britain, France, Italy, West Germany, and other West European countries.

Peaceful coexistence and peaceful economic competition, as identified by Premier Khrushchev, were thus ordinarily seen as the two major elements in the post-Stalin Soviet diplomatic and political offensive in the West and in the neutralist third world. Apart from its significance in what might be called the polemics of Soviet-Western relations during the Khrushchev era, the subject of peaceful coexistence had been on the agenda and had also been extensively debated at all the biennial reunions, since 1956, of the International Law Association — a worldwide, scientific association of international lawyers that had managed to transcend the ideological frontiers of the communist and capitalist blocs

6

Active International Cooperation

The doctrine of "peaceful coexistence" was the leitmotiv of Soviet foreign policy after the de-Stalinization campaign officially began in 1956, when Premier Khrushchev assumed political leadership in the Soviet Union. In his address to the 22nd Congress of the Communist Party on 17 October 1961, Premier Khrushchev assured his audience of top-level, Soviet decision makers that the principles of peaceful coexistence, which he attributed to Lenin, had "always been the central feature of Soviet foreign policy." Premier Khrushchev coupled his remarks on peaceful coexistence with a call for more extensive business relations with all countries, including Britain, France, Italy, West Germany, and other West European countries.

Peaceful coexistence and peaceful economic competition, as identified by Premier Khrushchev, were thus firmly linked as the two major elements in the post-Stalin, Soviet diplomatic and political offensive in the West and in the neutralist third world. Apart from its significance in what might be called the polemics of Soviet-Western relations during the Khrushchev era, the subject of peaceful coexistence had been on the agenda and had also been extensively debated at all the biennial reunions, since 1956, of the International Law Association - a worldwide, scientific association of international lawyers that had managed to transcend the ideological frontiers of the communist and capitalist blocs.

Beyond this, the United Nations General Assembly included peaceful coexistence on its agenda at its seventeenth session in the fall of 1962, albeit under the somewhat inelegant, Western-sponsored euphemism "friendly relations and cooperation among states." Under this same title, peaceful coexistence was debated exhaustively at every regular session of the UN General Assembly thereafter. In December 1963, friendly relations (coexistence) was given the UN's official imprimatur and institutionalized with the creation, pursuant to a General Assembly resolution, of a twenty-seven country (later thirty-one country) Special Committee charged with the "progressive development and codification" of what were essentially the original four principles specified in the Soviet Union's list of principles of peaceful coexistence.

In terms of the internal workings of the United Nations and its specialized committees and agencies, the debate over friendly relations (coexistence) could hardly have come at a better time. In 1960-61, when the matter was initiated in the Sixth (Legal) Committee of the General Assembly, that Committee had very little to do. The prestigious International Law Commission which it was the nominal responsibility of the Sixth Committee to oversee, was fully occupied with the necessarily slow codification of highly technical areas like the law of the sea, and diplomatic and consular relations.

There was a certain natural impatience on the part of the "new" countries with these more traditional processes of progressive development of law; joined with the Soviet bloc pressures for codification of peaceful coexistence, this gave a certain momentum to the work of the General Assembly's Special Committee, which was directed to the elaboration of the detailed, concrete, secondary principles that alone could give meaning to the abstract generality of the concept of coexistence. It must be noted that, even in Soviet juristic thinking, peaceful coexistence always had a somewhat ambivalent character. Thus, in January 1961, some months before his address to the 22nd Congress of the Communist Party, Premier Khrushchev explained the policy of peaceful coexistence to a Soviet audience as being no more than a "form of intensive economic, political and ideological struggle of the proletariat against the aggressive forces of imperialism in the international arena."

Here, Premier Khrushchev may have been appealing to that hard-line, neo-Stalinist remnant of Soviet juristic thinking that would use peaceful coexistence as no more than a convenient camouflage for achieving "proletarian internationalism" in the special sense of coordinated world revolution - in effect, using it as a sort of "Trojan horse" to lull Western suspicions while the Soviet Union proceeded quietly with preparations (again, in one of Premier Khrushchev's colourful phrases) "to bury the West." In its development in Premier Khrushchev's own personal thinking, however, as evidenced in the empirical record of Soviet foreign policy-in-action, peaceful coexistence increasingly took on the aspect of a somewhat static, even reactionary doctrine - redolent of Metternich and the post-Congress of Vienna "Holy Alliance" attempts to stifle political liberalism and political change in the name of "legitimacy."

In effect, Soviet foreign policy in this era became increasingly interested in the possibility, by bilateral arrangements or understandings with the West, of consecrating the political and military balance of power in the world as a formal juridical condition. For peaceful coexistence, in this sense, would amount to a virtual legitimation of the political and military status quo of the cold war era. Insofar as it would accept the factual cold war division of the world into the two great military blocs dominated by the Soviet Union and the United States, it would necessarily concede general control and responsibility by each bloc leader over its own sphere of influence.

It would further proclaim a principle of non-interference by either the Soviet Union or the United States in the other's bloc, however great the temptation to profit by the other side's difficulties, and however great the moral anguish at not being able to intervene in specific cases. We had this demonstrated most dramatically, as far as the West was concerned, in the frustrations of the West's own, self-imposed restraint in the Berlin and East German riots of 1953, and in the events in Hungary in the fall of 1956. By the same token, Premier Khrushchev must have experienced some of the West's bitter frustration over Berlin and Hungary in the circumstances surrounding the Soviet Union's withdrawal in the fall of 1962 - once President Kennedy had responded resolutely - from its Cuban adventure.

This is what was meant, in the somewhat cynical cold war vernacular of the time, by a Soviet-Western understanding to "balance" Hungary and Cuba. There was a significant development in Soviet-Western "friendly relations" in the years following the peaceful resolution of the Cuban missile crisis. While the standard Western interpretation of the Soviet approach to "peaceful coexistence" had once been the hard-line interpretation, by the middle 1960s it was fairly generally accepted among Western jurists that a working détente had developed between the Soviet Union and the West, and that it was worthwhile to take part in its further elaboration and concretization.

Looking back, it may now seem surprising that issues of nomenclature and the quarrel over peaceful coexistence versus friendly relations as the preferred legal "term of art" could loom so large in the mutually cautious approach to East-West détente. Writing to the author a few years after those bitter debates over words, Lord McNair remarked how the term "peaceful coexistence," once anathema to Western foreign ministries, had begun to lose its controversial quality. Part of the credit for this change must go to Western lawyers - particularly the "legal laymen," the university professors and practicing lawyers outside the various national foreign ministries' specialized legal departments - who refused to be constrained by traditional official positions.

In the various professional and scientific arenas for interaction between Soviet and Western lawyers in the late 1950s and early 1960s, Western lawyers pressed their Soviet counterparts to be specific, and to discuss actual problem-situations; it was not enough to talk of coexistence in cloudy generalities. Western lawyers suggested that the Soviet-Western legal dialogue could only be conducted usefully by eschewing bitter and largely futile debate over political ideology, and concentrating on current tensions in Soviet-Western relations together with the immediate range of practical solutions.

Here was the genesis of that step-by-step approach to Soviet-Western conflicts that was to be so strikingly vindicated a year later, by its direct employment to achieve the Moscow Partial Test Ban Treaty of August 1963. This same scientific method was accepted in a quiet, de facto manner by Soviet jurists (including the then Principal Legal Adviser to the Soviet Foreign Ministry, the very able and balanced Professor Gregory Tunkin), in place of the old-line, a priori, absolutist approach that had stressed the resolution of Soviet-Western conflicts through one comprehensive, law-making act that set out a universal, general code of principles of peaceful coexistence.

Their acceptance for the first time really permitted cooperative, Soviet-Western scientific effort towards the ending of the cold war and the relief of international tensions in practical ways. The emphasis on concrete problem solving, and the practical breakthrough achieved by replacing ideological debate with empirical methods, call attention to the fact that in the more technical, scientific areas, Soviet-Western cooperation (or at least recognition of common interests) had always been present - even before the political détente of Premier Khrushchev and President Kennedy.

We might even say that the most promising route to genuine Soviet-Western cooperation, transcending the somewhat negative condition of coexistence inaugurated by political détente, is through the approach to technical, scientific problems. For here the record suggests that the more demanding and difficult the problem, in scientific terms, the greater Soviet and Western reciprocity of interest is likely to be. It is the scientists themselves (construing this term in the broadest sense to include social scientists) who are best equipped, on both sides, to secure fundamental Soviet-Western understandings in these areas, since they are less bothered by the ideological preconceptions and a priori moral judgments that have generally so preoccupied or frustrated professional diplomats in the past.

This proposition can be illustrated by the substantial practical success of Soviet-Western scientific problem solving in concrete cases. We can examine and assess the record shortly. In the meantime, it is worth nothing that the problem-solving approach carries its own internal momentum, and at a certain point lends itself to the induction of general principles on a thoroughly empirical basis. In contrast the essentially a priori approach, with its emphasis on abstract principles, will often lag badly behind actual problem-situations and get caught up in largely sterile ideological debates.

The UN Special Committee on Friendly Relations, after the first enthusiastic response from Soviet bloc and third world countries following its formation in 1963, ran into seemingly endless difficulties in rendering precise and operational what was, in essence, a set of rather vague propositions replete with semantic confusions. Then, something rather strange began to occur. The original proponent of formal codification of peaceful coexistence, the Soviet Union, seemed to lose interest in the work of the Special Committee as Soviet differences with the West were resolved in concrete cases. As Soviet involvement in the Special Committee seemed to decline, Western foreign ministries could hardly see the need for continuing Western response.

The Committee's labours continued, however. The main political initiatives and the intellectual dynamism were supplied by jurists from politically more neutral, "middle" countries or from the third world. Some of these, like Milan Bartos of Yugoslavia, saw in the friendly relations exercise not simply a convenient vehicle for détente for the two bloc leaders, but also a juridical device which, imaginatively used, could help the cause of self-determination and pluralism within the blocs.

"Why not coexistence inside the blocs?" asked the Yugoslavs. By the same token, imaginative third world jurists like Krishna Rao of India saw in the elaboration and extension of the principles of friendly relations (coexistence) the practical possibility of protecting non-aligned, neutralist countries from big power "hegemony" - whether Soviet, or American, or even that joint (Soviet and American) condominium form of hegemony that seemed presaged as differences shaded off between the two bloc leaders.

The Special Committee finally completed its task in 1970, and its work is recorded in the Declaration on Principles of International Law concerning Friendly Relations and Cooperation among States in accordance with the Charter of the United Nations, embodied in a UN General Assembly resolution of October 1970. The Declaration enshrines seven principles, which can be briefly summarized as follows:

1. The duty of states to refrain from the threat or use of force against the territorial integrity or political independence of any state;
2. The duty of states to settle their international disputes by peaceful means;
3. The duty not to intervene in matters within the domestic jurisdiction of any state;
4. The duty of states to cooperate with one another;
5. The principle of equal rights and self-determination of peoples;
6. The principle of sovereign equality of states;
7. The duty of states to fulfill in good faith the obligations assumed by them in accordance with the Charter.

What did it all achieve? On first sight, the Declaration seems as abstract - some might unkindly say, as vacuous - as the original Soviet list of principles of peaceful coexistence from which it emerged a decade and a half later. An American delegate, unconsciously reflecting Southey's musings on the Battle of Blenheim that it was, after all, "a famous victory," publicly hailed it as "one of the major achievements of the

Twenty-Fifth Anniversary of the United Nations." He suggested that in his own and other countries' foreign ministries, legal advisers' perceptions of the issues had been "clarified and sharpened" in the whole process. That, perhaps, is the key.

When the Declaration was finally achieved in 1970, it had become a somewhat irrelevant footnote to historical changes long since established by more prosaic, essentially problem-oriented methods. But the process of negotiation between East and West (with some interesting neutralist and third world input, particularly towards the end), that lasted over a decade and was necessarily conducted in an intellectually disciplined way in yet another institutionalized international arena, may have helped in softening rival doctrinal positions that had been taken too categorically in the first place. In the end, détente was achieved progressively and empirically, prior to and without the necessity of the formalized Declaration of 1970.

To return to the problem-oriented approach with emphasis, now, on the area of science and technology, we may consider the quite substantial practical achievements in Soviet-Western cooperation - in highly technical areas demanding high technical skills - at times when, at a more strictly political level, further progress in ameliorating Soviet-Western relations might not have seemed very promising. First, the problem of the peaceful exploration and development of Antarctica. The United States Department of State, realizing the danger of international conflict caused by the welter of rival national claims in Antarctica, had taken the diplomatic initiative in 1948 and proposed to the countries then having competing claims to territorial sovereignty in Antarctica - Argentina, Chile, France, Norway, Great Britain, Australia and New Zealand - the desirability of calling an international conference looking towards possible internationalization of Antarctica.

The reaction of the seven states, however, was generally hostile to any surrender of national claims, and so the matter had to be dropped. At this stage, the Soviet Union came into the picture for the first time, demanding full participation in any Antarctic settlement. The US State Department had not, of course, included the Soviet Union in its list of interested states - 1948 being the year, by most counts, of the inception of the cold war. Following the Soviet bid, matters were allowed to drift for some years, though India proposed the question of Antarctica for discussion at the UN General Assembly in the fall of 1956.

The maturing of plans for International Geophysical Year brought Antarctica back as a subject for international scientific discussion, however, and also brought full-scale Soviet involvement. International Geophysical Year (1958), or ICY, was planned and administered by a special committee of the International Council of Scientific Unions. Though in some countries, particularly those of the Soviet bloc, scientific societies and academies are wholly or partly government controlled, the emphasis of the Council has been so clearly scientific that in the view of competent Western observers, it has been able to preserve a relatively independent, non-governmental character.

The Antarctic figured prominently in the Council's programme for IGY right from the outset. Regional conferences on the Antarctic, in connection with IGY, were held from 1955 onwards, with the Soviet Union sending official delegates and taking a leading part throughout. There was genuine concern, at the time, that the cold war might be extended to the South Pole, particularly since the Soviet Union had been assigned base sites and IGY responsibilities in the territorial sector of Antarctica claimed by Australia. During this period, governments were being urged from many sides to take steps to assure their own national claims in Antarctica; at the same time, there remained the countervailing scientifically based interests in maintaining freedom of inquiry in the Antarctic continent.

The IGY, in this sense, was a scientist-conceived and scientist-developed programme, operating under the clear understanding of all the scientists from the various national groups - Soviet bloc, Western, and "uncommitted" - that all activities conducted during IGY would be politically neutral in the sense of involving absolutely no ruling, one way or another, on the legal character of existing claims to territorial sovereignty in Antarctica. While it clearly would have been possible, legally, to conclude a final settlement of the political status of Antarctica prior to the Soviet participation in IGY, limited to Western countries that alone had international law-based territorial claims in that region, any such agreement was politically impossible because of the welter of competing Western claims and the mutual intransigence of those same Western countries in what was, after all, a non-cold war issue.

After Soviet participation in IGY, any future Antarctic régime that would exclude the Soviet Union had clearly become politically, if not indeed legally, impossible. The next political moves concerning Antarctica were clearly designed to build upon the era of inter-systems good feeling that had permeated the multinational effort in Antarctica during IGY. Some months prior to the termination of IGY, President Eisenhower foreshadowed a dramatically new approach to regulation of the Antarctic continent. In the American President's own words:

> The United States is dedicated to the principle that the vast uninhabited wastes of Antarctica shall be used only for peaceful purposes. We do not want Antarctica to become an object of political conflict.... We propose that Antarctica shall be open to all nations to conduct scientific or other peaceful activities there. We also propose that joint administrative arrangements be worked out....

President Eisenhower then proceeded to invite a group of twelve countries including all existing territorial claimants to Antarctica, plus the Soviet Union, and finally also Japan (which had itself formally renounced any territorial pretensions to Antarctica in the World War II Peace Treaty of 1951), to take part in an international conference in Washington designed to permit a direct transition from IGY to a new international régime in Antarctica. Some fifteen months of discussions then ensued, characterized by the same inter-systems cooperation that had been so notable throughout IGY. The chief Soviet delegate, Mr. Kuznetsov, expressed from the outset the Soviet Union's interest in settling the régime for Antarctica on an international basis. The final outcome of the conference was the Antarctic Treaty, signed in Washington on 1 December 1959.

The preamble to the new treaty expressly noted both the "substantial contributions to scientific knowledge resulting from international cooperation in scientific investigation in Antarctica," and the "establishment of a firm foundation for the continuation and development of such cooperation on the basis of freedom of scientific investigation in Antarctica as applied during the International Geophysical Year."

The key operational provisions of the Antarctic Treaty of 1959, for present purposes, are Articles 1, 3, 5 and 7. Article 1 provided:

Antarctica shall be used for peaceful purposes only. There shall be prohibited, *inter alia*, any measures of a military nature, such as the establishment of military bases and fortifications, the carrying out of military manoeuvres, as well as the testing of any type of weapons.

Article 5, in the same spirit (and anticipating by four years the Moscow Partial Test Ban Treaty of 1963), declared:

Any nuclear explosions in Antarctica and the disposal there of radioactive waste material shall be prohibited.

It was in Article 3 of the treaty, however, that the positive spirit of international, scientific cooperation, so successfully established in International Geophysical Year, was captured and extended. Article 3 provided for the exchange of information regarding plans for scientific programmes in Antarctica; for the exchange of scientific personnel between different national expeditions and stations in Antarctica; and for the exchange of scientific observations and the results of scientific investigation and research.

This was concretely followed up in Article 7, which provided for the designation of national observers, with authority to carry out detailed inspections of all areas of Antartica, including all stations, installations and equipment, and all ships and aircraft. Article 7, which also permitted aerial observations, was designed to ensure the proper carrying out of the provisions of the treaty. It remains to say that the Antarctic Treaty remains in full operation to this day, without any serious complaint as to violation of its terms or essential spirit.

The patterns of concrete, Soviet-Western cooperation in a technical, scientific area where Soviet and Western long-range interests were essentially the same, were followed four years later in the successful Soviet-Western negotiations leading to the conclusion of the Moscow Test Ban Treaty of August 1963. We have already discussed the Moscow Test Ban Treaty above. It is only necessary to note, in passing, that while the Khrushchev-Kennedy détente may have provided the political opportunity for discussing the banning of nuclear weapon tests, it was the weight of scientific evidence on both sides concerning their danger to human life that succeeded in communicating a special sense of urgency to the political leaders' attempt to reach a firm Soviet-Western agreement.

The common danger that acknowledged no ideological frontier, and was amply attested to by scientists from both main ideological systems, thus led inevitably to common acceptance of the control of nuclear weapon testing in the form of a firm international legal accord resting on the inter-systems consensus. The Moscow Test Ban Treaty of August 1963 had dealt tangentially with the peaceful regulation of outer space, insofar as its ban on nuclear weapon testing extended to outer space.

In January 1967, agreement was finally reached on a comprehensive treaty governing the peaceful regulation of outer space and space exploration. The text of the treaty had been worked out in the United Nations Committee on the Peaceful Uses of Outer Space, and in its expert legal subcommittee headed by Polish jurist Manfred Lachs. The immediate negotiations leading to the treaty lasted almost six months at the United Nations. They had been preceded by years of difficulty, and by protracted and seemingly fruitless discussions between lawyers and scientific experts from the Soviet Union, the United States, and other countries.

Agreement, however, had become certain - barring, of course, any major unexpected political development marring Soviet-United States relations, such as a marked or unexpected step-up in American military involvement in Vietnam - in June 1966 when, within a day of each other, first the Soviet Union and then the United States filed with the Secretary-General of the United Nations almost identical texts for a draft treaty on space. The Soviet version was for a treaty "On principles governing the activities of States in the exploration and use of Outer Space. The Moon and other Celestial Bodies," while the American version was for a treaty "governing the exploration of the Moon and other Celestial Bodies."

The final text, as approved by the UN Committee and then, formally, by the UN General Assembly, declared in its opening Article:

The exploration and use of Outer Space, including the moon and other celestial bodies, shall be carried out for the benefit and in the interests of all countries, irrespective of their degree of economic or scientific development.

The same article went on to affirm: "Outer Space, including the moon and other celestial bodies, shall be free for exploration and use by all states without discrimination of any kind." and that "there shall be free access to all areas of celestial bodies." and "freedom of scientific investigation in Outer Space."

The main operative provisions of the new treaty were contained, however, in two articles. Article 2 proclaimed:

Outer Space, including the moon and other celestial bodies, is not subject to national appropriation by claim of sovereignty, by means of use or occupation, or by any other means.

Article 4 read as follows:

States/parties to the treaty undertake not to place in orbit around the earth any objects carrying nuclear weapons or any other kinds of weapons of mass destruction, install such weapons on celestial bodies, or station such weapons in Outer Space in any other manner.

The same article went on to declare that "the moon and other celestial bodies shall be used...exclusively for peaceful purposes," and that "the establishment of military bases" and "the testing of any type of weapons" was forbidden (though the "use of military personnel for scientific research or for any other peaceful purposes" was not).

When one looks at Articles 2 and 4 - the principal constructive achievement of the new space treaty - one must acknowledge that the new treaty probably did not break much legal ground. The orbiting of nuclear weapons in space vehicles, for example, was expressly prohibited by the United Nations General Assembly resolution of 17 October 1963, which had originally been passed with joint Soviet and American backing. This had been one of the fruits of the Khrushchev-Kennedy détente highlighted by the successful signing of the Moscow Nuclear Test Ban Treaty in August 1963.

Though some formalistic lawyers might still deny the effect of law to a UN General Assembly resolution even where it rested, as here, on the consensus of the main competing political and social world systems, most of the world community had accepted the resolution on non-orbiting of nuclear weapons as binding international law from the moment of its adoption in the United Nations. And, of course, this particular principle was fully observed - in the spirit and in the letter - in the more than three years between its first adoption in the UN General Assembly resolution and its final incorporation in the Outer Space Treaty in January 1967.

As for the notion that the moon and other celestial bodies should not be subject to national appropriation or national sovereignty, that principle had been expressly conceded by Soviet international lawyers, both in the Soviet-Western discussions at the authoritative, if private, International Law Association and in Soviet scientific legal writings on space. The Soviet opinions on this issue were all the more interesting because first advanced at a time when the Soviet Union had a head start on the West in space explorations: it therefore seemed likely that the Soviet Union might try to apply customary international law rules governing territorial ownership and title, to the moon at least.

In the end, perhaps, the importance of the Outer Space Treaty of 1967 lay not so much in any legal novelty of the principles finally expressed in treaty form, as in its indication of two political realities. First, the achievement of a firm treaty on outer space confirmed what had been apparent to students of Soviet-Western relations over a number of years, namely, that in matters of a highly scientific character where the Soviet Union and the United States had achieved approximately the same level of technical development, it was not too difficult to record these facts in a formal agreement resting firmly upon mutuality and reciprocity of interests between the Soviet and American systems.

Hence, for example, the Moscow Test Ban Treaty of August 1963: hence, also, the original 1959 agreement on Antarctica, providing for its non-military use and for scientific cooperation in its exploration. The second and most significant reason for the importance of the Outer Space Treaty of 1967 was that it represented the first really substantial breakthrough, of a publicly acknowledged character, in Soviet-Western relations after the Moscow Test Ban Treaty of August 1963 and the United Nations General Assembly resolution on non-orbiting of nuclear weapons in space vehicles of October 1963.

The high hopes engendered by both these measures for a step-by-step progression to further concretization of the Khrushchev-Kennedy détente were shattered by President Kennedy's assassination in Dallas in November 1963, and by Premier Khrushchev's abrupt dismissal from office the following year. The next three years were rather bleak from the viewpoint of formal inter-systems accords going to fundamental issues of conflict, as new and apparently less sympathetic individuals than Khrushchev and Kennedy came to power in the Soviet Union and the United States. The Outer

Space Treaty reestablished the rhythm of inter-bloc accommodation between the leadership of the two main countries, leading in turn to the Nixon-Brezhnev détente and the Moscow "Summit" Accords of May 1972.

The progressive achievement of big power détente and the new era of scientific and technological cooperation seemingly inaugurated by the Antarctic Treaty of 1959 and the Outer Space Treaty of 1967, at first seemed to offer the prospect of a new international law of communications, particularly where it concerned the regulation and development of telecommunication satellites and telecommunication satellite broadcasting. The necessarily very high technological component of discussions limited effective participants, in the early stages certainly, to the Soviet Union and the United States.

The technical-scientific establishments in these countries had attained a level of professional expertise, confidence, and articulateness that allowed them to influence national policy making in ways hardly possible in other areas of East-West interaction, which were seemingly more open to and more readily comprehensible by lay decision makers. The legal specialists or legal technocrats, in their consummate professionalism, had dominated this area of Soviet-Western relations from the beginning at the expense of the legal generalists or legal laymen. But this, in turn, created some unexpected difficulties when political-ideological problems - involving difficult policy choices that might normally have been foreign to a highly technical area in which the main protagonists had relative parity - intruded into the debate.

While the antinomy of policy and function is of course present in other areas of international legal negotiation, the conflict between the two approaches, and between the generalists and the specialists sponsoring them, was more noticeable than ever in the approach to a new international law of communications. This was undoubtedly one of the factors inhibiting the development of a genuinely intersystemic, common law in spite of all the objective factors that seemed to favour a substantial and far-reaching Soviet-US accommodation in this area.

There is not, of course, any tidy blueprint for the international law of communications - no single constitutional document for a common international agency, setting out the institutional bases for international organization and international decision making in the field, as well as the main substantive legal principles or at least philosophical guidelines for their development and application. This is a direct consequence of the historical fact that the international law of communications did not emerge poetically, as the United Nations Organization did in 1945 with its brand new and purportedly all-encompassing fundamental charter, but more or less ad hoc, over the years.

It developed in response to problem-situations in the area of telecommunications and international broadcasting that seemed to demand not so much inter-national as trans-national solution or regulation. Its prime emphasis has been on functionalism. The resultant institutional structure has been particularly closely correlated with the technical-scientific needs of the individual problems being solved, and technical-scientific considerations have tended to dominate the process of decision making.

This explains why, when the use of space and space satellites for international broadcasting became both technically and commercially feasible, the first international control and development initiatives were not entrusted to the long- established, specialist, international agency already existing in the telecommunications field- the International Telecommunication Union (ITU) - but to an entirely new organization specially developed on an ad hoc basis for the purpose (INTELSAT).

While the ITU certainly had a high degree of specialist expertise within the general telecommunications field, it was an expertise limited essentially to posts, telegraphs, and telephones; at that time it did not include space technology. In addition, its specialized, international bureaucratic cadre had been recruited mainly from national posts and telegraph personnel. When the new problem of international utilization of space communications arose, therefore, the general consensus was that the ITU simply would not do Hence the decision to form the completely new international agency, INTELSAT.

But where the progress of disarmament was controlled by the major arms developers (the two superpowers), international telecommunications and its international regulation tended to be shaped from the outset by the prime space utilizer (the United States), which dominated the telecommunications field in terms of scientific knowledge, trained personnel, and the enormous capital required, at least initially, for its development. At the time of the Interim Agreements of August 1964, under which INTELSAT was formed, the post-cold war détente between the Soviet Union and the United States was still in its very early stages; moreover, there was a certain time lag between the Soviet Union and the United States in the telecommunications field.

When INTELSAT emerged, therefore, under the August 1964 agreements, it was possible to argue that it was not only politically inevitable but also necessary for effective telecommunications development, that the United States should assume both majority voting control in the new INTELSAT international organization, and effective management control through the United States' domestic common carrier for profit, COMSAT. These two key elements in INTELSAT - the weighted voting in the inter- national agency, and the use of a particular national agency as its executive component - were often strongly criticized in the years immediately after 1964. Weighted voting in an international agency is not, of course, unprecedented, for it also exists in the International Monetary Fund (IMF), in the UN Conference on Trade and Development (UNCTAD), in the International Coffee Agreement, and arguably even in the UN Security Council itself, with the built-in veto of big power, permanent members.

Indeed, it might be suggested that the principle of weighted voting, with effective decision-making power linked to financial or other relevant input, has become almost a norm in areas where the demands of functionalism are especially high, and where problem-solving competence demands special contributions, in terms of finance and skills, from certain countries.

The criticisms of INTELSAT usually looked to questions of degree rather than to questions of kind: the effective voting veto given to the United States, with its 53 percent financial investment in the INTELSAT system; the inevitable conflict of interests where the us Government agency COMSAT wore "three hats" at the same time - as a US domestic, common carrier for profit, as us national representative to INTELSAT, and finally as the general managerial authority within INTELSAT itself. The most serious indictment of INTELSAT, however, was that, as a functions-oriented, international organization established in the post-cold war era of détente, it did not include the Soviet Union - which had, of course, a significant presence of its own in space communications.

The responding argument would have to be that the United States had never barred the Soviet Union's entry into INTELSAT, and that the Us majority voting interest was hardly beyond renegotiation and possible downgrading in the event of a Soviet bid to join. Be that as it may, no direct Soviet initiative to join INTELSAT emerged. Instead, the Soviet Union proceeded to operate its own regional organization - INTERSPUTNIK, directed to the Communist countries - separate from, and in potential rivalry to, INTELSAT. The 1964 Interim Agreements on INTELSAT were eventually replaced, in 1971-72, by new Definitive Agreements that finally approved the phasing out of the US, COMSAT-based, management role over a six-year period, and also provided for the reduction of us majority voting control to a maximum of 40 percent in the new Board of Governors for INTELSAT.

It is possible that these measures, introduced in timely fashion as early as 1964, might have overcome Soviet reservations about the supposedly universal character of INTELSAT. By 1972, however, when the Definitive Agreements were finally ratified, it was too late. The two parallel organizations, INTELSAT and INTERSPUTNIK, were already firmly established, and any common principles in the new international law of communications would have had to be reached bilaterally, in negotiation between the two rival organizations. The failure to achieve a common, international organization is the sadder because, of all areas of potential East-West cooperation, communications seemed objectively to be among the most promising, given its scientific-technological component and the advanced academic training of its key participants.

This failure had important consequences that carried over from the strictly technical, functional areas to policy areas, where speech and communication interests seemed to conflict with national security and protection of national identity and culture. The Soviet Union, facing the problem of accidental or deliberate spillover of satellite television broadcasts from one country to another, sought express prohibition in treaty form - with a Draft Convention on Principles governing the use by States of Artificial Earth Satellites for Direct Television Broadcasting, submitted to the UN Outer Space Committee and then to the UN General Assembly itself - of "any material publicizing ideas of war, militarism, Nazism, national and racial hatred and enmity between peoples, as well as material which is immoral or instigating in nature or is otherwise aimed at interfering in the domestic affairs or foreign policy of other States."

A basic antinomy existed between the US, commercial television-influenced, "open society" approach to satellite television broadcasting and its regulation, and the more traditional, "protection of state sovereignty." "non-intervention in the internal affairs of states" approach of the Soviet Union. This conflict was reinforced by a quickly-emerging third world position concerned with the maintenance of indigenous civilizations, cultures, and ways of life, languages, and religions against alien, materialistic, and predominantly Western intrusions through television broadcasts spilling over from one country to another without the prior permission of the receiving country.

The antimony is a real one, and the conflict of social interests that it reflects can hardly be solved on an absolutist, either/or basis. It seems to call out, rather, for the kind of compromise based on mutual reasonableness and reciprocity of interest that characterized big power détente in its early, concrete realizations. In the absence of a common institutional forum where such accommodations could be developed through the application of pragmatic, empirical methods to concrete problem-situations, the resolution of this antimony has been made only slowly and conservatively - perhaps, in the result, favouring "content control" at the expense of the more liberal, "open society" values.

7

The Codification and Development of International Law

A 16-month study by UNITAR (the United Nations Institute for Training and Research), carried out by the undersigned and another, asserts that the International Law Commission" is no longer playing the central role in the law-making process that it could and should play." With such iconoclastic conclusions, the report instantly became the subject of heated debate in UN corridors in New York and Geneva and, to a lesser extent, on the floor of the Sixth Committee of the General Assembly.

While the Chairman of the Commission stoutly defended its work before the General Assembly's Sixth Committee, pointing out that the ILC "was constantly seeking to improve its working methods," others expressed doubts. Ambassador Rosenne, a leading authority on the subject, noted that a "certain malaise existed about the Commission, its work, its methods of work, its programme, its relations with the General Assembly through the Sixth Committee, its role with regard to the implementation of Article 13 of the Charter and many other matters." A British delegate to the Sixth Committee noted diplomatically that "it had occasionally been argued that in recent years it had allowed itself to concentrate unduly on topics of peripheral interest to the international community."

Some of the Sixth Committee's commentators endorsed UNITAR's criticisms and several of its proposed remedies, while others criticized the criticism. This dissonance is as it should be, since the primary purpose of UNITAR in preparing the study was to provoke reconsideration of the Commission's place within the UN system: its role, procedures, and institutional infrastructure. Such reconsideration stirs important political, as well as legal, sensitivities. The remainder of this Note will summarize the UNITAR study and its findings.

The ILC's mandate is derived from a 1947 General Assembly resolution that established the Commission and approved its statute. The General Assembly acted pursuant to Article 13(1)(a) of the UN Charter, which empowers it to "make recommendations for the purpose of: (a) promoting international co-operation in the political field and encouraging the progressive development of international law and its codification." The statute echoes that the Commission's task is "the promotion of the progressive development of international law and its codification."

Progressive development was defined as "the preparation of draft conventions on subjects which have not yet been regulated by international law or in regard to which the law has not yet been sufficiently developed in the practice of States." Codification was to be "the more precise formulation and systemization of rules of international law in fields where there already has been extensive state practice, precedent or doctrine." Although the ILC's statute recognizes the role of other official intergovernmental bodies engaged in codification and progressive development, the Commission rightfully claims pride of place as the intended principal legislative drafting organ of the United Nations system, much as the International Court of Justice is the premier adjudicative organ.

The ILC is also the only drafting body with versatile jurisdiction over any subject in the field of international law. Indeed, during its first two decades the Commission did succeed in producing draft conventions directed to a wide selection of the important legal issues of the day, including the law of the seas, diplomatic relations, consular relations, and the law of treaties. These were essential building blocks in the development of the postwar international legal system; and the system did not then seriously consider employing any other master mason.

The UNITAR study observes, however, that the ILC is now in danger of losing its preeminence because it has failed, in various ways, to accommodate itself to the inevitable concomitants of earthshaking changes in the community it serves. The emergence of a Third World majority in the state system has wholly altered the system's agenda: its priorities and it's a *prioris*. In the words of the study, the "Third World is not interested only in the codification and adaptation of existing international law; rather it is emphasizing the need for the dynamic evolution of international law and its extension to new activities.

The Commission has not adequately responded to these major changes in circumstances." The report charges that the Commission has eschewed new topics of interest to the Third World: for example, the elaboration of economic rights and duties pertaining to development and trade. The reason often advanced by ILC members, that these topics are not yet "ripened" by sufficient state practice to warrant codification, merely confirms the Third World's concern that the Commission is neglecting its duty to engage in the "progressive development," precisely, of topics that may not yet be ready for codification.

It is not widely appreciated that, to the Third World states, "progressive development" is the neglected and scorned - by the Western as well as the Communist world - halfway house along the path a principle takes in its tortuous and uncertain ascent from "ought" to "is." One consequence of all this is that many topics that the General Assembly might have assigned to the ILC have been handed, instead, to a proliferating gaggle of ad hoc bodies. The UNITAR report traces the beginning of this diffusionary tendency to the creation of the Committee on the Peaceful Uses of Outer Space. That circumvention of the ILC resulted in the conclusion of the 1967 Treaty on Principles Governing the Activities of States in the Exploration and Use of Outer Space, Including the Moon and other Celestial Bodies. In the UNITAR study's view:

> [I]t was the Commission's declining to assert its competence over the developing law of outer space that set the stage for the proliferation of more ad hoc bodies. Once launched, the tendency expanded to include even some of the areas which had customarily been considered to be within the domain of the Commission. Two examples are the creation of the committee on the peaceful uses of the sea-bed and the ocean floor beyond the limits of national jurisdiction, and the establishment of the Ad Hoc Committee on the Drafting of an International Convention against the Taking of Hostages.

Perhaps even more germane is the decision of the General Assembly in 1980 to entrust UNITAR, not the ILC, with the task of examining evidence of the emergence of legal principles applicable to economic relations between developed and developing states, an exercise in "progressive development" that involves research into treaties, state practice, and international conduct, leading to a draft restatement of evolving principles rather than to any legal codification.

While the UNITAR report cites the arguments of both those ILC members who do, and those who do not, wish to see the Commission deal also with questions where the law may be partially unsettled and political considerations abound, it accepts the view urged by the UN Secretary-General as early as 1971, that the Commission's long-term program of work should take into account the changing priorities of the international community, rather than confine itself to "safe" questions of little interest such as the codification of law applicable to the diplomatic bag and courier (which is currently on its agenda).

Why has this not happened? The study suggests that some of the fault lies with the Commission's membership, some with the structure of the Commission and its supporting bureaucracy, and some with the community of states as represented in the General Assembly's Sixth Committee. The UNITAR authors think that the ILC's problems have now become so entrenched that each of these causes must be addressed before the Commission can be expected to change direction. Unless some reforms are made, the ILC will merely replicate the UN system's wanton penchant for addressing institutional inadequacy and obsolescence by institutional replication and functional fragmentation - by setting up new little principalities to do the neglected tasks of the old without actually abolishing the latter. Naturally, it follows from this that the old and the new will become primarily engaged in inter se territorial disputes of arcane and unseemly futility.

Must legal draftsmanship stagger down this welltrodden, but dead, path? With the signposts so unambiguous, why has the ILC not recharted its own path? Inevitably, the members of the Commission disagree as to the direction its work should take. A significant number sided with Professor Paul Reuter: "Unless, of course, it was asked to do otherwise, the Commission would do better to choose less urgent topics, which might be of less direct concern to peoples and nations - which [are] more in need of peace and food than of legal texts - but were ripe for codification."

Others feel that, since the Commission is not a negotiating body of plenipotentiaries, its members are ill-suited to venture into areas where governments may disagree. These members cite the rejection of the Commission's draft on arbitral procedures as an instance of the fate that befalls works of the Commission that get ahead of the nations' will to agree. According to the UNITAR study, even if these views are not those of a majority, the "outcome of these cleavages among the members is that the Commission tends to follow the lead of those least interested in expanding the scope of Commission activities to the new areas of international law."

Collegiality and the Commission's preference for consensus allow "a minority of members opposed to the inclusion of a particular topic... to prevent the Commission from taking up such topics." Other members of the Commission freely concede that its agenda has, in this way, become a veritable what's what of drafting trivia, a parody of the world's urgent agenda. Currently before the Commission are codifications of law pertaining to succession of states in respect of matters other than treaties, state responsibility, treaties concluded between states and international organizations or between two or more international organizations, non-navigational uses of international watercourses, the status of the diplomatic courier and diplomatic bag not accompanied by diplomatic courier, relations between states and international organizations (second part of the topic), jurisdictional immunities of states and their property, and international liability for injurious consequences arising out of acts not prohibited by international law.

"With the exception of the topic of non-navigational uses of international watercourses," the UNITAR study concludes, "the Commission has maintained its previous basic commitment to the codification of topics of traditional international law." Inherent resistance to change, particularly by members from some developed countries, is compounded by absenteeism, especially among members from developing countries who tend to double as senior officials of their national governments or regional organizations. An agenda of esoterica breeds absenteeism and vice versa. And as the Commission's work becomes less and less relevant, its membership, perversely, becomes the more prestigious.

This is not illogical, for very important and busy international legal luminaries are willing and able to grace a commission that is engaged in codifying the immunities of the diplomatic bag - since it does not excessively tax the conscience or endanger the national interest to miss most of the meetings on such a topic-while they would be less likely to seek election if the topics were of sufficient importance to warrant their serious and continuous attention. Noting a "seven hat problem," the UNITAR study reports:

[M]any of these members find it hard to fulfill their responsibilities of attendance at Commission meetings because of conflicting professional commitments. In some cases, on the present Commission, members have been absent for the vast majority of meetings. Such poor attendance is lamentable and prevents the Commission from functioning up to its potential.

And it inevitably reinforces the urge towards the trivial. The procedures and bureaucratic infrastructure of the ILC do not promote self-reform. An example is the slow rate of progress on the topics being prepared for codification. The UNITAR study finds that the average time between the ILC's initial investigation of a topic and the production of final draft articles is 7 to 10 years. State responsibility has been on its agenda for over 25 years. "Except for specific, circumscribed subjects," the UNITAR study says, "the Commission, as a part-time body, cannot possibly cope on a regular basis with urgent demands of the General Assembly."

Such slow progress is virtually inevitable, given the Commission's penury. As early as 1951, the I LC recommended to the General Assembly that it become a full-time operation and was turned down, in part because of the cost. Almost certainly, the same response would obtain today. Yet the present fiscal arrangement pays members a per them barely sufficient to cover their stay in Geneva during the annual 12-week session of the Commission. All but those on pension or of great personal wealth must therefore be expected to hold fulltime posts elsewhere, which are likely to interfere with regular attendance at the Commission's session. The special rapporteurs receive a small additional payment that does not remotely compensate for the time they ought to spend on their topics between sessions in order to set a fast pace for the rest of the Commission.

These problems are not assuaged by the Commission's staff, which is drawn from the Codification Division of the UN Secretariat's Office of Legal Affairs. Since the division has many responsibilities, only five members can be spared on a relatively full-time basis to serve the ILC so little research support can be provided by the division that the special rapporteurs must look elsewhere for the help essential to their task. Those who come from foreign offices or universities able to provide a research base are thus much better positioned than others - primarily from developing countries - who can expect no such help. This may account, in part, for the relative paucity of rapporteurs from Third World countries.

Another share of the overall responsibility for the ILC's quandary rests with the Sixth Committee of the General Assembly, which reviews the Commission's work and may assign it topics. As the UNITAR study points out, this "oversight" function is less effective than it might be were not so many members of the ILC also their countries' representatives on the committee. Except for certain few members considered beyond the pale, the United Nations is surprisingly like a club. The membership hates unpleasantness and any criticism of what is being done is usually smothered under a bale of circumlocution. This clubbiness is particularly evident when the Sixth Committee of the General Assembly, consisting in part of the members of the ILC, is given the role of overseeing the performance of the Commission.

A study of the Commission's lapse raises many chicken-or-egg questions, which are probably of little prescriptive value. It is too late, for example, to ask whether the Sixth Committee does not assign important new topics to the ILC because it perceives the Commission as essentially unwilling and unable to deal with them, or whether the failure of the Sixth Committee to challenge (or trust) the Commission with important issues is responsible for the ILC's immobtlisme. Whatever their origins, two effects seem to have become welded into a *circulo inextricabills*.

The UNITAR study finds that the majority of United Nations members is thus unwilling to entrust important issues to the Commission. This is in part a reaction to the Commission's self-perception and in part a result of factors external to the Commission. The reluctance of the Third World nations to entrust their most sensitive and urgent concerns to the International Law Commission stems from a perception that the Commission is wedded in some fundamental way to a relatively static concept of international law. This perception has been a logical implication of, and has been re-enforced by, the Commission's own understanding of its role.

However, the "attitude of the Third World to the International Law Commission [also] partially developed as an extension of its attitude towards the legal organs of the U.N. as a whole [since the] decision of the International Court of Justice in the 1966 South West Africa case...." There is a feeling that legal institutions are unlikely to be sympathetic to the aspirations of those who seek to change the status quo, which breeds a reticence toward them. Moreover, these feelings have been reinforced "by the perceived lack of influence of the members from the developing countries" on the Commission. UNITAR's study attributes this to their being relatively inexperienced and overcommitted to other responsibilities, as well as to their lack of research staff support.

Until these perceived deficiencies are corrected, even the Third World countries that most desire the progressive development of law in areas of special concern are unlikely to refer those concerns to a body in which they see themselves as playing with an insuperable handicap. The UNITAR study concludes by considering a series of proposals for reform which are meant to address these three linked components of the Commission's condition: its membership, its procedures and bureaucratic infrastructure, and its oversight by the Sixth Committee. The study lays out a range of options, rejects some, and endorses others.

As to membership, the report reconsiders the case for a full-time Commission and, while admitting its advantages, rejects it primarily because it would be too expensive and, to a lesser extent, because the Commission might thereby lose the valuable services of senior officials and scholars unwilling to abandon all other responsibilities. Instead, the report proposes a compromise: a part-time Commission as at present, but with full-time rapporteurs.

Under the prevailing system, the study finds special rapporteurs who must also hold full-time posts elsewhere are overworked and find it difficult to spend the time needed to prepare their topics. As a result, many of the reports, which are supposed to be delivered to Commission members in advance of the annual session, are not finished until the session has already commenced. Members are thus unable to study the reports of the special rapporteurs at length before being asked to comment upon them.

Full-time rapporteurships would alleviate that inadequacy and would also make it easier for Third World members to serve as special rapporteurs by making it possible for them to afford a leave of absence from competing commitments. Changes in the procedures and infrastructure of the Commission include a proposal for abandoning the present practice of keeping items on a long-term program of work until they are completed. The report proposes a 5-year agenda, coinciding with the term of office of the commissioners and composed of items that could be completed during the period. Each 5-year cycle would be "zero based" in the sense that uncompleted items would not automatically be carried over.

Further to accelerate the ILC's working schedule, the study urges more use of topical chambers composed of a special rapporteur and a maximum of four other members. Such chambers could meet for one or two intensive weeks, between regular sessions of the full Commission, and would then report to the next plenary meeting. The use of multiple rapporteurs where a subject lends itself to subdivision is also urged. In particular, the UNITAR report proposes improvements in the research services provided to the ILC. At a minimum, the Codification Division must be able to augment the personnel available to assist rapporteurs.

In the opinion of the UNITAR authors, however, the overall problem of restoring credibility and cohesion to the process of progressive development and codification of law requires a system-wide response, particularly as this process has already become so fragmented through *ad hoc*-ery and institutional proliferation. They therefore propose the establishment of a UN legal research center, which could serve a number of functions. It would provide an enhanced research potential for the ILC, but also for the many other specialized and ad hoc bodies within the UN system, which currently develop their own - often inadequate - research staff or must do without. Such coordinate research, aside from providing better service with a more rational marshaling of resources, would also create a functional network linking those involved in many currently unrelated, overlapping, and sometimes contradictory efforts at research and drafting.

It could also provide a pool of technical, nonlegal expertise that would augment the capacity of the ILC to deal with the complex interdisciplinary problems that are so often high on the system's agenda, but are now thought to be beyond the ILC's narrow base of expertise. "There is no reason," the study says, "why a body like the International Law Commission cannot handle any legal topic regardless of its technical, scientific, or inter-disciplinary complexity," providing it is properly staffed.

The present tendency, of course, is strenuously in the opposite direction. The system required experts to support the decade-long Conference on the Law of the Sea, so a legal staff was assembled to develop an expertise exclusively on this subject. If and when those negotiations produce an Authority to administer the Area beyond national jurisdiction, some of these lawyers will form a new legal research staff. So proliferation occurs, unless a conscious effort is made to reverse the trend. Inexorably, the UN system will become a series of closed, unrelated legal research clusters: an uneconomic and inflexible use of a scarce and costly resource. There is no reason, for example, why the talents of a sea lawyer, whenever temporarily underutilized by the sea Authority, should not be redeployed to encompass research on the non-navigational uses of rivers for the ILC.

A final recommendation directed to reform of the ILC's modus operandi calls for greater variety in the form of its product. Having too long focused virtually exclusively on codification - producing draft articles for international conventions - the Commission should consider other kinds of output, including "model rules," restatements, and analyses of emerging trends in state and interstate practice. This could accelerate the disposition of topics. "State responsibility" could perhaps finally be laid to rest if it were agreed to issue the product as a restatement of principles rather than as a draft treaty for which nations no longer seem to be calling with discernible urgency.

The prospect of working on "progressive development" could also be improved if the ILC did not have to cap each research project with a treaty. "Progressive development" is almost a contradiction of the treaty form, since it implies some movement in the direction of, rather than a final arrival at, lawmaking. If such reforms, or a significant portion of them, or other viable options could be instituted, the Commission might again be eligible to serve as the principal instrument of legislative research and drafting in the UN system. It would then be up to the system to make proper use of it. This requires, above all, the cooperation of the General Assembly's Sixth Committee.

The committee must provide the political guidance as to what topics are urgent and deserve priority in the ILC's 5-year agenda. And, if the Commission is to work in areas that involve political sensitivity, the Sixth Committee, as an organ of plenipotentiaries, will have an essential role in reviewing and guiding the ongoing drafting process. This role cannot be discharged, as at present, by formal set-piece speeches of verbal back patting. The members of the committee must challenge and guide the work of the Commission by providing detailed critiques of its work-in-progress.

Such critiques could also compensate for the tendency of most states simply not to respond to the questionnaires sent them periodically by the ILC in an effort to elicit specific "feedback." In the words of the UNITAR study: "If the Commission is to take a bolder approach to the development of the law, the Sixth Committee must provide the parameters in which the Commission can work, by detailing the limits of political feasibility." While the UNITAR study does not say so, it would undoubtedly help if members of the ILC were not placed in the embarrassing position of reviewing their own work as members of the Sixth Committee.

The UNITAR study is by no means intended as an attack on the ILC. Given the extraordinary, change in the international agenda and the paucity of means at its disposal, the Commission has functioned remarkably well. Nevertheless, the UNITAR study concludes, it is gradually drifting from the centre of the international law-making process. As it completes the basic work of the codification of the fundamental areas of international law, the Commission will find itself with largely marginal topics on its agenda. Because the Commission has proved to be an efficacious and highly competent part of the law-making process this diminution in status is regrettable.

At the same time, there is a growing incoherence in the U.N. legislative system as a whole. The lack of coordination among the proliferating ad hoc law-making bodies is becoming an increasing problem. Returning the International Law Commission to its former importance may help to alleviate this problem to some extent by placing a strong actor at the centre. Of course, other steps must be taken as well. The report does not say so, but it implies that if the tendency towards legal fragmentation is not arrested, the system may soon have no further significant use for the ILC, in which case it should be retired.

THE 1981 U.S.-CZECHOSLOVAK CLAIMS SETTLEMENT AGREEMENT

THE AGREEMENT

After 35 years of on-again, off-again negotiations, on November 6, 1981, the United States and Czechoslovakia initialed an Agreement on the Settlement of Certain Outstanding Claims and Financial Issues. Congress approved the Agreement in a bill passed on December 16, 1981, which the President signed into law weeks later.2 Procedural arrangements required for the implementation of the Agreement were completed in January 1982, and in mid-February the basic reciprocal undertakings of the parties were performed.

The Agreement is conspicuous in several respects. It is the last in the series of U.S. claims settlements reached with the socialist countries of Central and Eastern Europe since the Second World War. For Czechoslovakia the settlement closes an era in which pending foreign claims often hampered the development of normal relations with Western countries. Finally, because it provides more than 100 percent of the principal of certified U.S. claims, the Agreement is unprecedented in the history of postwar claims negotiations and constitutes probably the most favorable settlement ever negotiated by the United States Government on behalf of its citizens.

Under the Agreement, Czechoslovakia recognized the validity of claims of U.S. nationals whose properties, rights, and interests in Czechoslovakia had been affected by nationalization, expropriation, and other measures involving takings of foreign property by the Czechoslovak Government between 1945 and the date of the Agreement; and it agreed to pay $81.5 million immediately in settlement to be distributed to the claimants. For its part, the United States Government consented to the return to Czechoslovakia of the remainder of its share of Nazi-looted monetary gold recovered by Allied armies at the close of the Second World War. The gold, which was in the custody of the American British-French Tripartite Commission, was held partly in the United States (8.2 metric tons) and partly in Great Britain (10.2 metric tons). The United States had withheld its consent to the return of this gold pending resolution of the claims issue. In addition, the Agreement resolved several other outstanding issues:

a. Czechoslovakia agreed to pay the United States $2.87 million immediately, and a further $2 million within the next 2 years, for surplus equipment it had purchased in 1946 from the U.S. Third Army but had never paid for.
b. Czechoslovakia also agreed to release about $1 million in U.S. bank accounts in Czechoslovakia that had been frozen.

c. Czechoslovakia's counterclaim of $16 million was effectively abandoned. The counterclaim had been made in response to the U.S. Government's confiscation of a steel mill purchased in the United States by Czechoslovakia in 1947, but never delivered.

d. The United States agreed to release its blocking control over Czechoslovak properties, rights, and interests in the United States and not to obstruct in any way their transfer to Czechoslovakia.

One outstanding issue that was not resolved by the Agreement concerned defaulted prewar Czechoslovak bonds. However, the Czechoslovak Government agreed to negotiate with the representatives of the American bondholders and, if no agreement was reached within 6 months, to discuss the matter with the U.S. Government at the diplomatic level.

THE ISSUE OF NATIONALIZATION

Postwar nationalization in Czechoslovakia was effected in two stages: first, in 1945, when President Benes signed decrees on nationalization of mines, certain industrial enterprises, banks, and insurance companies; second, in and after 1948, when the Communist Party under Klement Gottwald ousted from the Government its democratic coalition partners and decreed sweeping nationalization and expropriation of private property.

The legislation enacted in the first phase acknowledged the obligation to pay compensation for nationalized property, except in the case of property owned by German or Hungarian public and private corporations, persons of German or Hungarian nationality, and persons irrespective of nationality who had engaged before and during the war in activities detrimental to Czechoslovak statehood. An important provision stated that if compensation was refused to a legal person, natural persons that had a capital interest in the property and did not belong to the category of collaborators, traitors, and the like named in the exclusion, were to be recompensed in proportion to their shares.

No distinction between Czechoslovak nationals and aliens was made. Compensation proceedings were governed by administrative law, and claims were decided by administrative, not judicial, tribunals. The Government announced that it would negotiate compensation for nationalized enterprises in which foreign capital was invested directly with the governments of the owners, and in November 1946 it concluded an Agreement on Commercial Policy and Compensation Claims with the United States. Under the Agreement, nationals of each country were assured "adequate and effective compensation" by the Government of the other for properties it had nationalized or requisitioned.

The laws enacted during the second stage did not, in principle, deny compensation for nationalization: they even stipulated the basis for determining the amount of compensation payable. However, as could have been expected, the post-1948 Government did not subscribe to the view that prompt, adequate, and effective compensation was the norm of international law. The right to nationalize all private property was regarded as a sovereign right, and state sovereignty was deemed to empower the Government to determine the terms and conditions of compensation, if any, to be provided for foreign-owned property.

It was on this issue that a fundamental dispute arose between the United States and Czechoslovakia. It should be noted, however, that the United States Government never questioned the right of Czechoslovakia to nationalize private assets under its jurisdiction; the only disputed question was the amount of compensation. By its nature, the 1981 U.S.-Czechoslovak Agreement is a global settlement that covers all U.S. claims arising out of the nationalization and expropriation programs of the Czechoslovak Government after 1945; it does not deal with each individual claim separately. It is broadly based on the international standard set forth in the United Nations resolution of December 14, 1962 on permanent sovereignty over natural resources, but it is so drafted as to be without prejudice to either side's view of the applicable international law.

It has been maintained that the global settlements following the postwar nationalizations in the East European countries are "negotiated compromises and as such do not constitute a departure from the traditional international law principle"; yet, while they have created no new law common to the West and the East, their prevalence in the settlement practice cannot fail to undermine each side's case concerning the content of relevant international rules. Several scores of such global settlements have been reached through negotiation and compromise; it would surely be wrong to dismiss them as diplomatic decisions that are addressed to private pecuniary claims and have no legal effect beyond the unique circumstances giving rise to them.

In the absence of other precedents, it is difficult to see how international customary law could preserve the classical doctrine of responsibility for nationalization predicated on the existence of an unlawful act, or, on the other hand, how it could create a universal norm recognizing the right of the nationalizing state to determine unilaterally the conditions under which property is taken from foreigners and whether or not compensation should be paid. Common sense and justice require a reappraisal of the doctrines unsustained by practice, so as to enable international law to play its proper role in facilitating rationality in decisions.

THE ISSUE OF THE MONETARY GOLD

While compensation for nationalized properties was the primary aim of the American negotiators, the recovery of monetary gold was the main Czechoslovak concern. For peculiar reasons, the question was not entirely financial; both history and emotion, including memories of the Munich betrayal, were involved. The Czechoslovak monetary gold was at the center of a major political and legal row in 1939 when, shortly after the occupation of Prague by Hitler, the Bank for International Settlements in Basel, Switzerland, rashly acceded to the request of directors of the Prague National Bank, acting under duress, that all deposited Czechoslovak treasury gold be moved from Basel to the account of the German Reichsbank at the Bank of England in London.

When the news leaked a few weeks later, both the Basel-based bank and the Bank of England were accused in the British Parliament and in the press of collaboration with the Germans; quite naturally, the Czechoslovak government-in-exile and every Czechoslovak Government in power since the war have held that the gold was wrongfully transferred to the German Reichsbank. After the 1939 transfer, the gold never left London. The British Government froze the account when war broke out, and the gold coins and bullion were held as a German asset until 1946 when they came under the control of the Tripartite Commission.

The powers and functions of the Tripartite Commission for the Restitution of Monetary Gold included the duty to adjudicate upon any claim made by any country to a share of the gold found in Germany by the Allied forces, to determine the amount of the share if such a claim was admitted, and to carry out distribution. All decisions were by unanimous agreement of the members; when the Commission was in doubt about or unable to deal with a matter, it was referred to the Governments of the United States, Great Britain, and France for joint instructions, which served to preserve the rule of unanimity.

Czechoslovakia's share of the gold was determined by the Commission and a portion of it was transferred to Czechoslovakia in 1948. Further transfers were halted because the United States, the United Kingdom, and France refused to sign the decrees of release. When its claims were settled, France withdrew its opposition, and the United Kingdom also made known its willingness to release the gold. The United States, however, moved in the opposite direction. In 1974 U.S. consent was expressly linked by statute to the conclusion of a claims agreement satisfactory to Congress and in 1980 Congress attempted to enact legislation providing for unilateral action by the United States with regard to that portion of the Czechoslovak share held by the Federal Reserve Bank. These U.S. actions called into play certain fundamental legal issues, to which the discussion now turns.

The Question of Ownership. It was asserted that the gold involved could not be considered to be Czechoslovak property and that Czechoslovakia could not acquire title to it until its final allocation and delivery to Czechoslovakia. It is probably arguable that until the adjudication of the Czechoslovak claim by the Tripartite Commission and its determination of the amount of the Czechoslovak share, there was nothing to which Czechoslovakia could claim property rights (although its Government repeatedly rejected this argument during the negotiations by pointing out that the share deposited at the Bank of England was physically identical with the gold wrongfully transferred to Germany). But once this determination was made and the depositary institutions so notified, the title of property could be disputed only at the expense of inconsistency with the Commission's own decisions.

The precedent in question involved monetary gold deposited at two Italian institutions in Rome in the name of the Bank of Albania and seized by the Germans in September 1943. After the war the Italian Government stated that 88.5 percent of the share capital of the Bank of Albania had been the property of the Italian state, and it submitted a claim under the Paris Agreement on Reparation. The Albanian Government had submitted a similar claim to the Tripartite Commission. On November 17, 1950, the Commission referred the matter to the Governments of the United States, the United Kingdom, and France, which appointed an arbitrator to advise them on the question of ownership. The arbitrator determined that the gold "belonged to Albania, within the meaning of Part III of the Paris Act of January 14, 1946."

In anticipation of such a determination, the Three Powers had agreed to deliver the gold not to Albania itself, but to the United Kingdom in partial satisfaction of the earlier Judgment of the International Court of Justice in the Corfu

Channel case of 1949. Such a decision would have been inconceivable without the prior establishment of title by the arbitrator. In the Czechoslovak case, title was established by the Tripartite Commission itself in 1947, when the 24 tons of gold clearly became the property of Czechoslovakia. In fact, approximately 6 out of the 24 tons were delivered to Czechoslovakia shortly thereafter. The position of the United Kingdom and the United States, in whose custody the undelivered portions remained after the Second World War, is best thought of as analogous to that of custodian-trustees.

The Right of the United States to Dispose of the Gold. The Paris Agreement is silent on whether a member of the Tripartite Commission may withhold consent. But the right seems to derive from the consensual procedure used by the Commission in making its decisions and to apply especially to matters on which the Commission feels unable to act. The Paris Agreement does not provide for remedies, and as the Monetary Gold case demonstrates, no remedies are readily available unless the Three Powers extend an ad hoc offer to the aggrieved party to bring its case before an international tribunal.

Like other kinds of veto power, the right to withhold consent to an arrangement made under the Paris Agreement is practically unlimited; perhaps the only legal defense against it is the doctrine of the abuse of rights: "There is no legal right, however well established, which could not, in some circumstances, be refused recognition on the ground that it has been abused." However, aside from the impracticability of invoking it outside a judicial context, the doctrine is clearly inapplicable where the exercise of the right, though causing damage to another state, is in response to an abuse of rights by that state. The absence of objective international procedures for dispute settlement plainly makes it inappropriate to appraise the right to withhold consent on the basis of legal criteria and, instead, makes it subject to political considerations.

A related issue arose in 1980 when the U.S. House of Representatives considered requiring the United States Government, failing an agreement with Czechoslovakia within a reasonable time, to seize the gold allocated to Czechoslovakia by the Tripartite Commission, and to sell it and invest the proceeds for income with which to pay the claimants. Some proponents of this solution referred to the Albanian gold ultimately delivered to Great Britain in partial settlement of the Corfu damages. Earlier, a class action had been brought in the U.S. federal courts on behalf of the United States citizens whose property in Czechoslovakia had been nationalized.

The primary purpose of the action was to have the gold held in New York used to satisfy the unpaid portion of the awards granted under the Czechoslovakian Claims Program by the U.S. Foreign Claims Commission. The action also sought to have Czechoslovakia's share of the gold in England transferred to the United States and made available to satisfy the awards. In both instances, the administration took the position that the gold was not a conventional asset and that its unilateral seizure by the United States, while a negotiated settlement of U.S. claims was still possible and being pursued, would be contrary to international law. The Department of State asserted that it "recognizes and allows the immunity of the gold from the jurisdiction of the U.S. courts for the purpose of attachment, suit or other legal process in the action."

The Department of the Treasury further pointed out that "[d]omestic legislation which would require the Treasury Department to seize and sell the gold in the United States is certain to be controversial and could affect the willingness of foreign central banks to hold assets in this country." The British and French Governments made clear their opposition to the proposed U.S. legislation. The British Government asserted that the proposed sale of the gold held by the Federal Reserve Bank, if carried out, would be illegal under the terms of the Paris Agreement.... Since the gold is held in the name of the three governments on the Tripartite Commission Her Majesty's Government would regard any attempt by one party to the Paris Agreement to dispose of the gold without the consent of the other two parties as in disregard of its trustee obligations to the other signatories of the Paris Agreement.

According to the French Government, the Three Powers in that Agreement clearly set forth the principle of immunity regarding the gold in their custody; the United States therefore had "no claim" on the portion in the Federal Reserve Bank. "The mere fact that the United States Congress could claim its own competence to legislate on that issue would constitute a serious breach of the universally recognized norms of international law. It is out of the question for France to admit that domestic law overrules international commitments."

The Albanian gold case substantially differed as regards international law. First, there was unanimity among the Governments of the United States, the United Kingdom, and France that the gold should be delivered to Great Britain; that agreement was duly executed and, in accordance with international due process, enabled both Albania and Italy to contest the decision before the International Court of Justice. Second, the action was taken not in pursuance of a unilateral claim but in order to enforce and execute an earlier decision of the International Court; the Three Powers therefore acted within the limits of an internationally adjudicated claim. In the case of the Czechoslovak gold there was neither an agreement among the Three Powers nor any international decision to implement.

THE MOST-FAVORED-NATION CLAUSE

From the beginning, the Czechoslovak Government emphasized that the question of compensation depended partly upon the advantages granted to Czechoslovak export trade because its membership in the General Agreement on Tariffs and Trade (GATT) had not brought it most-favored-nation status. The 1974 tentative agreement was linked to possible most-favored-nation treatment for Czechoslovakia. However, the new claims settlement Agreement involves no such linkage.

Although it does remove one obstacle to more normal political and economic relations between the two countries, U.S. negotiators made clear that they considered claims an issue unrelated to trade, and that any agreement on claims would involve no commitment by the United States to offer most-favored-nation status or any other trade concessions. The human rights situation in Czechoslovakia obviously loomed in the background. The repressive measures taken by the Government against its citizens hampered the negotiations, particularly in light of the need for congressional approval of any agreement reached.

THE IMPLEMENTING LEGISLATION

In 1958, at the request of the administration, Congress enacted legislation establishing a pro special rapporteurs cedure for American citizens to file claims with the U.S. Foreign Claims Settlement Commission for the losses they had sustained from the nationalization of their property in Czechoslovakia. The Commission adjudicated 2,630 claims against Czechoslovakia in the amount of $72 million, plus $41 million in interest, by 1962. Under congressional authorization, approximately $8.5 million worth of the adjudicated claims were satisfied from the proceeds of the sale of the Czechoslovak steel mill equipment.

On two occasions, however, namely in 1963 and in 1974, Congress was responsible for the repudiation by the U.S. Government of tentative settlements with Czechoslovakia. Information regarding the 1974 arrangement reached Congress during its deliberations on the Trade Act of 1974; Congress promptly secured its control over the matter by inserting a new section 408 into the Act calling for the renegotiation of the arrangement and its submission to Congress as part of any agreement made with Czechoslovakia. It further stipulated that none of the gold in question could be released without congressional approval.

Congress did not oppose the previous settlements and issue this injunction in 1974 solely out of concern over the Czechoslovak nationalization case. As a supporting Senate report put it:

One-sided agreements of this nature are especially dangerous to the United 'States and its citizens at this particular time in history when nations in various parts of the world are threatening to expropriate or nationalize U.S. properties worth billions of dollars, while other nations have already taken valuable U.S. holdings without the payment of just compensation. The United States simply cannot afford to proclaim in the face of this trend that expropriations of U.S. properties will quickly be forgotten if the taking nation ultimately offers a mere pittance in return.

The time when these words were uttered was one of heightened sensitivity on all sides. In 1974 the emerging concept of a "New International Economic Order" was given normative expression in the Charter of Economic Rights and Duties of States by the UN General Assembly. Clearly, the proposed Czechoslovak settlement touched off a protective reaction in Congress, which not only perceived the immediate inconvenience to some 26 hundred individual claimants, but also grasped the long-term implications as justification for a new international principle. The view that only partial compensation is due for nationalization of foreign property would have received additional confirmation in the U.S.-Czechoslovak agreement.

The role assumed by Congress was not limited to monitoring the developments and reserving its approval for a final agreement: it also functioned as a spur to the negotiating process. When a stall developed and prospects for an early settlement receded, congressional determination to assure payment to the restive claimants intensified and led to a legislative proposal to liquidate the Czechoslovak gold so that they could be paid if a satisfactory negotiated settlement could not be reached promptly.

The Czechoslovakian Claims Settlement Act of 1981

The U.S.-Czechoslovak Agreement of November 6, 1981 provides that the U.S. Government will have exclusive competence to distribute the compensation received, in accordance with its legislation. The Czechoslovakian Claims Settlement Act of 1981, passed on December 16, 1981, constitutes the implementing legislation. In addition to giving the congressional approval required under section 408(b) of the Trade Act of 1974, it authorizes the Foreign Claims Settlement Commission to reconsider certain U.S. claims against Czechoslovakia and provides for the distribution and disbursement to U.S. claimants by the Treasury of the funds received under the Agreement.

The net sum of $81.5 million, minus a small sum for expenses incurred by the Department of the Treasury and the U.S. Foreign Claims Settlement Commission, is to be divided among three separate accounts in the Czechoslovakian Claims Fund established by section 402(b) of the International Claims Settlement Act of 1949:

1. An account of $74.55 million, to be available for payments on the unpaid balance of awards certified by the Foreign Claims Settlement Commission pursuant to section 410 of the International Claims Settlement Act of 1949;
2. An account of $1.5 million, to be available for payment of such new claims as may arise from the taking of property between August 8, 1958 and the date on which the Agreement entered into force; and
3. An account of $5.4 million, to be available for ex gratia payments of previously denied claims of the so-called Benes group of claimants.

Nationality and Ownership

The policy of the United States has been to espouse claims that have been "continuously owned" by its nationals from the date of the injury to the date the claim is presented. This principle is reiterated in the Agreement. The Czechoslovakian Claims Settlement Act, however, departs from this principle in one important respect: it sets aside a portion of the settlement for persons who were not U.S. citizens when their property was nationalized.

These claimants, who are referred to as the "Benegs" group, include persons (1) whose property was expropriated by the pre-February 1948 Government of President Benes on or after January 1, 1945 and before January 26, 1948; (2) who had become U.S. nationals by February 26, 1948; and (3) whose previous claims were denied by the U.S. Foreign Claims Settlement Commission solely on the ground that "such property was not owned by a person who was a national of the United States on the date of such nationalization or taking." The Commission is directed to re-determine the validity and the amount of any such claim that had been denied.

The idea to compensate these former Czechoslovak citizens and other persons, to whom the compensation promised in 1945 had never been made, first appeared during congressional consideration of the bill that contemplated liquidating the Czechoslovak gold. However, it was tempered by the reaction of the Department of State:

Under well-established principles of international law, to which the United States adheres, the United States cannot espouse claims against foreign governments for injuries inflicted upon persons who were not U.S. citizens at the time of the injury.... The United States view [is] that, under international law, the date of taking is fixed by the date of the expropriation decree and/or the date of physical seizure, and not by a subsequent date of repudiation of an undertaking to provide compensation.

Deviation from the established legal principles cited above would create a precedent with implications beyond this immediate case. It could open a broad range of new and marginal claims for the U.S. Government to pursue, without support under international law. At the same time, it could erode our ability to espouse legitimate claims of U.S. citizens in the face of worthless undertakings by a foreign government to provide future compensation. Despite this warning, when the time came to implement the negotiated settlement, Congress decided that payment had been denied to this group of claimants on grounds that were "faulty and inconsistent with the intent of Congress in enacting the 1958 law calling for the adjudication of claims against Czechoslovakia."

The fact that payment will be made *ex gratia*, as a matter of equity, may be psychologically important but seems to be irrelevant as a matter of law. That was probably why it was deemed advisable to create the legal fiction of "deferred" taking of property, which would make it possible to hold that injury was inflicted upon the claimants after they became U.S. nationals. The reasoning behind this legal construction appears in the report of the House Committee on Foreign Affairs:

> These claimants - the so-called "Benes" claimants - were U.S. nationals by February 26, 1948, when the Communists took power in Czechoslovakia. Action, however, had been taken against some or all of their properties by the previous government of Eduard Benes, albeit with public promises by that government of fair and just compensation.... The committee believes... that actions against property accompanied by promise of compensation should not, in this case, have been treated as takings, and that, in fact, the properties of these claimants were taken by the Communist government when that government took power and repudiated the promises of compensation made by the Benes government.

The position adopted by Congress refers to equality of lawful rights of the person and to protection in preserving these lawful rights when the person changes his nationality. Even though Congress did not intend to innovate insofar as international law was concerned, it helped raise the question of basic fairness in the dogma of nationality of claims.

The establishment of an international law of human rights, which depends substantially on intercession by other states in behalf of the rights even of a state's own nationals, and the fact that the rights of individuals are generally becoming less dependent on nationality make it necessary to reexamine certain assumptions underpinning the dogma of nationality. Even though property rights have lost much of their sanctity, the right of an individual not to be arbitrarily deprived of his property is a human right recognized in the Universal Declaration. In addition, since some countries take unnecessarily harsh measures toward their former citizens, it would be unfair to deny those persons protection by their new homeland.

The principle of nationality of claims was never regarded as absolute, and some have even doubted its reasonableness.

Sir Hersch Lauterpacht wondered what position the International Court of Justice would adopt if it were faced with the problem in a concrete situation. He concluded that there was no warrant for the assumption that the Court will invariably respect the claim of a sovereign State not to be made accountable for the infliction of an injury upon an individual, in a manner contrary to international law, except at the instance of the State of which that individual is a national at the time of the occurrence of the injury and of the institution of the proceedings before the court.

Consequently, the exception to the rule of nationality of claims made in favor of the "Benes" group of claimants is not in conflict with international law, and no legal fiction of the sort created by the congressional committee was needed to justify its adoption.

Dual Nationality

Under the terms of the United States-Czechoslovak Naturalization Treaty of July 16, 1928, "nationals of Czechoslovakia who have been or shall be naturalized in the territories of the United States shall be held by Czechoslovakia to have lost their former nationality and to be nationals of the United States." However, there is an exception to this rule: "The foregoing provisions of this Article shall not be applicable to a national of either country who obtains naturalization in the other while his country is at war." It is only in connection with this exception that a conflict of nationality may arise.

Technically, the state of war between Czechoslovakia and Germany during the Second World War was terminated by the unilateral declaration of the President of the Czechoslovak Republic of February 3, 1955. When it began is a matter of some controversy. On December 16, 1941, President Benes, then in exile, proclaimed that Czechoslovakia was in a state of war with all countries at war with the United Kingdom, the Soviet Union, and the United States, and that the state of war with Germany had begun the moment that the German Government had committed acts of violence against the security, independence, and territorial integrity of the Czechoslovak Republic.

Subsequently, the specific date was variously interpreted as September 17, 1938 (the day of the first incursions of irregular troops organized by Nazi Germany), September 29, 1938 (the day the Munich settlement was imposed upon Czechoslovakia), and March 15, 1939 (the day the German armies completed the occupation of the country). As could be expected, the Czechoslovak negotiators asserted that, for the purpose of determining eligibility for compensation, those persons that were naturalized in the United States between September 17, 1938 and February 3, 1955 could not be held to have lost their former nationality and were therefore dual nationals.

As such, they were not to be included in the negotiated settlement. However, the date of termination of war for the above purpose was later agreed to coincide with the cessation of hostilities in the European theater on May 8, 1945. As a consequence, the number of claims presented in behalf of American citizens thought to have dual nationality dwindled appreciably. Although no formal agreement has been reached on this particular problem, Czechoslovakia seems to accept the view that personal status is determined by dominant nationality.

It has been the theory of international law that when a state takes up a case of its national by resorting to international protection on his behalf, that state is actually asserting its own right. The espousing state therefore has the right to dispose of the claim, can compromise it, and can accept a settlement providing less than full compensation to its national. And strictly, international law does not require the espousing state to pay the recovery over to its nationals.

This theory is reflected in the U.S.-Czechoslovak Agreement of November 6, 1981. As from the settlement date, the Czechoslovak Government is released from all obligations to the United States or to its nationals relating to properties, rights, or interests affected by Czechoslovak measures of nationalization, expropriation, disposition, or other taking that arose prior to the date of the Agreement.

The U.S. Government undertook not to pursue or present any such claims to the Czechoslovak Government, and the latter agreed to refer any such claims presented directly to it to the former. The question arises whether these terms apply to unsatisfied portions of claims made by the "Benes" group. Although they were designated by Congress as beneficiaries of the lump sum settlement, their claims remain outside its scope as defined by Article 2 of the Agreement. This ambiguity, however, is more apparent than real. If such claims were ever presented to the Czechoslovak Government, it could not be prevented from referring them to the United States, and once before the U.S. Government, they would become inadmissible for having been satisfied already, albeit only partially.

The second segment of Part IV (Jurisdiction), which is included in Tentative Draft No. 3, includes an amended version of section 401 which had been laid over the previous year. In presenting the amended version the reporters reiterated their conclusion that the limitations that international law imposes on different aspects of a state's jurisdiction can best be understood under three headings: jurisdiction to prescribe, to adjudicate, to enforce. Comment explains that these are not presented as three discrete conceptual categories, since adjudication can be seen largely as a means of law enforcement.

But the three headings identify different aspects of the exercise of authority by a state, which, because they employ different means and have different consequences, have led to different principles of limitation under international law. In particular, while Tentative Draft No. 2 had presented the principles of limitation applicable to adjudication (whether or not used for what is commonly seen as law enforcement), sections 431-433, in this Tentative Draft, set forth limitations on enforcement other than through the courts, including limitations both on administrative action and on police action in foreign countries.

Sections 419-420 present additional United States applications illustrating the principles of jurisdiction to prescribe set forth in sections 402-403, Tentative Draft No. 2. These sections are applications in particular of section 403(3), which addressed the problem that arises when two states having jurisdiction to prescribe with respect to a person issue contradictory demands. Under section 419, prohibitions by the state in whose territory the act is to be carried out ordinarily prevail over orders of other states.

Section 420 applies that principle to requests for disclosure of information. It requires that an order to produce documents and information located abroad be issued by a court, not merely by a private party or by a U.S. agency as is possible under the Federal Rules of Civil Procedure and comparable State rules. Section 420 also requires that a request for production of documents or information located abroad meet a more stringent test of direct relevancy, necessity, and materiality than is required for comparable requests for documents or information located in the United States. If disclosure of information located outside the United States is prohibited by a law of the state in which the information is located, the person to whom the order is directed may be required to make a good faith effort to secure permission from the foreign authorities to make the information available. The court may not ordinarily impose sanctions on the person except in cases of deliberate concealment or removal of the information, or of failure to make a good faith effort to obtain permission to make it available.

Section 431 deals with jurisdiction to enforce law through executive, administrative, or police actions, including such measures as placing someone on a blacklist or restraining the transfer of assets. The Tentative Draft states that such measures, too, may be employed to enforce law against persons located outside the territory of the enforcing state only where the state has jurisdiction to prescribe, and if the person is given notice and a fair opportunity to be heard. Enforcement measures must be reasonably related to the violation and proportional to its gravity.

Sections 432-433 set forth the limitations on the means that a state may use outside its territory to enforce its laws.

International law forbids the exercise of enforcement functions in a foreign state without its consent, and if a person is abducted from another state without its consent, the other state may demand that the individual be returned. But if return is not demanded, the Tentative Draft accepts *male captus, bene detentus* as the general rule under both international law and the law of the United States.

In Part V, the reporters set forth so much of the Law of the Sea as seems desirable to include in this Restatement and which it seems safe to restate at this time. As the tentative table of contents indicates, we plan an additional chapter on the Resources of the High Seas but that, we have concluded, had better wait at least until the final outcome of the UN Law of the Sea Conference. The materials here presented rely heavily on the Draft Convention that has emerged from the Third Law of the Sea Conference, since, as regards the subjects we deal with, the Draft Convention largely reflects principles of customary law and previous conventions to which the United States is party [p. xxiv].

The Tentative Draft (§511), then, accepts as customary law a 12-mile territorial sea, an extended continental shelf, and a 200-mile exclusive economic zone, as well as a special status for archipelagic states (§511, Comment g). The draft is more tentative as to the principles of delimitation of the exclusive economic zone (or the continental shelf), which remained highly controversial, and their final articulation still uncertain, when the Tentative Draft was published.

When Part V was considered at the annual session of the Institute, the reporters indicated that the text would have to be looked at again in the light of developments, including the position taken by the United States during the final stages of the UN Conference on the Law of the Sea and after the conference was completed.

Part VII, Protection of Persons (Natural and Juridical) "looks substantially different from the treatment of those matters in the previous Restatement. It includes the international law of Human Rights which has developed considerably in the past decades" (p. xxiv). Particularly noteworthy is section 702, which sets forth as customary international law of human rights:

A state violates international law if, as a matter of state policy, it practices, encourages or condones

- Genocide,
- Slavery or slave trade,
- The murder or causing the disappearance of individuals,
- Torture or other cruel, inhuman or degrading treatment or punishment,
- Prolonged arbitrary detention,
- Systematic racial discrimination, or
- Consistent patterns of gross violations of internationally recognized human rights.

Section 703 sets forth the remedies for violation of human rights. It takes the position that a state party to an international human rights agreement has, as against any other state party violating the agreement, the remedies generally available for violation of an international agreement, as well as any special remedies provided by the particular agreement (§703(1)). Any state may pursue international remedies against any other state for a violation of the customary international law of human rights (§703(2)). As to "humanitarian intervention" by one state in the territory of another where human rights were violated, Comment e states:

It is generally accepted that a state may act to rescue victims or potential victims in an action strictly limited to the purpose, in circumstances not likely to involve disproportionate destruction of life or property in the state where the rescue takes place. Whether a state may intervene with military force in the territory of another state without its consent, not to rescue the victims but to prevent, terminate or suppress human rights violations, is not agreed or authoritatively determined. Such intervention might be acceptable if taken pursuant to resolution of a UN body or of a regional organization such as the Organization of American States.

Private remedies for human rights violations are available only where provided by international agreement or under a state's municipal law. The reporters cite (Note 7) the individual remedy found in Filartiga v. Peña-Irala for a victim of torture in Paraguay against the alleged torturer, under 28 U.S.C., section 1350, giving the U.S. federal courts jurisdiction of a "civil action by an alien for a tort only, committed in violation of the law of nations."

Sections 711-713 deal with state responsibility for injury to nationals of other states. In presenting these sections the reporters noted that the relevant law, especially as it relates to economic injury, is in some disarray, but the Tentative Draft does not differ from the previous Restatement in major respects on substantive issues (although the subject is presented differently and treated in briefer compass, in accordance with the overall plan of the revised Restatement). The reporters noted the turbulent history of that law and the vigorous attack on it, particularly the effort to have questions of compensation for expropriation governed by national law alone. They conclude, however, that expropriation of alien properties continues to be governed by international law and that international law requires, *inter alia*, that there be "just compensation." The reporters note that it has been and continues to be the U.S. position that just compensation means "prompt, adequate and effective compensation."

Tentative Draft No. 3 takes "an intermediate position" on the significance of an "internationalization clause" in a concession contract between a state and a private investor. According to the draft, if such a clause incorporates by reference the principles of international law or common principles, they are to be applied, but the clause does not convert the contract into an international agreement governed by the law of international agreements as reflected in the Vienna Convention on the Law of Treaties. That state would have a basis for claim under international law principles of responsibility for injury to foreign nationals if there were "discriminatory or other arbitrary repudiation" of the contract, or if, the contract being breached, the private party were not "given an adequate forum to determine the claim of breach or is not compensated for any breach determined to have occurred".

Tentative Draft No. 3 also includes sections 721-722, which restate selected principles of constitutional law particularly relevant to the foreign relations of the United States. Section 722 declares that while the Constitution expressly limits certain benefits to citizens, the safeguards of the Bill of Rights and of the Thirteenth and Fourteenth Amendments are enjoyed by aliens equally with citizens, generally even by temporary or undocumented aliens, although the equal protection of the laws does not preclude some distinctions between citizens and aliens, or between categories of aliens. The Institute did not have time to consider those sections at its annual meeting and they will presumably be presented again as part of Tentative Draft No. 4 in spring 1983.

8

Sustainability and the Right to Development

In recent years two ideas have gained prominence in international thinking about development-that of 'sustainable development' and that of the 'right to development'. The former has become particularly fashionable since the use of it in the Brundtland Report (1987), and the latter received its formal launch, after some years of gestation, in the United Nations Declaration on the Right to Development in December 1986. In this chapter I explore a number of philosophical problems to do with these two ideas and their juxtaposition, and conclude with a highly qualified endorsement of a 'right to sustainable development'.

Although the phrase 'sustainable development' makes no explicit reference to the environment, it is quite clear that the context in which the idea has gained prominence is that of environmental problems, both to do with the using up of resources and the problems of future shortages, and to do with the general effects of human activity, particularly industrial activity, on the natural environment - in terms of pollution, land degradation, alteration of the atmosphere, and so on.

Maybe in the abstract sustainable development is as much about sustaining the social, political and economic basis of development as about anything else. But the core idea of sustainable development in the modern context is that of a kind of development (i.e. socio-economic process), whether in poorer countries or in richer countries, which so treats the natural environment that the process of development, or at least the products or benefits of that process, can continue into the future in a sustainable way, both for ourselves and our children, and for future generations. As the Brundtland Report puts it: 'Humanity has the ability to make development sustainable to ensure it meets the needs of the present without compromising the ability of future generations to meet their own needs.'

Given then the value assumption, based on sheer collective enlightened interests if not on moral concerns for the future, that development ought to be sustainable, the key practical challenge has become that of working out strategies for development that satisfy this condition of sustainability. It is fair to say that the Brundtland Report, the Pearce Report (advocating sustainable development for the UK) and most political parties which have adopted a 'green' agenda assume that such policies are about economic growth, i.e. a new kind of economic growth which is environmentally friendly. As we shall see later, this assumption that sustainability is combinable with economic growth may turn out to be highly suspect.

THE RIGHT TO DEVELOPMENT

The Declaration on the Right to Development asserts that all human beings have an inalienable human right to development, which it characterizes as follows:

> Development is a comprehensive economic, social, cultural and political process, which aims at the constant improvement of the well-being of the entire population and of all its individuals on the basis of their active, free and meaningful participation in development and in the fair distribution of benefits resulting therefrom.

What is interesting is that it clearly grounds the 'right to development' in the idea of human rights as expressed in earlier UN declarations and covenants. It is because development is a process in which human rights are progressively realized that people have a right to it. The right to development so to speak makes explicit what has been implicit in earlier human rights assertions, namely that if people have rights they have rights to the conditions necessary for the realization of those rights. What the word 'development' indicates is that, if those necessary conditions cannot now be met, at least a process of moving towards them and thus progressively realizing them is something which people have a right to. This is especially evident with regard to a whole range of rights such as economic rights and rights to subsistence, which require economic resources and institutional infrastructures, which simply may not be available in many poorer countries.

Second, the operational context of this declaration is that nation-states have a right to development, and that governments have special obligations to realize the right to development, both nationally and internationally. Indeed, subsequent work in the UN Commission on Human Rights is precisely concerned with finding ways of implementing such rights and obligations in international law. The whole UN process of declaring and implementing a right to development can thus also be seen as a way of making explicit (and effective) the idea that human rights generate moral obligations which are international or global in scope, not just national.

Why cannot the two ideas briefly sketched above be fused together? After all, if what the idea of 'sustainable development' really brings out is the fact that the forms of development that should be pursued are sustainable forms, and the idea of a right to development simply stresses that development is based on human rights and on duties, national and international, to promote it, surely we can acknowledge that people have a right to sustainable development. This would be then a right to the kinds of social, political and economic changes which both improve the well-being of people now and preserve the conditions (environmental, institutional, etc.) so that people in the future can achieve well-being as well.

Now such a synthesis does seem to make intuitive sense. Indeed, if one accepts that there are human rights and that sustainability is a necessary element to a satisfactory definition of development, and that a right to development is grounded derivatively in the realization of human rights, then intellectually there seems no alternative. And this broadly is the conclusion I reach at the end of the chapter. What on the face of it is problematic about fusing the two ideas of sustainability and rights together in this way is this:

a. Whatever the merits of the attempts to bring together the concerns of the environmentalist with the concerns of the developmentalist under the umbrella of one phrase, there remain deep divisions between them. The former are concerned to contain or even question development as growth, for the sake of their concerns for future well-being or their concerns for the natural environment or biosphere in its own right. The latter are concerned with the current economic well-being of people, and, in the case of poorer countries, with strong international commitment to further such development. The phrase 'sustainable development' already contains this tension, but the phrase 'right to sustainable development' only accentuates it.
b. The agenda behind 'rights' discourse is essentially that even if all basic human rights are not now realizable in the world (because of economic limitations) then at least they will be realizable once sufficient economic and institutional changes in the world have taken place. (Development generally is premised upon the real possibility - though not inevitability - of progress.) This simply comes up against a very different worldview of many who are impressed by the seriousness of our environmental predicament - the idea that universal growth is not possible and that the extensive failure to meet basic human needs will remain part of and indeed will become a larger part of the human predicament.

These problems are genuine problems for anyone wishing to assert a right to sustainable development. But they can be met, once our ideas of sustainability and development and the right to development are more fully developed. To say they can be met does depend upon certain broad empirical assumptions in addition to certain lines of philosophical argument and analysis, and as a philosopher cannot authoritatively assess those assumptions. The chapter is premised upon a broad 'middle ground' set of assumptions about the developmental and environmental possibilities before us and the fact that they present us with real choices which require careful moral thought. The relevance of these reflections would be much reduced if one adopted a wholly optimistic scenario which renders the philosophical 'problem' otiose, or a wholly pessimistic scenario which renders it academic and irresolvable.

DEVELOPMENT

Central to the discussion is the question: what is development? One common view has been that development is essentially economic growth, and that the way to achieve economic growth is through modernization, i.e. the general introduction of and increase in industrialization, advanced technology and modern bureaucratic and economic mechanisms. What developing countries need to do is to catch up with and essentially imitate developed countries, which, even if they haven't achieved full development, are well on the way to doing so, and provides the model which poorer countries are to copy.

It is well recognized by many that development cannot simply be about economic growth. For we can imagine countries in which economic growth occurs and the GNP goes up, but certain other things do not occur, like improvements for the very poor who are left out, or maintenance of civil liberties and democratic freedoms. Concern for the position of the poor, the improvement of which was not seen as occurring as a result of a 'trickle-down' effect of general prosperity, led to ideas of development like 'development with equity', i.e. economic growth coupled with appropriate distribution of wealth so that the poor had a fair share, not to say a priority in the general increment of economic benefits. Consider, for instance, the 'basic needs' approach to development as a way of giving expression to this concern.

What this suggests is that at root the idea of development is about a process of change which occurs in a society in which the well-being of people is increased. This begins to look like the UN definition given above, for the UN definition talks of a comprehensive process aiming at the constant improvement of the well-being of the entire population and of all individuals. The UN definition in fact makes reference to well-being in two rather different ways: first, it talks of well-being in terms of a number of dimensions, social, cultural, political, as well as economic well-being. Second, it refers to certain characteristics of social life such as free participation and fairness in the distribution of benefits, i.e. to certain moral characteristics of a society, such as justice and liberty.

Now we might want to argue about the details of the values indicated here, but the essential point to make about this UN definition is that it makes it very clear that 'development' as a goal of human endeavour is essentially the label we use for the processes of change which are seen as good, or even seen as what ought to occur. Indeed, this reflects the fact that much discussion about the nature of development is about the values which we believe in. Disagreement about what development is turns out often to be disagreement about what values we think ought to be instantiated in the process of change which we advocate.

In one respect, however, I do want to comment critically at this stage on the UN definition, namely for its omission of any direct reference to the priority of alleviating extreme poverty within development. Is this accidental? After all, it talks of improvements for all individuals and also of fairness of distribution, so one might think that commitment to the reduction of poverty was clearly implied by these ideas. This would be a generous interpretation, I think, since the general tenor of the document is on development for all countries and on the more rapid development of poorer countries as such.

It is important to make explicit the difference between the right to development and the right of poor people to such development as will enable them to escape from extreme poverty. Any doubts which may be raised about the general right to development should not be seen as raising doubts about the rights of poor people to the basic necessities of life, and thus to a right to the kind of development which is essential to this.

DIFFERENT KINDS OF OBJECTIONS TO THE RIGHT TO DEVELOPMENT

a. There might be a general objection to the whole idea of human rights. If the right to development is seen as an expression of the conditions necessary to human rights, and there are no human rights, then the argument has lost its basis.

b. There might be a slightly less general but still broad objection based on doubts not on human rights in general but on certain kinds of human rights in particular, such as the sorts of socio-economic rights which are seen as 'recipience' rights. Since the right to development is primarily based on economic progress, it might be seen as logically underpinned by certain kinds of rights which are denied.

c. While it may be granted that human rights do exist, the right to development goes well beyond the assertion of human rights in ways which are problematic. For instance:

   i. It asserts the existence of international obligations and/or global obligations, i.e. obligations on the part of other countries to further development and/or obligations on the part of other people in the world to help further development.

   ii. In stressing general improvements in well-being in a country it goes well beyond what it is appropriate for any community to impose on itself or its government (let alone other countries or peoples). Protecting and promoting rights are one thing, improving general well-being (economic or otherwise) is another.

d. In so far as the right to development is actually asserted in the present international system, it raises problems:
   i. About the extent to which countries have a right to define development in their own ways (the autonomy condition) and at the same time impose obligations on other countries;
   ii. About why nation-states, as opposed to smaller sub national units or larger supranational units, or as opposed to other institutional arrangements for managing world affairs, should be seen as the obvious units of development anyway.
e. Disagreements about how to define development make it inappropriate to assert a right to development.

It is of course clear that a central prop to talking of the right to development would be taken away if one took away the commitment to human rights. There is much debate in the philosophical literature, which I will do no more than touch on, as to whether human rights exist and in what sense they do. Whatever else may be a matter of dispute it would generally be accepted that a human right is a right asserted to belong to all human beings as such anywhere and that the assertion of it is the expression of some moral claim - and that its existence does not depend upon positive social morality or established law.

Thus it is clear that the assertion of human rights is in some sense the assertion of a universal or global moral standard-and the Universal Declaration of Human Rights (1948) is often taken to be an embodiment of such a global moral perspective. The chief objection to this comes from ethical relativism which denies that there is an extra-cultural perspective from which to assert universal rights qua human or indeed any other universal values.

If, however, one is prepared to assert that human beings have rights, there is no good reason to restrict those rights to the so-called 'negative' rights such as liberty, and not extend them to subsistence rights. Indeed, as Henry Shue has well shown, the positive/negative distinction is unhelpful since all types of rights have positive and negative aspects to them. It is as true of liberty rights as it is of security rights and subsistence rights, the human rights that Shue has defended as basic, that the duties correlating to them are of three kinds: duties not to deprive (of that to which someone has a right), duties to prevent from being deprived and duties to aid the deprived.

On Shue's argument, the right to subsistence and security is basic in the sense that if it is not realized all other rights are meaningless. Assuming then that human rights exist, it seems plausible to include social and economic rights with their heavy emphasis upon the duty to protect from economic deprivation and aid the economically deprived. Since much of development is about precisely that, a right to development can be seen as based on this, if not other considerations.

INTERNATIONAL/GLOBAL OBLIGATION

One of the key questions which now arises, though, is the question of whose duty it is, if people have rights, e.g. to liberty, security and subsistence, to realize those rights? It is commonly recognized that within an organized community (or more generally a country under one legal system) all people have a duty to refrain from depriving individuals of what they have a right to, but that governments have a special duty to protect people from deprivations, by enforcing law and by providing social security, a free health service, etc., and to aid the deprived in similar ways. However, in circumstances where governments and institutional agencies cannot for lack of resources realize basic human rights (the typical situation of poorer countries), or do not from indifference or connivance, or actually thwart their realization, fellow citizens have not merely duties not to deprive, but also duties to protect and aid as well.

What, however, of the wider context, internationally or globally? The Declaration on the Right to Development is certainly seen as entailing obligations in the international community and in other states to help promote development. What is the source of these obligations? Do the human rights, which the right to development expresses, themselves generate international obligations? The following argument, which I call the Cosmopolitan Model, is promising:

a. Global obligation - Human rights are asserted as part of the commitment to a global moral community, i.e. to one moral domain of relations, responsibilities and obligations. We are all responsible in principle for the realization of human rights anywhere.
b. International obligation as the expression of global obligation - Governments, whether acting on their own or multilaterally, ought to reflect, as far as is possible, the moral imperatives and priorities of the global moral community.
c. Conclusion - Governments therefore have duties to other governments to support efforts to realize global values, e.g. the realization of basic human rights.

COSMOPOLITANISM AND GLOBAL ETHICS

Do human rights generate international obligations via global obligations? The answer to this depends upon whether one accepts the two crucial premises above. First, it has to be recognized that the claim that human rights are universal, i.e. applicable to all human beings everywhere, does not entail that the correlative obligations extend in principle to all people in the world. It may be insisted (mistakenly) that human rights, though universal in character, essentially generate only local obligations, local in the sense that the obligations which arise in the context of an ongoing community, and in the sense that a government of a country stands in a special relation of protection and aid vis-à-vis the rights of its citizens (for contractarian reasons or whatever).

Certainly ethical universalism is not the same thing as cosmopolitanism. The latter idea is, as I understand it, the idea that we all belong morally to one community in which responsibility and obligations for one another in principle extend across the globe. (Cosmopolitanism is in fact consistent with acknowledging a degree of diversity in values in different societies.) The idea of a 'global ethic' is no doubt normally intended to cover both universalism and cosmopolitanism, but we have to acknowledge that they are distinct strands. (The distinction is valid whether the universal values in question are about rights, duties or well-being.)

If human rights are to function as the direct generator of international obligations then they must at least be seen as asserting in principle obligations on the part of people anywhere in the world to do something about them.

David Luban makes use of an intriguing claim made by Shue that socially basic human rights are 'everyone's minimum reasonable demands upon the rest of humanity'. He reads this (which seems to me to be right anyway) as asserting that any human being anywhere may in principle have obligations to realize human rights. Thus, although it has to be granted that the idea of a human right on its own without a wider theory behind it does not strictly entail cosmopolitan responsibility, it is difficult to see what the function of human rights discourse is, if it is not to assert the oneness of humanity and the idea of global solidarity and moral community.

It is likely that the kinds of reasons advanced for defending human rights will be the kinds of reasons for seeing the scope of morality in global terms. At any rate the assertion of subsistence rights seems as good a way as any for showing why those who are well off in richer countries have duties to help alleviate suffering in other parts of the world. The second crucial premise is that international obligations, i.e. the obligations which governments or nation-states have towards one another, are derivative of this cosmopolitan/global perspective. But this can be denied, and, if it is denied, then human rights play no special role is underpinning international obligation.

THE INTERNATIONALIST TRADITION

This takes us into the heartland of normative international relations theory. The idea that there is a morality of states, as

Beitz calls it, which is distinct, both in content and in rationale, from ordinary moral norms, has been popular in the so-called 'internationalist' tradition - and in many ways is to be welcomed as an alternative to harsher forms of realism, i.e. to the idea that moral norms have no relevance or application in international relations at all. Its characteristics have been an emphasis on the importance of principles of sovereignty, non-intervention, honouring international pacts and agreements, rules of war, and so on.

This is very much what has been called the 'international analogue of nineteenth-century liberalism', for within the framework of moral restraint lies the idea that each nation-state has the right to pursue its interests, including its economic interests, as best it can. Now one might say that this chimed well with the idea of a right to development. For is not a right to pursue the national interests and in particular the economic interest of a country another way of saying that each country has a right to development?

The answer is that it is not; for the essential import of asserting a right to development is not just to say that there is nothing wrong in a country's pursuing its own development, and that if it fails to do so because of competition from other countries bent on the same, there is nothing wrong about that either. It is rather that countries have a right to certain forms of co-operative behaviour on the part of other countries, which permit if not actively promotes their development. That is, the right to development asserts a duty in other countries in the international community not to hinder - and in the case of the right to development of poorer countries, actively to assist in-their development.

Now it has to be granted, even stressed, that within the framework of the international tradition, there is room for the development of co-operative norms-and one of these areas has been that of environmental protection in recent years. Likewise one can see the commitment of the richer countries in the early 1970s to give 0.7 per cent of GNP as aid and the more recent Declaration on the Right to Development as helping to establish a duty to further development in poorer countries (by appropriate aid, favourable international trade regimes, etc.).

But we should note, on the one hand, that the traditional right of countries to pursue their interests including development had nothing particularly to do with human rights. The relevance of social and economic rights (with their emphasis on recipience) was often not acknowledged and the civil and political rights of citizens were seen as an alien intrusion into the smooth running of international relations. As Hedley Bull noted, international order was seen as inimical to the demands of human justice. (By 'human justice' he meant appeal to human rights.)

On the other hand, what think has to be acknowledged is that the extent to which co-operation in order to further development in poorer countries has become accepted as a norm of international relations is a reflection of the extent to which the norms of international relations have become influenced by wider moral norms of a cosmopolitan kind. This could be presented as the Internationalist Model alternative to the Cosmopolitan Model given earlier:

a. Autonomy of international morality - The moral rules which ought to govern the relations of states are those which by and large have evolved in the 'society of states' to suit the mutual interest of states in their external relations.
b. Indirect influence of global values via international actors- Global ethical values such as human rights have an influence on the morality of states in proportion to the extent that past and present consideration of them by international actors informs the formation of international law, customary rules and particular policy decisions.
c. Conclusion - Governments therefore have obligations to support development, including development directed to the realization of basic human rights, to the extent that the international morality of states has endorsed it.

This is arguably an unsatisfactory way of grounding an international obligation, precisely because it relies on the moral views of international actors themselves and conservatively upon the state of established international norms, whereas the cosmopolitan approach appeals directly to basic moral norms that are rationally defensible-norms which reflect the fact that human beings are morally primary (in relation to states), that we live in one moral community and thus that the norms of international relations between states ought to, even if they do not, reflect these more basic norms of a global ethic. Human rights contribute an important part of that wider moral framework which should be used to evaluate and criticize the behaviour of states and the norms they have come to accept.

If development is seen as a process in which there is a steady increase in well-being for all the population, the question might be asked: is there a right to this? There is a difference between saying that people have a right to seek a further increase in their well-being, and saying they have a right to get it, in the sense that others should not hinder them or should aid them in so doing. It seems odd to say that a person who is already well off has a right to a further increase in his or her standard of living, or that someone who is well educated has a right to further learning, or that someone who has an adequate social life has a right to an even richer one.

A definition of 'development' as general improvements does not really discriminate between the improvements (in income, learning, social life) for people who are economically, educationally or socially deprived or disadvantaged and the improvements for those who are not. The point is not just that the rights of the former are more important than the rights of the latter. It is that it makes less or little sense to talk of the rights of the latter group-at least in the same sense of requiring action of others. The trouble with a blanket definition of development as general improvement, although it may capture something of what development means, is that it somehow creates an overstatement when coupled with the assertion of a right to it.

We should remember that the right to development is asserted not just as a right of poorer countries but also of richer countries. Once we attend to what a right to continued improvement in economic well-being means as applied to rich countries, we can see what a strange idea it is. Indeed, it seems clear that a richer country may not even have a right to development in the weaker sense that there is nothing wrong in its seeking further development-especially if that is linked to continued economic growth within environmental constraints, as discussed below.

What, however, about poorer countries? It certainly seems clear, if there is anything in the line of thought being developed here, that people have rights to a reasonable standard of living, and so, given the fact that hundreds of millions of people in poorer countries live clearly below that level, their rights require urgent action. In so far as development programmes are either targeted towards the improvement of their situation or are such as clearly to have such improvement as a significant part of the process, development in poorer countries can be seen, instrumentally or derivatively, as a process in which these rights are increasingly realized. So the right to development is generated by these rights and in turn transmits obligations to people and governments generally.

But are the goals of development in poorer countries necessarily of this kind-i.e. targeted wholly or significantly on poverty eradication? The answer is: never wholly, and sadly sometimes not significantly. My point is not here to criticize the policies of Third World governments; rather it is to point to the fact that their development policies have quite legitimately other goals as well, including economic growth and general improvements in many other areas.

The question nevertheless remains: in so far as these development goals lie beyond the meeting of basic rights and aim at general improvements, do these countries have a right to development against the international community? The 'right to development', unless otherwise qualified, explicitly does not discriminate between different development goals. While all these goals might well be legitimate goals for a country to pursue, it does not follow that all these goals are such that that country has a right that other countries help it achieve them.

This argument may seem a bizarre one, given the evident fact that poorer countries in the world are so much poorer than rich countries. Surely it is self-evident that poorer countries have a right to development precisely in the sense that economic development, indeed rapid economic development, is something the international community has a duty to help further (and is in fact doing little about) in poorer countries. And it may also seem self-evident that this is not just because basic rights are not currently being met on a large scale, it is also because there is an immense gap between rich countries and poor countries which is morally unacceptable.

Now the gap between rich and poor countries is indeed a matter of grave moral concern, but we have to ask ourselves what the basis of this is. Is it simply because there are significant inequalities between countries' wealth or their levels of economic development? Is it the fact that economic exploitation, past and present, has created and sustains the great gap between countries? Is it the fact that the level of economic well-being of poor countries is simply too low for them to meet the basic needs of their people?

The first argument has to be handled with care. There do not seem to be any good reasons for claiming that all countries should have the same per capita wealth any more than there are for saying that all individuals in a society (or the world) should have the same level of wealth. Indeed, the argument is less plausible since one can readily imagine a world in which the average per capita wealth of all countries was the same but there were still unacceptably wide ranges of income/wealth distribution within countries. Though inequality as such may not be wrong, great inequalities generally ought to be reduced, but this is usually for the other reasons mentioned.

What makes inequalities of wealth unacceptable to the extent that they are is arguably (i) the fact that those inequalities reflect exploitative or unjust economic relations (e.g. where workers because of their weakness do not get a fair wage, or where discrimination such as racism or sexism operates) and (ii) the fact that the outcome of such inequalities is that some people live in unacceptable poverty, i.e. are denied their basic rights. This applies as much to relations between countries as to relations within countries. The unacceptability of these inequalities thus underpins a right to development of a country as a means of rectifying a situation in which the rights of its people are denied by these inequalities.

Poorer countries, then, do have a right to development and one that generates international obligations to assist them in realizing it. It turns out to be a right to general improvements in economic well-being, not because they have a right to catch up fully with the level of economic well-being in richer countries, but just because this would be a consequence of a fairer, less exploitative global economy and because it is required for the meeting of basic needs. (Since it is justified in terms of justice and rights, it must in consistency be development directed to goals justified by moral argument.)

In operational terms, i.e. in terms of what it means in practice in the world, the right to development is very much understood to mean the rights and duties of governments. Now if we think of governments as having a duty to promote the development of their country, there is an implication here (i) that the process of development is the process of change in the whole country, i.e. that the unit of development is at the level of a country; (ii) that governments are in control of that process; and (iii) that governments are as it were entitled to define what the development process is for their countries. There is also the implication (iv) that governments can make demands on other governments in the framework of international agreement and law to further development.

The present reality of the world is of course that governments play a large part in defining both the content of and units of development. Development is often assumed to be national development-understandably inasmuch as national governments have, if any institutional actors have, the power to influence the way things go in areas of the world. But it is clear that this need not be the only level of description for development. All sorts of entities can be the object of planning, from small communities, farms, cities, regions, to supranational areas such as the EC or even, from the perspective of UN agencies or thinkers who take as their concern 'world development', the world as a whole as a developing system.

The amount of interest we focus on these different levels is in part a function of how much power actors have to influence or control change at these different levels; and in part a function of how much power and influence we think ought to exist at these different levels. There is nothing inevitable about the current concentration of planning power at the level of national governments. Greater devolved decision-making to communities and regions is perfectly possible, as is the transfer of decision-making to larger bodies (thereby chipping away at the sacred cow of absolute sovereignty), or a combination of the two.

If governments do have de facto great control over the development processes that occur within their borders, then of course if people have a right to those development processes, governments, as representing those interests, both have duties to further them and rights (up to a point) against the international community not to hinder them. But governments only have those rights on the assumption that they do further the genuine development needs of their people. A government cannot legitimately define its own development goals without taking into account the genuine development needs of its people. If it fails to do so, morally the basis for a claim against other countries simply lapses.

DEFINING DEVELOPMENT

The preceding discussion leads us to look more generally at a difficulty with defining development. The problem philosophically with saying that someone has a right to development, where it is left open what development is, is that a right surely needs a content which seems to be missing.

If one has correlative obligations to support it, it would be like signing a blank cheque. Politically it is also problematic granting other countries a right to development, especially if one's country is seen as having an obligation to support their development, if it is possible that the country may define its own development in ways which are judged to be (say) inappropriate, contrary to the ideal of development one's own country has itself, or even contrary to one's own country's development interests.

On the other hand, 'development' is like certain other concepts such as liberty, self-determination, autonomy, participation and empowerment. The ways these ideas are interpreted and expressed vary considerably from individual to individual and are expected to do so. That, one might say, is the point about these important social concepts. Yet we accept that people have rights to these - not just in the sense that there is nothing wrong in their exercising these rights, but in the sense that others have an obligation not to hinder such exercise and indeed to help such exercise where circumstances thwart it. Indeed, these concepts are not merely parallel to the idea of development; they are for many thinkers part and parcel of the idea of development itself.

Other countries may have duties to assist if external assistance is needed. But there are limits to the extent that countries are free to determine their own development-limits which may apply to rich countries whose policies may not be fair in relation to the rest of the world, as much as to poorer countries whose policies it would be unfair to expect donor countries to support. This political limitation is paralleled by the philosophical point that, granted that development is that process of socio-economic change which ought to happen, it will not do to translate this as: any process that those involved think ought to happen. For instance, an environmentalist is unlikely to accept a growth paradigm just because most people think it desirable. From the point of view of any thinker a right to development must be constrained by the thinker's own view of what genuine development is (including the degree of self-determination which he or she endorses).

The general thrust of my argument has been that poorer countries have a right to development as a condition of reducing extreme poverty and as a consequence of removing global economic injustice. But I have raised a doubt about defining development as general economic growth (for rich or poor countries alike), at least in the sense that this implies a right to it, either in the strong sense (as implying a duty in others to aid or not to hinder) or in the weaker sense (as implying that it is not wrong to seek/pursue it). These doubts are confirmed if we turn to the environmental constraints of sustainability.

SUSTAINABILITY

The idea of sustainability seems fairly clear: an activity, state of affairs or process is sustainable if it is capable of being sustained, that is, capable of continuing in the future without change. A pattern of agriculture on a given area of land is sustainable if it can be maintained indefinitely; i.e. the same pattern of agriculture could occur in ten years' time, fifty years' time, etc.

A pattern of agriculture, for instance one reliant on high inputs of chemicals, or a monoculture, might not be sustainable if it turned out that after some years the soils had become ruined. An industrial practice would be sustainable if there were an indefinite supply of the materials needed to run it and if the effects it had on the local environment were not such as eventually to damage it so as to undermine the industrial practice.

What I have just said illustrates the idea of sustainable development, since agriculture policy and industrial activity are two key ingredients of development. What makes development sustainable has a lot to do with the levels and kinds of agricultural and industrial activity which are generally involved. However, the above account of development simply in terms of what is capable of being sustained is not in fact adequate for several reasons. It is not sufficient that an activity be capable of being sustained. There must also be a will/ commitment to sustain it.

The future is not just foreseen; it is also planned for. Furthermore one key assumption of even greater significance needs to be brought out into the open. It is assumed that sustainable agriculture, industry and development generally ought to be pursued; that it would be wrong to pursue policies which were not sustainable. Why is this? The assumption must be that if certain kinds of agriculture or economic activity are good now, they will be good in the future, whether that is the future of ourselves, of our children or of future generations unknown to us. This evaluative component to the idea of sustainable development points up the weakness already noted in thinking of sustainable development (or anything else that may be the object of commitment or planning) as merely that which is capable of being sustained.

For, there are many kinds of activity which can be sustained in themselves but only at great costs. Indeed, to apply a point which G. E. Moore used in connection with J.S. Mill's use of the word 'desirable', what is perhaps significant about sustainability is that it is about what 'ought to be' sustained rather than what merely 'can be' sustained. This is already implicit in the point made above that a practice which is unsustainable ought not to be carried out. But this gives merely a negative reason to do with the need to continue the value of the activity itself. The wider point is that there may a number of different respects in which sustainable development should be evaluated as what ought to be pursued or what is worth pursuing. A form of development worth sustaining will at the very least not only protect the future, but also be:

a. Just in terms of the present social structures and practices of the society;
b. Non-damaging to the natural environment;
c. Non-damaging to people in other countries; and
d. Fair in relation to the like aspirations of other countries.

(Not everyone will of course accept these evaluative positions. What is important, analytically, is that any form of sustainable development which someone is prepared to endorse will be a form which satisfies the range of moral criteria which that person accepts, whatever those may be.)

What I mean by this check-list is that if a country was pursuing a form of development which could be sustained into the future but which either (a) was manifestly repressive or indifferent to its own poor now, or (b) destroyed either within its own borders or in other countries the natural environment, or (c) involved economic policies, perhaps because of the country's economic power, which actually damaged other economies or helped to cause or perpetuate poverty elsewhere, or helped to create unsustainable situations in other countries, or (d) manifestly involved policies which, if generally practiced, even just by those countries with the resources to do likewise, would create unsustainable conditions in the world-then, if any of these consequences were the case, we would not want to endorse that model of sustainable development.

An example of (d) would be this: it might well be the case that if one industrial country were to continue emitting carbon dioxide (CO_2) at present rates and all other countries stopped altogether, the effects on the atmosphere would not be significantly bad. But the fact is that many other countries are emitting at similar levels and yet more countries would like to do so and are moving into a position to do so. Here the test 'what if other countries do what you are doing?', given that other countries have as much reason or interest in selfishly doing so, becomes a critical test.

But this 'generalization' test is ambiguous. Is the test merely 'what if all other countries that wants to and is in a position to do so, do so' or is it really 'what if all countries everywhere were to do so'? Either way, it can be argued, major changes in the levels of western economic practice are called for; but the latter test has much more radical consequences.

Take, for instance, the general standard of living and general level of economic activity in rich countries. Suppose that all countries were like that. Imagine a world in which all countries have our average level of economic well-being. Many would accept that we are imagining impossibility. It has, for instance, been estimated that if all the world had achieved the typical energy consumption of rich countries, energy consumption globally would be (in 2025 AD) over five times, or 55 terawatt years (Twy), what it was in 1980 (10 Twy). It seems reasonable to suppose that we would have created a total environmental catastrophe from CO_2 -induced global warming, general pollution, increased radiation problems from increased reliance on nuclear energy, etc.

Suppose then we are imagining impossibility. Does it follow from this that because we cannot generalize western levels of economic activity (either literally or because the effects would be too bad), that we in the west ought to reduce our levels of economic activity (energy consumption, etc.) to that level which could be generalized on a sustainable basis for all countries in the world? While there are good reasons for saying that the west ought to cut back somewhat, it is not clear that the simple generalization argument provides the right basis or the right prescription. If there is nothing intrinsically wrong in differences of wealth between countries (as noted earlier), then the fact that the levels of wealth and economic activity of rich countries cannot be universalized in it does not make it wrong.

There are, however, plenty of other reasons why a commitment to continued growth might be questioned. Briefly, and in the absence of space to argue the points properly, these are that the actual practices of industrialized countries, taken together (the limited generalization argument above), if not taken individually, are (a) damaging the global environment - i.e. the environment for Third World countries (and non-human life) as well as for future generations-and, (b) controlling the global economy in ways that are economically either damaging to countries in the South or failing to further their development, including the reduction of extreme poverty. There is therefore ample reason for richer countries (a) to share their wealth through better aid and more general trade arrangements and, (b) to reduce their contribution to the unsustainable levels of resource use, pollution, CO_2 emissions, and so on.

If, for instance, it is the case that continued economic growth by rich countries is sustainable if poorer countries do not catch up at all (and continue to be economically exploited), but that it is not sustainable if poorer countries make significant improvements essential to their escaping the problems of extreme poverty (and get a fairer deal from the international economy), then poorer countries would have every right to feel that the maintaining of that growth was unjustified.

What really suggesting is this: the only real way to get a handle on the problem of whether a form of sustainable development for a country is justifiable (assuming it is sustainable for that country itself) is to consider it from a global perspective, i.e. from the perspective of world development. That is, to consider the situation of all countries in the world, and to ask what levels and kinds of economic activity, i.e. what kinds of development, could consistently be put together into a sustainable global package. If talk of the 'new world order', popular since the ending of the cold war and the Gulf crisis, is to mean anything it will have to do with the willingness to subsume national interests, which as I have noted include development objectives, under broader considerations.

There are therefore a variety of reasons for arguing that if sustainable development is to be taken to be sustainable economic development or growth, the idea, though internally coherent, is not realizable in the real world - certainly for rich countries. On the other hand, real economic growth for poor countries would be realizable in the real world, if only richer countries changed their ways to allow it. Indeed, economic growth for poorer countries especially that was targeted on the very poor would actually be beneficial to the environment since extreme poverty is often a cause of environmental degradation.

If, then, one recognizes that development need not, and should not, be defined in terms of general economic growth for all but as a process of improving well-being (broadly defined) in conditions of justice and freedom, and with commitment to such real economic growth as is necessary for the sake of the poor, then the idea of a world in which development can occur for all peoples seems wholly realistic. Although I have expressed reservations about the right to development partly because of the difficulty of saying that countries or peoples could be said to have a right to continued general improvements in well-being, the reality of the world is one in which the pressing need to ensure that all people achieve a reasonable life to which they have a right exists almost everywhere, in poor countries to a great extent as well as in rich countries to some extent.

Our environmental predicament, and the concern to sustain what we have achieved into the future, will only make the problems of development in the present that much more urgent. Therefore in practice the right to development, where development is suitably qualified in the ways I have indicated and puts emphasis upon what is needed to enable people to realize their basic rights, is worth articulating and defending. Is it a right to sustainable development?

Well, if sustainability is one of the attributes that an adequate definition of development must contain, it follows that if there is a right to development there is a right to sustainable development. If we assume the point of view of an agent whose interest is in their life and the lives of those around them we might be better to say: it is a right to development which is at the same time sustainable. If, on the other hand, we assume the point of view of an agent who sees it as part of their own objectives in life that their life harmonizes with that of their neighbours distant in both space and time, then the very sustainability of development, far from being a constraint, is precisely part of what we each have a right to, and can demand of our governments and of ourselves to be realized.

9

The Temporal Dimension of International Law

The temporal dimension of international law denotes the problem of the claims to legitimacy and continued application today of legal principles and rules manifestly developed in an era now past. The antinomy between an "old" and a postulated "new" international law has its historical roots in the Soviet-Western legal "great debate" occurring at the end of the 1950s and the beginning of the 1960s at a time when, with all the benefits of retrospective wisdom, we can now recognize that the Cold War was ending and a new era of Big Power coexistence and détente was succeeding it. The term "new" international law was used, innocently enough, by the then principal legal adviser to the Soviet Foreign Ministry, Gregory Tunkin, in a context in which he seemed to call in question the adequacy, in contemporary terms and having regard to the vast changes in the membership of the world community since World War II and the new range of societal interests emerging as a result, of the whole corpus of classical international law principles and rules.

To Western jurists, who immediately joined issue on the basis of a perceived threat to Western political, economic, and military interests which any challenge to classical international law would represent, Dr. Tunkin replied elegantly that he was advocating "new international law" only, and that he had certainly called "neither for 'a new international law' nor for a 'revolution' in international law"; and that he had "no intention of overthrowing the international law now in force." That answer, allowing for the debater's skill with which it was formulated, says something-as any empirical examination of Soviet practice over the years will surely confirm - for the long-range continuity, even conservatism, of Soviet international law and its interest in essentially incremental change rather than any fundamental act of novation.

The gap between abstract legal doctrines-what Ehrlich called the law-in-books - and law-in-action or actual legal practice in concrete cases is as marked in regard to Soviet international law as in the case of any other "regional" system of international law, Western or other. Soviet international law doctrine is the heir to a revolutionary past, and the principles of the Great October Socialist Revolution of 1917 certainly operate, by way of what Harold D. Lasswell called legal folklore, to influence and shape the formulation of many current policy options; but the actual choice between those different options-legal decision making-will tend to operate in Soviet society, not less than in Western society, on a rational calculation of the national interest, short-range as well as long-range, in any problem situation.

The dynamic element in the intellectual campaign on behalf of a "new" international law comes a little later than the Soviet-Western legal "great debate" that inaugurated détente; and when it comes it is with other actors, newly or recently admitted as legal members of the world community and with interests in the world public order system that quite transcend the essentially bipolar, Soviet-Western issue of détente. The movement for a "new" international law, challenging the "old" or "classical," putatively Western or Eurocentric international law, is essentially a Third World-led movement.

It draws some direct inspiration, to be sure, from the ideological inheritance of the Great October Socialist Revolution of 1917, and it would be rather surprising if it did not. Classical international law in its heyday was certainly enriched by the French Revolutionary and Napoleonic inheritance; and the great principles of nationalism, independence, and liberalism that stemmed from it were certainly reinforced and extended, in their turn, by the principles of the Great October Socialist Revolution. There is, in fact, a direct linear development to be seen, from the French Revolution through the October Revolution to the declaratory resolutions of the United Nations General Assembly, from the 1950s onwards, of the international law principles of national self-determination, decolonization, and independence.

The principal reason, however, for the contemporary Third World-based challenge to classical international law is that it is viewed, rightly or wrongly, as an instrument for preserving a world political and economic order in whose creation the Third World did not participate and which is still oriented to the interests of those dominant postindustrial societies of today (Communist and Western) that so largely made it. The challenge to classical international law as an "old" law, reflecting an "old" world public order system now under challenge and in process of disappearing, is also helped by the new legal teachings, strongly influenced as these are by theories of historical relativism and by the application of rigorously empirical methods to the study of the origins of legal principles and rules.

The new teachings demonstrate clearly enough that, so far from being a body of timeless absolutes, good for all seasons and all places, and postulated a priori in advance of actual problem situations, the main principles and rules of classical international law were developed ad hoc and experientially, in response to concrete international conflicts and the need for accommodation of the rival parties and the diverse interests that they represented. Most classical international law is, in fact, of comparatively recent historical origin. If there are strictly doctrinal borrowings, extensive enough in certain areas (notably as to territorial title), from the Roman law, classical international law is still, by and large, the creation of the foreign ministers and supporting jurists of the host of small Western European succession states to the old dyarchy of Holy Roman Empire and church, whose claims to universal temporal and spiritual authority had received their legal quietus with the ending of the Thirty Years' War.

The Treaty of Westphalia in 1648 had confirmed the claims to legal sovereignty of those new European societies, founded on the rise of commerce, which looked for their political and economic self-aggrandizement in trading relationships with other countries and in the assertion, by military power where necessary, of claims to territorial title and political sovereignty over newly discovered lands overseas and their aboriginal peoples. Grotius's celebrated *mare liberum* doctrine, which declared the high seas open to the ships and the commerce of all countries and incapable, therefore, of national appropriation, was to become the foundation of the "classical" Law of the Sea and to endure for more than three hundred years until our contemporary era.

But it was, in fact, in its origins a particularist response, by an early seventeenth-century jurist, to the particular legal needs of the then new state, Holland, which had retained him as a juris- consult against the historically older *mare clausum* doctrines developed by Spanish and Portuguese jurists in direct response to the legal needs of the two original European colonial empires, whose political condominium overseas had been given spiritual, if not legal, sanction by Alexander VI's celebrated papal bull dividing the New World territories between Spain and Portugal. The immediate political success of the Grotian doctrine of the Law of the Sea at the time of its formulation undoubtedly owed much to the political and military power of those states that actively sponsored or espoused it.

Its extension and acceptance as *lex lata* on a well-nigh universal scale thereafter stemmed from its innate reasonableness and common sense, corresponding to the political self-interest of all the dominant actors involved in the smaller, "European" world community of that era; just as the challenge to the doctrine's legal authority in the 1970s and the 1980s resulted from the emergence of new, economic interests not present or perceived at the time of creation, and the emergence also of new, non-"European" actors in the latter-day world community.

The implications of historical relativism and recognition of the particular space-time dimension in which particular principles and rules of classical international law emerged have not yet been realized in any comprehensive reordering or rewriting of those principles and rules so as to accord with new societal conditions or needs in the world community today. Classical international law did, however, recognize and accept- albeit very late in the day and in embryonic form only - a special doctrinal category seeking to incorporate the time element into international law- namely, intertemporal law.

INTERTEMPORAL LAW

In a celebrated ruling more than half a century ago, in the Island of Palmas case, the arbitrator, Swiss jurist Max Huber, noted that "manifestations of territorial sovereignty assume ... different forms, according to conditions of time and place." He identified as the "so-called intertemporal law" the question "which of different legal systems prevailing at successive periods is to be applied in a particular case?"

Arbitrator Huber's actual, concrete application of the concept of intertemporal law in this case was a modest one. The dispute itself was wholly polite-between two Western, European or European-derived imperial states, the Netherlands and the United States (the latter as recent legal successor to imperial Spain under the treaty of peace that ended the Spanish-American War of 1898). The limited, European "family compact" aspect of classical international law and of the rules that it specially developed or extended for those Western European commercial, trading societies that had sought their main political expansion in the establishment of colonial empires overseas, is amply reflected in the arbitrator's passing comments as to the legal rights of discovery and acquisition of "uninhabited regions or regions inhabited by savages or semi-civilized peoples."

For the arbitrator, distinguished jurist as he was, this latter phrase denoted all those peoples not of European stock or culture. The step made by classical international law, over the several and more centuries preceding Arbitrator Huber's ruling, of legally equating territories inhabited by such peoples with uninhabited regions and regions therefore open to effective acquisition by the first European visitor, was perhaps logically inevitable, granted the basic Eurocentrism of those in a position to make the legally authoritative and binding decisions concerned.

The cultural particularity or relativism of the special international law categories as to acquisition and retention of territorial title developed in that earlier "colonial" period of world history is obvious enough, just as is the case for their imaginative rewriting or reordering today, now that the main legal imperatives of the post-World War II era, of decolonization, independence, and national self-determination have been so largely achieved in the main political arenas of the contemporary world community.

THE SEARCH FOR A MODERN RESTATEMENT

The Institut de Droit International, responding to all the pressures for fundamental legal change in a world community clearly in an era of transition from an "old," classical, Western-based public order system to a "new" one, whose exact contours and directions are not always clear, established a special research commission to report on the "problem of intertemporal law" in time for its centennial session, held in Rome in 1973. In the report, and in the formal resolution adopted by the Institut at the Wiesbaden session in 1975, the problematic is identified modestly as intertemporal problems, the Institut thereby eschewing the invitation from some of its more adventurous spirits to proceed to the development of general rules of intertemporal law.

Judge Manfred Lachs, as a member of the Institut's research commission, had warned against any approach to the role of time in relation to law that was too strictly confined to the study of positive law alone. In rejecting the suggested dichotomy between the time dimension "from the philosophical viewpoint" and the time dimension in its effects "in the field of positive law," he rightly reminded other members of the commissiion that, even in the natural sciences, erstwhile purely static conceptions of the time component had been sundered in modern times by the development of the theory of relativity and the more sophisticated latter-day comprehension of the whole space-time continuum.

The explanation for any juridical conservatism inherent in the Institut commission's approach to one of the key legal problems of an era of transition such as our own - how to adjust, creatively and in timely fashion, the legal order of yesterday to the new societal conditions and demands of today and the emerging tomorrow - surely is not to be found in intellectual timidity on the part of its members, for it was a very strong commission with an innovatory and forward-looking rapporteur, the late Max Sorensen.

The existing positive law base, the point of departure for any venture in the progressive development of international law, was, quite simply, too narrow in its original formulation, since it was developed at the apogee of classical Western international law, in a purely intra-Western dispute, with deliberately narrowed-down issues determined by, and corresponding to, the self-interest of the two, then only notionally adversary, colonial powers, the Netherlands and the United States, actually involved in the dispute that they had agreed to submit to arbitration.

The problem of creative restatement, half a century later, of the culturally relativist and intellectually deliberately narrow and restricted positive law principles therein laid down was compounded by the asymmetrical character of the legal-doctrinal categories involved; as Judge Pescatore pointed out, such conflicts in a contemporary context would often concern treaty and custom, or bilateral and multilateral treaty, the default in parity between the categories of legal norms for which one must determine the field of temporal applications thus adding to the complexity of the problem.

The Institut's attempt to define the problem, contained in its final resolution as adopted in Wiesbaden in 1975, expressly recognizes the central antinomy of international law of our times, between the status quo and the forces of change. In its preamble, it states that "any solution of an intertemporal problem in the international field must take account of the dual requirement of development and stability."

It completes the purely definitional exercise by declaring that "the general intertemporal problem...relates to the delimitation of the temporal sphere of application of norms"; and that the problem "arises whenever a rule refers to a concept the scope or significance of which has changed in the course of time."

The prescriptive part of the Institut's resolution seems to adhere rather closely to Arbitrator Huber's original formulation:

1. Unless otherwise indicated, the temporal sphere of application of any norm of public international law shall be determined in accordance with the general principle of law by which any fact, action or situation must be assessed in the light of the rules of law that are contemporaneous with it.

The openings of the future, however, are contained in Article 3 of the Institut resolution, which, while expressly reserving to "States and other subjects of international law ... the power to determine by common consent the temporal sphere of application of norms," makes such liberty of contract nevertheless "subject to any imperative norm of international law which might restrict that power." Such "imperative norms" are, on the precedent of the Vienna Convention on Treaties, in no way defined, and will therefore in the future remain open to creative interpretation of historical evolution of norms.

The attempted hedging in of this *jus cogens* limitation on the parties' liberty to contract out of the intertemporal law dating (or updating, as the case may be) of their mutual, treaty-based obligations, by the provision, in paragraph 2 of the same Article 3, that it is all to be "without prejudice to obligations which may ensue for contracting parties from previous treaties to which they are parties and from the provisions of which they cannot depart even by common consent," seems otiose and legally irrelevant and ineffectual, since, *ex hypothesi*, an "imperative norm" of international law (*jus cogens*) must be hierarchically superior to and legally prevail over any contrary rule or obligation, whether flowing from customary international law or from the parties' own self-legislation in treaty form.

CREATIVE JUDICIAL LEGISLATION: THE WORLD COURT

NAMIBIA (1971)

The Namibia advisory opinion, rendered by the International Court of Justice in 1971, represented one of those very rare instances of a second chance accorded to an international institution to correct political damage resulting to it from an earlier decision. In this case, the decision was the narrow 8-7 judgment (determined on the second, tie-breaking vote of the court's president) in 1966 in South West Africa, Second Phase, which many liberal-minded Western jurists, likening it to the United States Supreme Court decision more than a century earlier in the Dred Scott case, which was thought to have hastened the onset of the American Civil War, characterized as one of the court's "great, self-inflicted wounds." In South West Africa, Second Phase, in 1966, the court majority finely limited its earlier, 1962 ruling in South West Africa, Preliminary Objections, in which it had held that the complainant states, Ethiopia and Liberia, had *locus standi* to raise the issue of the legality of the white minority-ruled Republic of South Africa's continued control over South West Africa, by now holding that they did not have legal standing to receive judgment, a legal distinction that would certainly have baffled the ingenuity of the medieval schoolmen. In the angry political criticism that followed its 1966 ruling, the court was denounced in the United Nations General Assembly as a "white man's tribunal."

The opportunity for political atonement by the court came when the United Nations Security Council voted to refer to the court the general issue of the Legal Consequences for States of the Continued Presence of South Africa in Namibia (South West Africa), this in the light of a series of United Nations-based measures following the 1966 court decision, of which the most striking perhaps was General Assembly Resolution 2145 (XXI) of 1966, declaring the Republic of South Africa mandate over Namibia (South West Africa) to be forthwith "terminated." In a judicial volte-face startling in both number and extent after no more than five years, the court in 1971, by 13-2 and 11-4 votes on the substantive issues, agreed that the mandate was effectively terminated and the Republic of South Africa's presence in Namibia was in consequence illegal, these two decisions being opposable to all states in the sense of barring *erga omnes* the legality of a situation maintained in violation of international law.

The ruling of the court is a multi-opinion one, with no less than seven different, separate (majority) opinions filed, in addition to the official opinion of the court. The court majority's conclusions rest on a number of separate grounds, of which, in the present context, the issue of the time dimension in legal interpretation is of special interest to us. The Republic of South Africa's claimed legal title to Namibia derived from its original League of Nations Class "C" category mandate, conferred in 1919. The Republic of South Africa's legal argumentation before the court in the Namibia hearing covered, as the opinion of the court noted, "a wide field of history, going back to the origin and functioning of the Mandate," and designed to demonstrate that such mandates were "in their practical effect not far removed from annexation."

While cynical opinion at the time of the creation of the League of Nations mandates system no doubt viewed the mandates concept as a polite euphemism or legal fiction to veil the postwar division of defeated imperial Germany's colonies on a "to the victor the spoils" principle, a now contemporary World Court, deciding the issue in a contemporary context, flatly rejected any such assimilation of the post-World War I mandates to classical international law's colonies because that would be "tantamount to admitting that the relevant provisions of the [League of Nations] Covenant were of a purely nominal character and that the rights they enshrined were of their very nature imperfect and unenforceable." Borrowing from its own earlier advisory opinion of 1950 on the International Status of South West Africa, the court reiterated that in the setting up of the mandates system "two principles were considered to be of paramount importance: the principle of non-annexation and the principle that the well-being and development of such peoples form 'a sacred trust of civilisation.' "

It is here that the World Court reaches out and embraces the concept of intertemporal law. The relevant international law to apply today is not a closed body of principles, conceived and applied as in time past, the actual time of entry into force of the League of Nations' mandates system back in 1919; but something rather more dynamic, lending itself to progressive, generic interpretation and reformulation over the years since that time, in accord with the changing conditions and expectations of a world community that is today vastly more representative and pluralistic in character than that narrower, "European," special legal community that imposed its Carthaginian "victors' peace" at Versailles in 1919 and set up the League of Nations as an integral element of the postwar world public order system that it sought to use to maintain the spoils of that victory against defeated imperial Germany and its erstwhile allies in World War I.

...The Court is bound to take into account the fact that the concepts embodied in Article 22 of the Covenant...were not static, but were by definition evolutionary, as also, therefore, was the concept of the "sacred trust." The parties to the Covenant must consequently be deemed to have accepted them as such. That is why, viewing the institutions of 1919, the Court must take into consideration the changes which have occurred in the supervening half-century, and its interpretation cannot remain unaffected by the subsequent development of law, through the Charter of the United Nations and by way of customary law. Moreover, an international instrument has to be interpreted and applied within the framework of the entire legal system prevailing at the time of the interpretation. In the domain to which the present proceedings relate, the last fifty years, as indicated above, have brought important developments. These developments leave little doubt that the ultimate objective of the sacred trust was the self- determination and independence of the peoples concerned. In this domain, as elsewhere, the corpus *iuris gentium* has been considerably enriched, and this the Court, if it is faithfully to discharge its functions, may not ignore.

WESTERN SAHARA (1975)

The Western Sahara problem came to the World Court on reference from the United Nations General Assembly. Like Namibia (1971), it was at root a "colonial" issue-the attempt by the new Third World majority in the main parliamentary organs of the United Nations to compel a "parent" European, imperial power to recognize the winds of change in the world community and to concede national self-determination, independence, and decolonization to an original, indigenous, aboriginal people. Spain, through failure to decentralize and devolve its colonial administration in timely fashion, had lost almost all of its first, Latin American colonial empire within the first few decades of the nineteenth century, and had then turned, painfully and awkwardly, to build a much more modest second empire out of the morsels of Africa that had by that time been left over, forgotten, or rejected as worthless by far more rapacious or ruthless imperial powers.

When the historical moment finally could not be postponed for disposing of its second, African empire, Spain seemed to have learned nothing and forgotten nothing from its earlier historical experience. For it accepted the "new" international law principles of decolonization, independence and national self-determination for subject colonial peoples only tardily and then seemingly most reluctantly and because there was no politically viable alternative available. On Spain's behalf it can be noted that there were certainly other imperial powers which had also decolonized either very, very late in the day and with no particular goodwill, or else on a highly partial and selective basis with only the, by then, politically and militarily indefensible colonies being yielded up in timely fashion.

By comparison with these other old imperial countries, Spain had a stagnant national economy and was arguably incapable of easily and quickly recovering from the extra financial blow of loss of the revenues from the rich phosphate deposits in its Western Sahara colonies. In this context, Spain now proposed that it should go ahead and hold its own referendum in the contested West African colonial territory, a political stratagem that was viewed, perhaps correctly, by the United Nations General Assembly majority as a device for further delaying and frustrating the original people's approach to independent nationhood. Hence the Third World activism for a General Assembly reference to the court for advisory opinion, as a method of triggering or speeding up Spanish decolonization. The key question posed to the court in the General Assembly's reference directly implicated the classical Western European-derived international law rules as to acquisition of territorial sovereignty by an imperial state in relation to colonial territories and aboriginal peoples overseas: "Was Western Sahara (Rio Oro and Sakiet el Hamra) at the time of colonisation by Spain a territory belonging to no one (terra nullius)?"

The court, in the Western Sahara advisory opinion in 1975, divided 13-3 on this question, and the court's ruling, once again, sees the official opinion of the court accompanied by a plethora of separate (majority) opinions or declarations-no less than nine of these, in fact. It is thus a multi-ground majority ruling with, in common-law terms, no clear ratio *decidendi* or majority ground of decision apparent in the official record. Nevertheless, the issue of intertemporal law and its application in a contemporary problem situation is a core element in the court holding, and one on which a clear line of intellectual demarcation or differentiation is apparent between the more orthodox, conservative, "classical" majority within the overall court majority and what might be categorized, without any hidden value judgment being intended, as the court's more avant-garde or front-running members, with their deliberate openings to the "new" international law.

Thus the official opinion of the court decided that, for purposes of responding to the *res nullius* question, the critical time period was that beginning in 1884, when Spain proclaimed a proctectorate over the Rio de Oro. While Spain had indeed mentioned certain earlier acts of alleged display of its sovereignty in the fifteenth and sixteenth centuries, it had done so, the official opinion of the court suggested, only to enlighten the court as to the remote antecedents of the Spanish presence on the West African coast and not with the design of proving any continuity between those acts and the Spanish proclamation of a protectorate in 1884. The period beginning in 1884 thus constituted the temporal context within which the two substantive questions addressed to the court by the General Assembly should be answered.

It was on this basis that the official opinion of the court reasoned that the question whether or not Western Sahara was terra nullius at the time of colonization by Spain was to be interpreted by reference to the law in force at that period, 1884. But a determination that Western Sahara was terra nullius in that case would be possible only if it were established that at that time the territory belonged to no one. On the specific facts, the court found that, at the time of colonization by Spain, Western Sahara was inhabited by people who, if nomadic, were socially and politically organized in tribes and under chiefs competent to represent them. Indeed, in colonizing Western Sahara, Spain itself purported to base itself legally on various agreements entered into between the king of Spain and the chiefs of local tribes. The court was thus able to respond fairly easily and quickly to the main question posed to it by the General Assembly and to conclude that at the time of Spanish colonization Western Sahara was not a "territory belonging to no one (*terra nullius*)."

A second question referred to the court by the General Assembly asked the court to state what were the "legal ties" between Western Sahara and "the Kingdom of Morocco and the Mauritanian entity." This second question, the court majority opined, would also have to be decided in the temporal context of the actual act of colonization by Spain-that is, 1884. At the time of such colonization, the court found, Western Sahara, as an area of desert with low and spasmodic rainfall, was being developed almost exclusively by nomads, who traversed very wide areas of the desert, not confined to Western Sahara, the links between the different nomadic communities being essentially tribal rather than territorial ties or ties of allegiance or vassalage.

Morocco had argued, on a basis of the old Permanent Court's ruling in Legal Status of Eastern Greenland, that a series of events stretching back to the seventh century A.D. and the Arab conquest of North Africa, even though having a "far-flung, spasmodic and often transitory character," were sufficient, in relation to a territory geographically contiguous to itself and desert in character, to establish a claim to title based "upon continued display of authority." The legally novel aspect of the Moroccan case, however, was posited upon asserted common ethnological, cultural, and religious ties between Western Sahara and Morocco, the argument being that the common religious bond of Islam existing among the peoples concerned could form legal ties of sovereignty where the essentially Western, ethnocentrist notion of territory might not. While seemingly not accepting these arguments as such, the court did conclude that the available evidence provided indications that a legal tie of allegiance had existed at the relevant period between the Sultan of Morocco and some, but only some, of the nomadic peoples of the Western Sahara territory.

As for the legal ties, at the time of Spanish colonization, between Western Sahara and the "Mauritanian entity" (the latter, concededly, something that did not exist as a state at that particular point in historical time), the then contemporary state of Mauritania laid emphasis on the special characteristics of the Saharan area and the nomadic existence of many of the tribes, each of which had its own well-defined migration area with well-defined migration routes determined by the location of water holes, burial grounds, cultivated areas, and pastures. As the Mauritanian government contended, "the colonial Powers...in drawing frontiers took no account of these human factors and in particular of the tribal territories and migration routes, which were, as a result, bisected and even trisected by these artificial frontiers."

The Spanish government, in reply, rejected any notion of a "nation" or "people" in the Western Sahara "formed of tribes, confederations and emirates jointly exercising co-sovereignty," characterizing the Mauritanian government's case as resting on "the mere sociological facts of nomadic life." This was a position that the court seemed eventually to embrace in ruling that there was no "tie of sovereignty, or of allegiance of tribes, or of 'simple inclusion' in the same legal entity."

The official opinion of the court in Western Sahara, as we have suggested, is conservative or cautious in regard to a rather novel fact situation that seemed to invite legal innovation, since it provided unusual opportunities for the judges to move toward a progressive development of old international law categories to meet the new political and societal facts of life of the post-World War II world community. Not so the separate (specially concurring) opinions, which, while filed in support of the official opinion of the court, make, in several instances at least, such determined openings to the "new" international law as to amount almost to veiled dissents from the opinion of the court in the range and quality of the substantive law critique that they advance.

The strongest and most sustained of the special opinions is that of Vice-President Ammoun, which adopts, with approval, remarks contained in the written pleadings before the court by the Zairian jurist Bayona-Ba-Meya. Such pleadings served in Vice-President Ammoun's words, to dismiss the materialistic concept of terra nullius, which led to this dismemberment of Africa following the Berlin Conference of 1885. Mr. Bayona-Ba-Meya substitutes for this a spiritual notion: the ancestral tie between the land, or "mother nature," and the man, who was born therefrom, remains attached thereto, and must one day return thither to be united with his ancestors. This link is the basis of the ownership of the soil, or better, of sovereignty. This amounts to a denial of the very concept of terra nullius in the sense of a land which is capable of being appropriated by someone who is not born therefrom. It is a condemnation of the modern concept, as defined by Pasquale Fiore, which regards as terra nullius territories inhabited by populations whose civilisation, in the sense of the public law of Europe, is backward and whose political organisation is not conceived according to Western norms.... This is the reply which may be given to the participants in the Berlin Conference of 1885....

Judge Ammoun then adopted with approval the reasoning of the Algerian jurist Mohammed Bedjaoui, who in his written pleading before the court had identified three distinct epochs in the development and evolution of the "classical" international law as to acquisition of title to territory:

- Roman antiquity, when any territory which was not Roman was characterised, legally, as being nullius;
- The epoch of the great Western European "discoveries" of the sixteenth and seventeenth centuries, during which any territory not belonging to a Western European Christian sovereign was characterised, legally, as nullius;
- The nineteenth century, during which any territory which did not belong to a so-called civilised state was characterised, legally, as nullius.

Judge Ammoun concluded:

... the concept of terra nullius, employed at all periods to the brink of the twentieth century, to justify conquest and colonisation, stands condemned. It is well known that in the sixteenth century Francisco de Vittoria protested against the application to the American Indians, in order to deprive them of their lands, of the concept of *res nullius*.

Judge Ammoun was joined, in his discussion of the spatially and temporally limited "Western" or "classical" international law character of the concept of terra nullius, by

Judge Forster, who in a separate opinion indicated his own disagreement with the opinion of the court insofar as it had concluded against ties of territorial sovereignty between Western Sahara and the Kingdom of Morocco and the Mauritanian entity. Judge Forster thought that the opinion of the court had gone too far in minimising the exceptional importance of the geographical, social and temporal contexts of the problem.... It is Africa of former times which is in question, as to which it cannot arbitrarily be required that its institutions should be a carbon copy of European institutions, for on that basis almost the entire African continent would have to be declared terra nullius.

This was a theme recurred to by ad hoc Judge Boni, who, in a separate opinion, also reproached the authors of the majority opinion of the court for their essentially static conception of the "classical" international law cluster of legal concepts as to acquisition of territorial title. The intellectual joinder of issue was thus made clearly and coherently and interestingly, in Western Sahara, between the "old," essentially Western, Eurocentrist international law rules in this area, and the "new," with their openings to the much more inclusive and richly pluralist world community of today. The relativism, in space-time terms, of the "old" or "classical" rules, with their origins in that limited, family-compact era of those European societies founded on the rise of commerce and consequently in search of territorial conquests and colonies overseas, thus stands sharply demonstrated, as is also the case for the imaginative restatement and rewriting of these "old" rules, so that they may better accord with contemporary societal needs.

CONTINENTAL SHELF (TUNISIA/LIBYAN ARAB JAMAHIRIYA), (1982)

Continental Shelf (Tunisia/ Libyan Arab Jamahiriya) is one of those rare instances in World Court jurisprudence-of the "old" Permanent Court of the between-the-two-wars era and of the "new" International Court of the post-World War

II era-of a dispute between two states from outside that limited Western European, family-compact group of states that had so largely written "classical" international law and its detailed rules. In this case, it was two recently decolonized Third World countries, Tunisia (a former French colony) and Libya (a former Italian colony), that were directly involved. The conflicts between the "old" and the "new" international law that we have seen in earlier cases that produced the opportunities for progressive development of international law, symbolized in the conflict of the actual parties-usually a parent European or European- derived imperial state and its former colonial territories-are not so clear-cut and obvious.

Nevertheless, the range of opinions filed in the case, from the official opinion of the court to the three separate opinions and the three dissenting opinions (Judges Gros, Oda, and ad hoc Judge Evensen), reveal clearly enough that the essentially static conservative approach to restatement of the "old" or "classical" law tended to favor one of the two parties rather than the other. By comparison, a more imaginative judicial opening to the "new" international law would be needed for that other party to succeed. The historical contradictions inherent in a court process and a court judgment rendered in an era of transition and rapid change in the world community are plentiful and obvious. We may note in passing the fact that counsel for the two parties were overwhelmingly drawn from the "old," Western European countries, notwithstanding that the client states were both newly decolonized Third World countries.

The "European" character of the handling and presentation of the case before the court seemed to carry over into the judgment and judicial opinions rendered, giving it at times a jejune quality redolent of an earlier historical era in the world community; as if the two original, parent colonial states, Italy and France, were carrying on, by some quirk of the time machine and through the proxies of their erstwhile colonies, Libya and Tunisia, their old imperial rivalries and battles of yesterday.

Our present interest in the case lies in those aspects of the judgment (concerning the delimitation of the continental shelf between the two adjacent states) that involve recourse to "new trends" in international law, as exemplified in the then still continuing Third United Nations Conference on the Law of the Sea and its project for a draft convention (particularly Articles 76 and 83), and that involve application of equitable principles with a view to achieving an equitable solution (particularly proportionality).

These deliberate judicial openings to the "new" international law as a viable alternative option to the simple restatement of the "old" or "classical" law, such as it might be are perhaps best reflected in the dissenting opinion of the Japanese jurist Judge Oda. Judge Oda noted that while the basic legal concept of the continental shelf had been strongly confirmed by the 1958 Convention on the Continental Shelf and further endorsed by the court's own judgment in 1969, in North Sea Continental Shelf, as being established under customary international law, the actual extent of the legal continental shelf had been left indeterminate, because of the introduction of the equivocal notion of exploitability which suggested that the area could eventually expand under virtually the whole of the high seas. This trend was halted by the rise of the new concept of the international sea-bed area late in the 1960s. The realisation that the concept of exploitability could be interpreted to mean that all sea-bed areas of the world would eventually be divided among separate States led Malta to take the initiative by introducing the concept of the common heritage of mankind, to be applied in the area beyond a redefined continental shelf.

If this, then, was the dominant new trend in the concept of the continental shelf, confirmed in United Nations General Assembly Resolution 2340 (XXII) of December 18, 1967, establishing the United Nations Sea- Bed Committee, the legal definition of the outer limits of the continental shelf for purposes of national appropriation was subject to fluctuating criteria, with many landlocked and shelf-locked countries, acting as a group, taking a position in 1972 opposing the idea of wider continental- shelf and / or narrower international sea-bed areas. The background to Article 69 of the so-called Informal Composite Negotiating Text of the ensuing Third United Nations Conference on the Law of the Sea was the "fact of geography that the formation of the continental shelf can be extremely inequitable for some coastal States."

In the result, we find the compromise proposal that the continental shelf would be divided into two areas, the first being the area within 200 miles from the coast, where the exclusive interests of the coastal state would be established, and the other, the area beyond that, where a portion of the profits would be dedicated to the international community, in particular the developing nations. This parallelism is retained, with some modifications, in the draft convention as Article 82. It cannot be over-emphasised that this formula never founded part of the traditional concept of the continental shelf.

Judge Oda went on to conclude, from this, that parallel with the change in the outer limit of the continental shelf-the clear trend in the evolution of international law since the 1958 convention-the notion of natural prolongation by which the concept of the continental shelf was embellished in the [Court's] 1969 Judgment has greatly lost its significance, particularly with the introduction of the criterion of the 200-mile distance under the strong influence of the concept of the exclusive economic zone ..., not to mention the parallelism between that zone and a possible inner-continental shelf of 200 miles, coupled with the possibility of a different régime applying to the continental margin beyond that distance.... The concept of the continental shelf cannot have escaped change as a result of the fading-away of the geomorphological notion of natural prolongation. This notion may be said to have remained in the case where the (geomorphological) continental shelf or slope extends farther than 200 miles, yet it must be said that the concept of the continental shelf, which had been sustained by scholarly views and the imperious necessities of the 1950s, has, early in the 1980s, changed.

Judge Oda's dissenting opinion represents an intellectual tour de force by a jurist who, on his sustained experience as adviser and member of his own country's national delegation to the various international conclaves on the Law of the Sea from 1958 onward, might fairly be described as a founding father of the modern Law of Sea. The extensive and detailed survey of all the travaux préparatoires undertaken by Judge Oda might, in and of itself, be enough, on strictly historical grounds, to dispose of the Libyan Arab Jamahiriya's case as to a "natural prolongation" of its continental shelf accepted by the court majority.

Judge Oda's excursus, in his dissenting opinion, on the role of equitable principles in contemporary international law was also interesting in the present context, insofar as he refused to regard equity as a closed juridical category incapable of further growth through time.

The court in its 1969 judgment in North Sea Continental Shelf had refused to accept the concept of "a just and equitable share," preferring to restrict itself to the "delimitation and not to the apportionment of the areas concerned, or their division into converging sectors."

While prepared to accept that "the sea-bed area is not meant to be parcelled out like so many fiefs," Judge Oda was at pains to distinguish and limit the 1969 court holding where it refused to embrace the idea of equitable apportionment. This part of the earlier 1969 holding, in Judge Oda's view, was now overtaken by events. There was thus insufficient reason for the present Court, in 1982, to be inhibited from realising that the present delimitation was simply a question of equitably dividing, or apportioning, between the Parties, by means of a justifiable line of demarcation, those submarine areas which either could potentially have claimed.

The opening up of the time dimension in international law was thus explicit, even if in the end Judge Oda would draw back from any court- based formulation of a "geographical equity" involving "global resource policies" or even "world social justice." This part of Judge Oda's discussion goes, however, beyond our present concern with the operation of the time factor in international law, and will be canvassed more fully in the analysis of the role of equity today among the formal sources of law.

The contemporary acceptance of the relevance of the time dimension in international law stems from the increasing recognition of the historical relativism of so many of the rules of "classical" international law. These rules arose, of course, in particular eras in world history, in response to particular societal conditions, needs, and expectations, as perceived and recorded by the dominant political forces of those times. It is on this basis that so much of "classical" international law-both old treaties and old rules of customary international law-is now rejected or questioned by the "new" countries of the Third World as "Western" or "Eurocentric" in character and hence as no longer authoritative and binding in the new, more richly pluralistic and inclusive world community of today, which has transcended its original, narrowly Western political base with the successful legal achievement of national self-determination, decolonization, and independence on a by now nearly universal scale.

The normative quality, in legal terms today, of the old international law rules is increasingly subjected to the test of reason: those rules are to be critically reexamined in the context of the historically limited space-time dimension of their origins, and then tested in terms of their claims, such as they may be, to continuing relevance and reasonableness in the larger world community of our time. What is less clear is the exact doctrinal-legal basis on which those old substantive legal rules can be, according to the contemporary test of reason, either accepted in their original sense and meaning, or else restated and updated in symbiotic relationship with a changed (and much expanded) international society, or, finally, rejected altogether as historically anachronistic and incompatible with the evolving juridical conscience of mankind.

Karl Doehring, a jurist of the Federal Republic of Germany, correctly identifies a certain ambiguity in the concept of the time factor in international law and suggests that it first be broken down into its various elements for the purpose of separate analysis and calculation of the juridical consequences. One such element is clearly the "classical" formulation of intertemporal law represented by Arbitrator Max Huber's ruling in Island of Pal-mas in 1928. The emphasis here is clearly on the time at which the particular rule in question first arose.

Since the actual conflict was between two Western powers, the arbitrator's emphasis on time of origin is not loaded in ethnic-cultural terms with regard to its consequences when applied; nor is there any particular cause for reproach of the arbitrator for his focus on time past to the exclusion of time present or even the emerging time future. Objective certainty as to the content of the claimed rule at its time of origin was the value sought by the parties, the Netherlands and the United States, both then, in Weberian terms, at the apogee of their own particular economic and legal development; and this is what the arbitrator rendered to them. It would be itself anachronistic to apply to arbitrator Huber's seminal ruling of more than half a century ago the legal standards and values of the present world community, which is in transition and fundamental conflict.

Less certain, however, is the case for the relatively traditional or conservative restatement adopted by the authoritative Institut de Droit International in 1975 in its Wiesbaden resolution. Allowing for the fact that the Institut operates essentially by consensus and that its resolutions are the product of compromises within its specialized commissions and very often acquire thereby a watered-down or lowest-common-denominator character in which the status quo ante tends to prevail, the political and legal challenge to "classical" international law and the transition from the "old" postwar world public order system were already apparent at that time.

The distinguished rapporteur, Judge Sorensen, was fully aware of the problem, as is manifest from the thoughtful argumentation he developed in his provisional and final reports. But the final resolution, while identifying the basic antinomy between stability and change in contemporary international law, offers no particular help in its solution to concrete cases. It gives, indeed, a prime emphasis to the voluntarist approach and the power of the parties to "determine by common consent the temporal sphere of application of norms," subject only to "any imperative norm of international law which might restrict that power." The resolution does not provide any criteria for identifying such imperative norms that would restrict the law-making power of the original parties as to the time factor.

It might be suggested, of course, that the resolution's voluntarist emphasis, which makes the will of the original contracting parties determinative of the time factor, is not an adequate response to the interest in change in the stability-change legal antinomy postulated in the resolution's preamble; for it will normally be a latter-day third party, extrinsic to the original contractual obligation, who will be making the case, in contemporary terms, for imaginative rewriting and updating of the old rules and their novation in legal terms today. On legal interpretation, the Institut resolution suggests that it is "appropriate to have recourse to the usual methods of interpretation," without, however, defining these or even listing them by way of example; and it remains unclear whether the Institut envisaged these as including progressive, generic interpretation, along the lines of the International Court of Justice's advisory opinion in Namibia 1971.

Apart from intertemporal law *stricto sensu*, as defined by Arbitrator Huber and the Institut's Wiesbaden resolution, there are other examples of the relevance of the time factor as recognized and applied in international law doctrine and jurisprudence. Doehring, in his imaginative study published in 1964, points to Jellinek's concept, Die normative Kraft des Faktischen, first developed in 1922, and its potential to create concrete legal consequences in problem situations of that time, such as the post- World War II territorial frontiers in Central and Eastern Europe. These particular problems may now have been finally resolved, in legal terms, by the supervening Ostpolitik mini-accords between the Federal Republic of Germany on the one hand and the Soviet Union and Eastern European countries.

But the general philosophical problem of the duality of the Sein and the Sollen remains, for the final attribution of normative legal consequences to the factual, existential condition amounts to a form of international legal determinism. It is no doubt on purely pragmatic considerations that the International Law Commission would confer such sanctity on treaties establishing a territorial boundary, exempting them from the ordinary rules as to fundamental change of circumstances, even though so many such treaties have been imposed under duress, at the conclusion of a war or in a European "colonial" context. Granted this newly created gap in its application today, *clausula rebus sic stantibus* remains one of the more potentially interesting and creative legal- doctrinal bases for adjusting old legal rules-here, treaty-made rules - to meet new societal conditions and also new values in the plural world community of today.

By and large, however, the best opportunities for imaginative application of the time factor in the progressive development of international law would seem to lie in the ordinary processes of legal interpretation, especially as applied by the International Court. As the Institut de Droit International special rapporteur, Judge Sorensen, expressly noted in his provisional report, Verdross and before him Baade had accepted a qualitative difference, for purposes of legal interpretation, between limited, normally bilateral, treaties - which ought, it was suggested, normally to be referred to the law in force at the moment when the treaty entered into force - and the larger, usually multilateral "normative" conventions - which, it was suggested, lent themselves to "evolutionary notions" by which the contracting parties had "wanted to keep the door open to the development of international law"; such a larger, "normative" convention "acquired its own life, independent of the will of the parties at the moment of its conclusion."

Beyond that, the International Court of Justice has shown the way-albeit more usually in dissenting opinions like Judge Jessup's in South West Africa, Second Phase in 1966, but sometimes in the majority opinion of the court itself, as in Namibia, 1971-to "progressive, generic interpretation which, as an instrument of judicial activism, quite as properly belongs among the traditional or "classical" techniques of judicial construction as that strict or literal, positivist interpretation manifested by the court majority in the opinion of the court in the politically unfortunate and much criticized one-vote-majority South West Africa, Second Phase opinion.

What may be needed to continue to spark such creative judicial interpretation in the future is a more imaginative and dynamic approach to history on the part of counsel appearing before the court and preparing the *legal factum*, much as counsel Bayona-Ba-Meya and Mohammed Bedjaoui, appearing in argument in Western Sahara in 1975, refused to accept past history as exercising a dead-hand control today and insisted instead, in Jean Jaurès' phase, in "taking from the altars of the past the fires, not the ashes." It is a concept well known to common lawyers, and summed up in Mr. Justice Oliver Wendell Holmes's maxim that "the life of the law has not been logic, but experience."

The concept of intertemporal law, imaginatively updated and applied today, seems comprehensive enough, as a doctrinal-legal category, to encompass modern, evolutionary approaches to the interpretation of past history and their application, through the judicial process, to the novation of old legal categories through the techniques of progressive, generic interpretation. Intertemporal law, viewed now as a formal juridical category, is, it is submitted, still inchoate but fully capable of further organic growth and development. The requirement, in analytical jurisprudential terms, is to conceptualize it into a larger, more comprehensive category encompassing at once intemporal law *stricto sensu*, at least as restated by the Institut de Droit International in its Wiesbaden resolution in 1975; that special juridical process whereby the factual or existential becomes normative, through and with the passage of time (Die normative Kraft des Faktischen); and the authoritative manifestations of the "progressive development of international law" effectuated in the judgments and assorted opinions of the International Court of Justice and in the law-making decisions of other legally competent United Nations organs (declaratory resolutions of the United Nations General Assembly, agreed texts of international codifying conferences, and the like).

10

International Court of Justice and Judicial Policy Making

COURT JURISDICTION

The Charter, in its Article 92, establishes the International Court of Justice as the "principal judicial organ of the United Nations," and also declares the statute of the court (based on the statute of the old, between- the-two-world-wars Permanent Court of International Justice, to which the new International Court succeeded) as "form[ing] an integral part of the present Charter." All members of the United Nations are, according to Article 93 of the Charter, ipso facto parties to the statute of the International Court; and the annual report of the court for 1981-1982, submitted to the thirty-seventh annual session of the General Assembly, noted that the total was then 157, plus Switzerland and two mini- or quasi-states.

Articles 36(1) of the court statute provides that the jurisdiction of the court "comprises all cases which the parties refer to it and all matters specially provided for in the Charter of the United Nations or in treaties and conventions in force." Under Article 36(2) of the court statute, the states party to the statute may declare that they "recognise as compulsory ipso facto and without special agreement, in relation to any other state accepting the same obligation, the jurisdiction of the Court in all legal disputes...." The annual report of the court for 1981-1982 noted that at that time there were forty-seven states which had opted to recognize the compulsory jurisdiction of the court in terms of Article 36(2) of the court statute, though a number of these states had attached reservations to their acceptance of such compulsory jurisdiction, particularly (as with the United States) reservations excepting from such acceptance matters within their own domestic jurisdiction as they themselves might choose to interpret that.

A potentially fecund source of jurisdiction for the International Court remains the advisory opinion jurisdiction established by the Charter, Article 96:

1. The General Assembly or the Security Council may request the International Court of Justice to give any advisory opinion on any legal question.
2. Other organs of the United Nations and specialised agencies, which may at any time be so authorised by the General Assembly, may also request advisory opinions of the Court on legal questions arising within the scope of their activities.

The annual report of the court for 1981-1982 noted that, in addition to the General Assembly and Security Council, the list of United Nations organs and specialized agencies at present legally authorized to approach the court for advisory opinions included the Economic and Social Council, the Trusteeship Council, the Interim Committee of the General Assembly, the Committee on Applications for Review of Administrative Tribunal Judgments, and specialized agencies such as the ILO, FAO, UNESCO, International Bank for Reconstruction and Development, International Monetary Fund, and others.

COMPARATIVE REGIONAL ATTITUDES TO INTERNATIONAL ADJUDICATION

The central dilemma in international adjudication in our times concerns the dwindling away of the effective working jurisdiction of the International Court of Justice since its inauguration in 1946, in comparison, certainly, with the rich years between the two world wars, when the old Permanent Court of International Justice was in operation. Part of the explanation for the latter-day crisis in the work load of the International Court-too few cases, too few client states - is indeed to be found in the comparison between the two periods of international adjudication, that of the "old" court and that of the "new" court.

For the old Permanent Court was in operation in that earlier, European "family compact" era of international organization when the League of Nations, as the embryonic world government of the time, reflected the interests and aspirations of the politically dominant Western European states that had imposed the Treaty of Versailles of 1919.

Judicial settlement of disputes, in this context, reflected the special cultural attitudes and intellectual outlooks of Western European society in the golden years of its political, military, and economic power; and the notion of "judicializing" international conflicts and their concrete resolution had a special appeal, therefore, in what was an essentially homogeneous, limited, special legal community, whose key members shared the same essential values. The expansion of the world community after World War II to take in-particularly as decolonization and national self-determination began to be achieved on a near worldwide basis-so very many new, non-Western European, Afro-Asian states presaged a decline in the erstwhile prestige and authority and popularity of the court-based approach to conflict resolution, even though so many of the "new" states had, for their own part, very substantial "received" European (whether Anglo-Saxon common law, or French or German civil law) legal traditions.

It was not only a matter of basic legal-institutional method and process involved in the concept of judicial settlement of disputes, but also one of the substantive legal values and value choice thought likely to emerge if the fundamental political-legal conflicts of the post-World War II era were referred to the courts for arbitrament. We have already noted the Soviet opposition to any expanded role for the International Court within the United Nations system, and a fortiorito any form of judicial legislation or judicial policy making for the future.

Such Soviet attitudes toward the World Court, which have the merit of consistency and avoidance of any purely ad hoc response in pursuit of temporary national advantage in the instant case, stem historically from pre-World War II Soviet doctrinal positions in regard to the old Permanent Court and to the League of Nations as a whole, and reflect that defensive "holding operation" style of approach that the Soviet Union has always felt to be appropriate for itself and its political allies in their approach to international organization, in view of their more or less permanent minority voting situation in each and all of the main international organs and specialized agencies. But the Soviet special position on the International Court also reflects purely internal, municipal Soviet legal doctrinal writings on "Western" separation-of-powers concepts, denying, as "undemocratic" and as an infringement of the prerogatives of the other, "popular", elected organs of government, any asserted power of constitutional review or constitutional control on the part of the judiciary in relation to the executive and legislative branches of government.

In Certain Expenses of the United Nations in 1962 as we have noted, the two Soviet-bloc judges on the International Court, President Winiarski and Judge Koretsky, took care to insist that the United Nations Charter was not a constitution, to be interpreted and applied in any broad, creative. expansive way, but rather a multilateral treaty, in terms of which the contractual parties had given up some of their own powers for certain quite limited purposes but no more, and which was therefore to be treated and interpreted restrictively, without regard to the claimed "purposes" of the Organization or, for that matter, to supervening practice of the Organization, whatever it might be.

The Soviet-bloc approach to the role-strictly, non-role- of the International Court in the international law making process thus denies any form of judicial policy making and certainly any form of teleological interpretation - even of the style recommended by Gény at the close of the nineteenth century as a necessary, alternative approach to "grammatical" and "logical" interpretation of the Napoleonic Civil Code if the civil law were to maintain its historic quality of a "living law" in constant relation to changing societal needs.

The comparisons with the analytical positivists or "black letter" lawyers of the English Common Law are clear, and it is not by accident, therefore, that Judge Winiarski could feel free to join with the court president, Sir Percy Spender, and that great classical common law jurist Sir Gerald Fitzmaurice in making the bare majority's-8-7, on the second, tie-breaking vote of President Spender-in South West Africa, Second Phase in 1966, whereby the court denied to the two complainant states legal standing to obtain a decision. The states in question-Ethiopia and Liberia - were protesting the white-minority-governed Republic of South Africa's continued apartheid administration over the former German colony and later League of Nations mandate over Namibia (South West Africa).

Since the court, by an 8-7 majority, had earlier, in 1962, conceded to the same two states full legal standing to bring the suit in the first place, the purported legal distinction in 1966 that their legal standing did not extend to receiving judgment would have baffled the ingenuity of the medieval schoolmen. It says a good deal for Judge Winiarski's sense of fidelity to law and consistency in the application of his legal principles that he was prepared to participate, as the logical consequence thereof, in a majority judgment that clearly ran counter to the "new" imperative principles of international law-decolonization and national self-determination - so actively sponsored by Soviet-bloc delegates in all the main political arenas of the United Nations since its founding in 1945. South West Africa, Second Phase in 1966 was a watershed decision for the International Court, and for many external observers of the court's work a political disaster-one of the court's "great, self-inflicted wounds," as Chief Justice Charles Evans Hughes once said of the American Supreme Court decision in the Dred Scott case, which hastened the onset of the American Civil War.

It confirmed, in one single blow, all the suspicions and fears - however ill- founded they might be in fact or as a matter of historical record-of the "new" Afro-Asian countries in the General Assembly that international organization as a whole and the court in particular were politically loaded in favor of maintenance of the political-legal status quo. The angry denunciations in the General Assembly that the court's 1966 judgment was a "white man's" decision, rendered by a "white man's" tribunal, were only partly assuaged by political action in the General Assembly itself, whereby in October 1966 a resolution was adopted, by 114 votes to 2, with 3 abstentions, declaring the Republic of South Africa's original League of Nations-conferred mandate to administer South West Africa to be legally "terminated," and also declaring that the territory now came under the "direct responsibility" of the United Nations.

The political backlash to the court's 1966 decision also brought a Security Council vote in 1970 to request an advisory opinion from the court on the "legal consequences for States of the continued presence of South Africa in Namibia (South West Africa)," and thus a rare second chance for the court to retrieve a prestige and authority already severely compromised politically, if not indeed lost, by the 1966 decision. But the political damage had been done already, and it could not have come at a worse time for the court in terms of an opportunity lost for encouraging the wave of newly decolonized states entering the United Nations in the late 1950s and throughout the 1960s to bring their disputes and conflicts to the court for peaceful settlement. It would prove to be a long and difficult road back for the court, in spite of courageous and avant-garde law-making decisions like that rendered by the court in 1971 on the Security Council request of 1970 for advisory opinion on Namibia (South West Africa).

POLITICAL-LEGAL FACTORS

In some senses, of course, the "new" countries may have exaggerated the inbuilt quality of permanence within the court itself, as to basic conceptions of the judicial decision-making role in great political-legal causes célèbres and also of the degree of respect and deference to be accorded by the judges to the existing corpus of "old" or "classical" international law. More, perhaps, than any other final tribunal, national or international, of our times, the court can be made responsive to fundamental change in societal conditions within the world community (including that marked expansion of the membership of the United Nations that made it more nearly "representative" or universal by the end of the 1960s) through the processes of selection of its judges.

The constitutional legitimacy of the International Court as a law-making institution flows from the election of its members by absolute majority vote in the General Assembly and in the Security Council, sitting separately - as stipulated in Article 10(1) of the court statute. The stipulation for the double majority, General Assembly and Security Council, gives some weighted voting advantage to the five permanent members of the Security Council insofar as, if they were ever to remain united, they would amount to a one-third voting bloc in the council. But, contrary to popular impression, the permanent members have no right of veto in Security Council elections of judges, Article 10(2) providing expressly that the Security Council vote is to be taken "without any distinction between permanent and non-permanent members of the Security Council."

There is thus absolutely no power on the part of the permanent members, acting individually or collectively, legally to block election of the candidate from any state or legal or ideological system, or a fortiori to impose the election of their own national or nationally favored candidates. World Court elections are thus subject, like any other United Nations elections, to the skills of coalition building and the political give- and-take and bargaining inherent in any composite, compromise list of agreed candidates. The fact that four of the five permanent members of the Security Council (the People's Republic of China excepted) have managed to maintain continuing national representation on the International Court since its inauguration in 1946, through political success of their candidates in the periodic elections of the judges, is due to a number of different factors.

The virtually unanimous endorsement of the official Soviet and American candidates, over the years is clearly due to the acceptance by all Member States of the basic political fact of life of post-World War II international organization, namely the Soviet-American balance and the need for an effective presence of both superpowers in all main United Nations institutions and agencies. As to the two remaining permanent members of the Security Council, the United Kingdom and France, their unbroken record in maintaining their official candidates- though with sharply declining majorities in the most recent elections in the case of the United Kingdom. -an no doubt be attributed to the high technical-legal qualifications of their candidates, and perhaps also to the continuing bureaucratic momentum of past General Assembly-Security Council habits of voting quasi-automatically for permanent members, irrespective of whether they were the two superpowers or simply the two other European vestigial survivals of the wartime Big Five.

The triennial elections to the court, with a third of the membership retiring at each election, have seen the emergence of complicated but politically sophisticated customs or conventions as to the division and allocation of the fifteen seats on the court on a "regional"-mixed legal-systemic, linguistic, political-ideological, and geographical-basis, with the only real contests being internal ones within each of the "regions" as to the filling of the particular regional seat involved; or, more rarely, interregional conflicts calling for marginal readjustment in the exact numbers of seats to be awarded to one region rather than another under the "gentlemen's agreement" on voting.

With the belated seating in the United Nations, in 1971, of the People's Republic of China, it seems certain that the customary "Chinese" seat on the International Court will be restored whenever the People's Republic decides to present a candidate, this both because of the People's Republic's quality as a permanent member of the Security Council and also the political fact of life of China's political status today as a world power. But the seating of a Chinese judge will mean, on a fifteen-member tribunal, loss of a seat for one of the existing "regional" groups. Should the Chinese seat be created out of the existing Asian regional group, or out of the Latin American group, or out of the Western European group (which already includes Japan)?

The one thing that seems clear is that the African regional group can hardly be called on to make the sacrifice. Much behind-the-scenes political maneuvering and a good deal of political anguish can be expected when the existing "gentlemen's agreement" on voting has to be rewritten to take account at least of the Chinese fact. It is not impossible, of course that the International Law Commission precedent of simply increasing the number of judges on the court will be resorted to, to resolve the dilemma of choice. Whatever the merits, on purely technical and institutional grounds, for reexamining the composition and internal organization of the court, including its members, it would be a pity if purely expedient considerations were to produce such a short-range political solution, without any prior consideration of its effects upon the court in terms of long-range efficiency and work capacity.

The filling of casual vacancies on the court arising from the death or retirement of an incumbent judge before the end of his regular nine-year term offers the occasion, since usually only one vacancy is involved, for ordinary "regional" considerations to be influenced or overwhelmed by larger East-West or even North-South conflicts intruding into the electoral processes. There has been a custom or convention-it is only that, and not a positive law requirement-of replacing a deceased or retired judge by another of the same nationality, to fill the unexpired judicial term still remaining.

But with almost 150 Member States of the United Nations now competing at the regular triennial election for the five seats open on the fifteen-member court, a contemporary reinterpretation of that custom or convention might suggest filling the vacancy from the same "region" as the judge being replaced, but not necessarily by a judge of the same nationality.

All these considerations came to the fore early in 1982, with the election to fill the vacancy on the court created by the death of Judge El-Erian of Egypt in late 1981. In "regional" terms - which sometimes offer the advantage of not being too precisely and hence too rigidly, defined-the seat was an Arab, Islamic seat, with the extra sub regional refinement of being North African and also involving a country with a French civil law, internal municipal law base. The official nominations for the election saw candidates from Egypt itself, Algeria, Libyan Arab Jamahiriya, Benin Madagascar, and Israel, but most of these were purely honorific nominations, and the actual choice soon narrowed down to one between the Egyptian candidate (nominated by twenty-five countries, including, most prominently, the United States), and the Algerian candidate (nominated by thirty-five countries, predominantly Third World and headed by Brazil, Mexico, Saudi Arabia, and Yugoslavia, but also including France and the Soviet Union.

The behind-the-scenes lobbying was intense, and so the characterization of the contest as a North-South one, with the United States and West-backed candidate losing out to the Third World candidate, is no doubt a fair one, in spite of the obvious crosscurrents presented by the French and other politically farseeing Western states' support for the Algerian candidate, Dr. Bedjaoui. The result of the partial election of March 1982 may have served as an index of the increasing political sophistication within the United Nations ranks as to the affirmative law-making role of the International Court and, in consequence, the relevance and propriety of inquiry into a judicial candidate's legal values and his degree of commitment to the principle of the progressive development of international law.

It also indicated that, in a contest for a particular seat from the one regional bloc on which compromise has not been reached by diplomatic arrangements within the bloc before the public stage of the General Assembly-Security Council vote, all things otherwise being equal, the intellectually and professionally more qualified candidate is likely to prevail. Dr. Bedjaoui of Algeria, who was elected to the court, had already won his spurs internationally - as a distinguished academic jurist and writer and as a professional legal diplomat- in the universities, and as his country's representative to UNESCO and in the United Nations General Assembly's Sixth (Legal) Committee and in the ILC.

THE JUDGES AS LEGAL HONORATIORES

The different "regional" attitudes to the nature and character of the International Court and of the international adjudication in general, and the impact on them of the time factor and the shifting balance of political forces within the United Nations are amply reflected in the distinctive national approaches to selection of official candidates for election to the court and to the support of candidates from other states. Article 2 of the court statute speaks of a body of independent judges, elected regardless of their nationality from among persons of high moral character, who possess the qualifications required in their respective countries for appointment to the highest judicial offices, or are jurisconsults of recognised competence in international law.

If the principle of judicial settlement of disputes be viewed as an ethnocentrist, distinctively Western one, it is, within the Western legal family, even more American than Western European. One remembers the enthusiastic, perhaps somewhat simplistic, American-based "world rule of law" campaign for extension of the jurisdiction of the World Court, launched in the immediate postwar years, notwithstanding the basic political inconsistency that the United States government, by reason of its own self-defining "domestic jurisdiction" exception to its acceptance of the compulsory jurisdiction of the International Court under Article 36(2) and (3) of the court statute, had created a major effective legal gap in the court's jurisdiction and any hopes of establishing it, as law-in-action, on a nearly universal basis. As the pro-Western automatic voting majorities in that smaller United Nations of the late 1940s and early 1950s have disappeared into history, the deemed "politicization" of the main United Nations organs, the Security Council and General Assembly has brought about a revision, albeit in a somewhat belated way, of dominant attitudes to the court and to international adjudication.

The United States and other Western countries seem to be moving more and more toward basic Soviet and Soviet-bloc positions on the court and its potentialities for radical novation of international law under the impulse of Third World-initiated legal processes decided by new and regionally more representative court majorities, in which Third World judges will increasingly predominate. This has meant more and more a Western defensive or "holding operation" conception of the court, paralleling that of the Soviet Union, and a tendency, again paralleling that in the Soviet Union, to nominate professional foreign ministry lawyers or longtime advisers, rather than the "independent judges" or "jurisconsults" perhaps too idealistically envisaged under Article 2 of the court statute.

Many of these same foreign ministry professionals and advisers will, of course, be distinguished jurists in their own right, and in fact some of the intellectually most sparkling members of the court in recent years, from both East and West, fall into this category. But to have the two superpowers and their supporters apply such a frankly realistic political approach to selection of candidates for the court hastens the disappearance of the legal fiction of yesteryear that judicial adjudication is inherently neutral in substantive, philosophical terms, and that international law itself can be reduced to Rudolf von Ihering's "heaven of juridical concepts," remote from social and economic reality.

The de facto operation of the international law-making processes in international diplomatic conferences, in the United Nations General Assembly, and in its specialist Sixth (Legal) Committee, as a form of resolution of competing interests pressed by contending states according to their own special political, social, and economic advantage, warrants in measure the increasing conception of the path to the court as a progression from Sixth (Legal) Committee to the ILC and then on. What Max Weber called the legal "honoratiores" will thus have changed from the academic-legal jurisconsult, more nearly intended by the court statute, to the professional-legal jurist who has refined his foreign ministry experience by some substantial direct United Nations experience.

It is another unconscious historical irony that the Third World pressures for remaking the International Court into a more affirmative law-making posture, to which these changes in judicial selection criteria in the West respond, have drawn a principal intellectual inspiration from the American internal, municipal constitutional law teachings of the 1940s and 1950s on judicial activism and judicial legislation for societal change, within the United States Supreme Court.

LAW AND POLICY

The International Court reflects, in fact, not less than the United States Supreme Court or other major final appellate tribunals of our times, the polar doctrinal positions as to the role of courts in community policy making summed up in the antinomy of judicial self-restraint and judicial activism. The distinction, under other names, is well known to both common law and civil law schools of legal interpretation-the difference, in common law terms, between strict "black-letter law," analytical, positivist approaches to legal construction, on the one hand, and purposive, policy, sociological approaches on the other; the difference, in civil law terms, between grammatical or logical interpretations which try to hew to the words of a charter, code, or statute as written, and teleological interpretations which look rather for a larger social purpose behind the original legislative formulation.

In terms of the International Court and its actual practice, the differences in basic judicial approaches are better represented less as a strict dichotomy than as a philosophical-methodological continuum, with one judicial approach shading off into another and with certain intellectual cross-currents created by special procedural, adjectival law factors present in the court's jurisdiction. The International Court also started off in 1946 with a substantial backlog of analytical positivist, jurisprudence-of-concepts style of case law precedents inherited from its predecessor, the old Permanent Court, which, with a relatively stable and ideologically homogeneous group of states adhering to its jurisdiction in the limited "West European"-dominated world community of that era, could afford to limit itself to a strict and literal interpretation, in which policy elements were consciously subordinated by the judges and indeed hardly sought or welcomed by the parties invoking the court's jurisdiction in the first place.

South West Africa, Second Phase, rendered in 1966 by the 8-7 majority, was, as already noted, a watershed decision for the court, looking both backward to the old and honorable analytical positivist tradition, and also forward to the newer policy imperatives of the progressive development of international law in an approaching era of fundamental political, social, and economic change in the world community.

Though heralding the end of the old, the South West Africa, Second Phase opinion of the court is a masterly exercise in the classical self-styled neutral approach to judicial interpretation, as befits its distinguished authors, the court's president, Sir Percy Spender of Australia, and the British judge Sir Gerald Fitzmaurice, whose hand is obvious in the reasoning and drafting of the opinion. The criticisms of the opinion of the court in South West Africa, Second Phase go not to its intrinsic legal logic, which can hardly be faulted, but to legal logic unsparingly pursued to the bitter end, to the absolute exclusion of policy in law and indeed everything else-an exercise in logic and not in life!, as the British political theorist Harold Laski remarked in another context.

After this politically charged and controversial decision, which brought a great wave of criticism of the court in the General Assembly, the court began its difficult journey back into public political approval and confidence. The way back had been foreshadowed already in the 1966 decision itself, by the dissenting opinions, particularly that of the American Judge Philip Jessup," which, fulfilling the traditional role of a judicial dissent as an appeal to the future in law, ventured unashamedly into natural law in its appeal to the "views and attitudes of the contemporary international community" and the "accumulation of expressions of condemnation of Apartheid...proof of the pertinent contemporary international standard, in order to reject the Republic of South Africa government's case and to strike down governmentally practiced racial discrimination.

Judge Jessup, in correctly sensing winds of change in the world community, functioned in the full spirit of judicial liberal activism, while the court majority, in contrast, practiced an extreme form of judicial self-restraint in the face of a burning social issue on which the world community, through its main parliamentary organs, had made its own moral position quite clear and categorical from the early 1950s onward. But it was the dissent by Judge Jessup, rather than the more orthodox majority opinion of the court of the 1966 decision that served as the inspiration for the International Court's volte-face five years later, in Legal Consequences for States of the Continued Presence of South Africa in Namibia (South West Africa) (1971).

There, by lopsided majorities of 12-2 and 11-4 on the substantive legal issues, the court reached out for the concept of intertemporal law and the time dimension in legal interpretation to conclude that, whatever the character in 1919 of the League of Nations mandate then given to South Africa over the former German colony of South West Africa, progressive, generic interpretation dictated that such a mandate be regarded as evolutionary rather than static, particularly in respect to that "sacred trust of civilization" that mandates connoted. So far from being a closed body of principles that had become fixed once and for all in 1919, when the League of Nations system came into force, the notion of mandate was something rather more dynamic, lending itself to contemporary reformulation in accordance with changing societal conditions and expectations.

Specifically, the court found that fifty years of important historical developments since 1919 leave little doubt that the ultimate objective of the sacred trust was the self-determination and independence of the peoples concerned. In this domain, as elsewhere, the *corpus iuris gentium* has been considerably enriched, and this the Court, if it is faithfully to discharge its functions, may not ignore.

If the court majority in Namibia (South West Africa) in 1971 thus embraces openly for the first time judicial activism and the cause of judicial law making in general, the advisory opinion majority holding is not without its own built-in antithesis - specifically a strong dissenting opinion by the British judge Sir Gerald Fitzmaurice, who quoted with approval comments by the American law professor and one-time judge on the old Permanent Court, Manley Hudson, on the necessity of the court to keep "within the limits which characterise judicial action," especially when exercising the advisory opinion jurisdiction. The court, in Manley Hudson's words as adopted by Judge Fitzmaurice, must always be at pains to act "not as an 'academy of jurists' but as a responsible 'magistrature.'"

CONTRADICTIONS AND CONFLICTS

After Namibia (South West Africa) in 1971, the International Court majority seemed prepared to move boldly and chart out new legal frontiers, without too many inhibitions left over from its earlier "strict and complete legalism" approach. The practical problem, however, was that it had virtually no cases in which to expound and develop its new liberal activism.

The "new" countries, still distrustful of the court after South West Africa, Second Phase of 1966, and slow in taking note of the political changes already brought about by the triennial election processes to the court's membership, were not yet prepared to bring their problems to the court for judicial solution; while the "old" countries, who were politically more sensitive, perhaps, to the intellectual transformation already under way on the court in terms of basic legal philosophy and legal thinking, seemed less and less inclined to venture their legal fortunes on a politically more and more uncertain and changing majority coalition within the court's ranks. The result was a few cases, widely scattered in time and often with flawed procedures-not a very happy base on which to build new experiments in judicial policy making.

Nuclear Tests (Australia v. France; New Zealand v. France), which arose in the early 1970s, might have seemed to present a glorious ready-made opportunity for the court to place itself on the side of the angels and to participate, if not indeed lead, in the progressive development of the new international law for the protection of the natural environment. Newly elected Socialist administrations in Australia and New Zealand, in spite of several decades of continuingly uncritical and enthusiastic cooperation in American and British nuclear test explosions in the South Pacific region on the part of their predecessor right-of-center governments, moved in the International Court to try to halt high-altitude nuclear test explosions in the South Pacific launched by the French government.

The court's approach to decision on the case was complicated procedurally by the French government's denial, in legal terms, of the court's jurisdiction and its consequent refusal to participate in the proceedings before the court or to present oral argument (though it did issue a White Paper corresponding in many respects to a written factum). The court's approach to preliminary jurisdictional objections in the past has resulted from precedents and its own decisions, the matter not being elucidated in the court statute itself. One approach, and that invariably applied by municipal, national tribunals, both common law and civil law, has been to regard the preliminary jurisdictional objection as a prior question that must be answered in favor of jurisdiction before the court can venture on to the merits and substantive law issues - in the court's own jurisprudence, the Mavrommatis precedent.

A looser, more facultative approach has been to permit simultaneous proceedings on the prior jurisdictional issue and on the merits, on the pragmatic argument that sometimes these two questions would be inextricably intertwined and incapable of separation. The intellectual dilemma for the court had seemingly been resolved in its 1972 rules-new Article 67(1) (6) and (7) - which lays down that the court must resolve the question of its jurisdiction before entering upon the merits, and that as to other (non jurisdictional) preliminary objections going to other grounds, the court should either uphold the objection, reject it, or declare that it "does not possess, in the circumstances of the case, an exclusively preliminary character." If this latter decision is taken, the court then enters upon the merits, and the preliminary objection, now ruled to be not "exclusively preliminary," simply becomes one among the various defenses to be invoked by the respondent.

The preliminary jurisdictional question complicates the analysis of the International Court's two judgments in Nuclear Tests-the 1973 order granting interim measures of protection, which was decided by an 8-6 majority (with an official opinion of the court and four other, individual majority opinions, and four individual dissenting opinions); and the 1974 final judgment, which ruled that the issue had become moot (and therefore would not need to be decided on the merits), which was decided by a 9-6 majority (with an official opinion of the court and four other, individual majority opinions, and one joint dissenting opinion signed by four judges, and two other, individual dissenting opinions).

The plethora of individual judicial opinions, (specially concurring opinions on the majority side and dissenting opinions on the other) present in the two judgments of 1973 and 1974, plus a complete change in the composition of the judicial majorities between the two cases, point to profound philosophical disagreements, quite apart from any incidental personality clashes, within the ranks of the court. Though the preliminary jurisdictional issue is a complicating factor in those internal court disputes, since it constitutes procedural cross- currents to the substantive law differences, it does not appear that the final judgment in 1974, which addresses itself to questions essentially of procedural, adjectival law, is limited in its implications to that issue. In a significant judicial role reversal, some of the more liberal activist-inclined members of the court combined to make the final majority in 1974, ruling the issue to have become moot and so passing up the opportunity for ruling on "new" international law substantive issues otherwise dear to them.

The key judicial holding, in the final judgment in 1974, was that the issue had become moot with the unilateral declarations of intention by the French president and by French ministers, indicating the termination of any further above-the-ground nuclear tests by France in the South Pacific. This particular judicial holding was at once innovative in terms of legal doctrine and conservative, in that it applied the doctrine of judicial self- restraint and avoided ruling on substantive policy issues where lesser, procedural issues could provide a solution. The dossier in French Nuclear Tests was not completely satisfactory for purposes of a major policy ruling by the court.

The key complainant, Australia, then seeking the court's aid in developing and applying "new" international law principles of environmental protection to strike down the French government action, did not come into court "with clean hands" in view of its past association and endorsement (albeit through a different government) of similar American and British government action. There was also a not altogether explained incident involving an unauthorized leak by the Australian prime minister of the court's interim ruling of 1973, prior to its official release by the court.

The two judgments in Nuclear Tests, of 1973 and 1974, are better seen, it may be suggested, as examples of the trial-and-error testing inherent in ventures in judicial law making on the part of courts not as yet fully experienced or confident in that domain. The prime lesson from Nuclear Tests, 1973 and 1974, therefore, would be that judicial activism requires, for its effective exercise, a proper procedural, adjectival law base and a dossier uncluttered by matters extraneous to the key policy choice involved.

Both these elements-proper procedural base and uncluttered dossier - were present a year later in the Western Sahara case of 1975. Once again the court's judgment was accompanied by a plethora of individual judicial opinions and this in a case where the verdict was reached by lopsided judicial majorities. However, in Western Sahara the openings of judicial activism were patent and unequivocal, perhaps because the occasion-a conflict between "old" international law categories invoked by a European "colonial" power, and "new" international law principles invoked by Third World "decolonized" countries-presented the opportunity for a clear-cut policy choice, while Nuclear Tests, as a dispute between wholly Western postindustrial "colonial" societies, did not. The issue of the legal title to former Spanish colonies in the Western Sahara (Rio de Oro and Sakiet El Hamra) provided, in fact, the opportunity for a far-reaching reexamination and updating of classical international law rules on the acquisition of territorial title by colonization, in respect to lands previously occupied by non-European indigenous or aboriginal peoples (*terra nullius*).

The issue came to the court by way of a United Nations General Assembly request for an advisory opinion. The colonial power, Spain, in anticipation of United Nations action, had announced a decision to hold its own referendum within the colony; this move was viewed by the neighboring Third World countries and potential successor states- Morocco, Mauritania, and Algeria - as a clever stratagem designed to maintain Spain's political and economic influence over the Western Sahara after its by now inevitable decolonization and independence.

The individual judicial opinions annexed to the court's holding in Western Sahara have an importance that transcends the particular issues of that case. Was the Western Sahara territory, at the time of its colonization by Spain, terra nullius?

The court noted that Spain itself relied for its original claim to title on agreements, "documents," and "deeds of adherence" signed by the chiefs of the local communities with Spain and confirmed by the king of Spain; for these reasons alone, the argument that the Western Sahara was terra nullius at the time of colonization would be refuted.

But three of the specially concurring judicial opinions in particular go beyond the necessities of the case to dispose of the concept of terra nullius itself - those of Vice - President Ammoun, Judge Forster, and ad hoc Judge Boni, all of them distinguished Third World jurists. Vice-President Ammoun in particular rejected as a purely Western, ethnocentrist conception "classical" international law's formal categories as to the legal modes of establishing sovereignty and sovereign title over territory. Thus the legal category of terra nullius had been effectively employed until the beginning of the twentieth century to justify European military conquest and colonization overseas.

Given the time dimension in international law, these were outdated legal categories that corresponded, in historically relativist terms, to an era of Western and European domination in the world community, now past. Six years earlier, in 1969, in his specially concurring opinion in North Sea Continental Shelf, a strictly intracontinental Western European dispute, Judge Ammoun had taken the opportunity to reject in passing the unconscious juridical "racialism" inherent in such well-accepted "classical" international law categories as that cited in Article 38 (1) (c) of the World Court statute-"the general principles of law recognized by civilized nations."

Judge Forster, in his specially concurring opinion in Western Sahara, echoed Judge Ammoun in his strictures upon the spatially and temporally limited "Western" or "classical" concept of terra nullius. He pointed out that "It is Africa of former times which is in question, as to which it cannot arbitrarily be required that its institutions should be a carbon copy of European institutions." Ad hoc Judge Boni went a step further in suggesting that, in determining the character of territorial sovereignty today, the modern principle of self-determination of peoples required obligatory consultation of the inhabitants of the territory concerned.

Western Sahara, 1975, not merely in its lopsided judicial majorities (16-0, 14-2, and 15-1, on the substantive issues) but in the very intellectual range and breadth of the special opinions filed in support of its rulings, provided an admirable vehicle for judicial activism in the progressive development of international law, and for the successful passage from the "old" to the "new" in terms of international law doctrine. One would have to wait until the end of the decade for a case presenting a comparable interrelation of law and politics, and opportunity, in consequence, for a judicial policy ruling. This was United States Diplomatic and Consular Staff in Tehran, but the case was complicated, as Nuclear Tests had been before it, by preliminary procedural questions and the fact that the Iranian government, like France before it in Nuclear Tests, chose not to be represented before the court in answer to the United States' complaint (though the Iranian government did send a letter to the court).

It might, of course, be suggested (and this was confirmed by the actual experience in the court decision making in United States Diplomatic and Consular Staff in Tehran) that absence of representation before the court may not in fact be too much of a practical disability, the judges, following precedents well observed by municipal, national courts, seeming then to be at pains to take up initiatives on behalf of the absent party; and that, in terms of fact-finding and the taking of judicial notice of political events bearing on the political issues, the absent party may turn out to be more advantaged than if he had actually been present and had to carry the burden of proof of such facts and leading evidence in his own behalf.

And so, perhaps, it was in United States Diplomatic and Consular Staff in Tehran. This case, brought by the United States against Iran, arose from the taking over of the United States Embassy in Tehran and the forcible detention of United States diplomatic and consular personnel by Iranian demonstrators in November 1979, immediately after the United States government's decision to admit the ex-Shah of Iran to the United States for medical treatment. The Iranian government chose not to be represented before the court.

In its interim order of December 1979, the court took note of a letter received from the Iranian foreign minister, contending that the issue of the American hostages represented only ... a marginal and secondary aspect of an overall problem, one such that it cannot be studied separately, and which involves, *inter alia*, more than twenty-five years of continual interference by the United States in the internal affairs of Iran. The American government's application to the court, in the Iranian foreign minister's view, could not be divorced from its proper context, namely the whole political dossier of the relations between Iran and the United States over the last twenty-five years...in particular the coup d'état of 1953 stirred up and carried out by the C.I.A., the overthrow of the lawful national government of Dr. Mossadegh, the restoration of the Shah and of his regime which was under the control of American interests, and all the social, economic, cultural, and political consequences of the direct interventions in our internal affairs.

The response of the court to these averments was, first of all, a technical one. It insisted that it was for the Iranian government to bring forward all the requisite proof and clearly establish the facts alleged, to the satisfaction of the court. This, of course, Iran had not done, since it had chosen not to present its case before the court. The court's second line of argument was that, even if the allegations of persistent American government misconduct had been established, they could not be regarded as justification for Iran's conduct and a defense against the United States' claims in the present case.

This conclusion was reached on the basis that the Vienna Convention on Diplomatic Relations of 1961 and the Vienna Convention on Consular Relations of 1963 provided their own built-in remedies against abuses of diplomatic privileges and immunities by way of espionage or interference in the internal affairs of the receiving state- namely, declaring the offending diplomatic staff *persona non grata* and thus compelling their recall. This last-cited remedy was well known and well used, from the Cold War era onward, by the Soviet Union and the United States. It has certainly been practiced often enough by the two bloc leaders, with almost jovial good humor, and usually on a quid pro quo basis. It may have been somewhat unrealistic for the court to suggest it as a meaningful remedy in bilateral relationships other than Big Power ones, or in situations where the same relative parity of political-military strength does not exist.

Perhaps, again, the two Vienna conventions are already somewhat dated and unresponsive to the political facts of life of the post-Cold War era, when the diplomatic missions of the Big Powers are actively used as agencies of quiet diplomacy to influence events within smaller countries. The judges of the World Court were unanimous in holding that the Iranian government must immediately end the detention of American diplomatic and consular personnel allow them to leave Iran, and restore diplomatic premises, property, and archives to the United States. Several of them went beyond the official opinion of the court to base such an obligation on sources outside "classical" Western-based international law. Judge Lachs, in his separate opinion, expressly cited the large number of Afro-Asian states that had ratified the two Vienna conventions; and Judge Tarazi, in his dissenting opinion, referred to Islamic law on the inviolability of diplomatic envoys, to the teachings of Muhammad, and to the practice of Arab states from the seventh century. Judge Lachs felt, however, that the court majority should have applied "sound judicial economy" and not gone into the issue of Iran's obligation to make reparation, apart from the return of the diplomatic personnel, premises, and property.

Judge Tarazi, in his dissent, adverted to the court's affirmative duty of judicial fact finding. He felt that the American government's actions in Iran in 1953, on behalf of the shah, were sufficiently in the public domain to have been made a subject of judicial notice. Judge Tarazi also considered that the American government was perfectly aware that its authorization for the ex-shah to enter the United States in October 1979 "might have untoward consequences"; therefore, any responsibility on the part of the Iranian government had to be envisaged "in the context of the revolution which took place in that country and brought about, as it were, a break with a past condemned as oppressive."

Judge Tarazi was finally very critical-as was Judge Morozov in his dissenting opinion - of various American government actions before and after the court was seized with jurisdiction in the case: the freezing of Iranian economic assets in the United States, and their preparing to satisfy various private American claims, and the abortive American military operation of April 1980. All of these actions were undertaken while the court was embarking on its deliberation prior to judgment, and in Judge Tarazi's view they "constituted an encroachment on the functions of the Court."

The court thus unanimously reaffirmed the inviolability of diplomatic personnel and premises. Though it could hardly do otherwise, since the two conventions concerned were very recent and quite explicit, the character of the opinion of the court and the three individual opinions is such that the principle must be considered an imperative one, ranking almost as *jus cogens*.

Beyond this point, however, the individual opinions-the separate opinion of Judge Lachs and the dissenting opinions of Judge Morozov and Judge Tarazi - properly introduce additional nuances not fully present in the official opinion of the court and important to the progressive development of international law doctrine. This is just what special judicial opinions are supposed to do, and with proper balance in their exercise they are fully compatible with the court's maintaining its collegial quality while it ventures on judicial law making.

SPECIAL CHAMBERS

Criticism of a malaise in particular institutions within the United Nations Organization usually brings a demand for institutional reform or novation, sometimes confused, as in the case of the International Law Commission in 1981, with an increase in the numbers in the institution concerned. The case for the institution of special chambers within the International Court of Justice has, however, as Judge Lachs pointed out, historical roots that long precede the present court and go back to the original Permanent Court of International Justice and to the Treaty of Versailles, particularly Articles 336 and 376, and the provisions of the peace treaties dealing with questions of navigation, transit, and communications, the intention being to establish chambers of five judges to deal with these cases. There was also provision for a chamber of summary procedure composed of three judges.

These provisions, not acted upon in regard to the old Permanent Court, were taken up in the 1946 court statute, Article 26 of which authorized the formation of chambers of three or more judges for dealing with particular categories of cases, labor and also transit and communications being mentioned specifically. The court is also given a general authority under its statute to form chambers to deal with particular cases, "the number of judges to constitute such a chamber [to] be determined by the Court with the approval of the parties" (Article 26 [2]); and with cases to be heard and determined by the chambers "if the parties so request" (Article 26 [3]). It is expressly stipulated that a judgment given by any such chamber "shall be considered as rendered by the Court" (Article 27), and there is also provision for the formation annually of a chamber of five judges which, at the request of the parties, may hear and determine cases by summary procedure (Article 29).

The idea of activating special chambers of the court was taken up and reinforced in the 1972 rules of court, particularly Articles 24 to 27 of those rules, and restated in the current rules of court, adopted in 1978, particularly Articles 15 to 21 of those rules. The case for such special chambers appears to have hinged, then, upon arguments that there were very many small cases that were unworthy of being handled by the full court of fifteen judges or that hardly warranted the lengthy and costly procedure involved in such plenum hearings. The emphasis in the argument here is upon the relative importance or unimportance of a case and its financial burden.

There is no reference to the irritation, voiced sotto voce in a number of capitals after North Sea Continental Shelf, 1969, that a regionally limited Western European case, between Western European parties, was being decided by a court that was numerically dominated by "strangers" to the special Western European family, who then compounded their putative offense by insisting on filling their own individual separate or dissenting opinions. Apart from any latter-day nostalgic desire to turn back the clock to an earlier "European family compact" era of international adjudication between the two world wars, such an objection draws attention to the spatial dimension of international law and its increasing regionalization today in legal - systemic, linguistic, ethnic, cultural and ideological terms. Does it make good sense, then, today to recognize and institutionalize this regionalization of international law, in international adjudication, by conferring on states from the one regional system the ability to regionalize their dispute settlement by opting to create their own special regional chamber within the framework of the International Court?

It might certainly encourage a greater readiness to have recourse to the court if the parties, sharing common regional values, could thus opt in advance to exclude the "wild" judicial votes that they might fear to be present in the larger forum of the full court. But, as against that, it might simply accentuate and exaggerate the current historical tendency to fragment international law into a plurality of different subsystems and deny its claims to universality. What would this do, in any case, to the stipulation in Article 27 of the court statute that the judgment of any such limited, regional chamber "shall be considered as rendered by the Court" and thus of equal legal authority to the full court's jurisprudence? The 1972 rules of court, in many respects, appear designed to increase the role of the parties in the selection of the members of the special panel or chamber: while Article 26 (2) of the court statute speaks merely of the "number" of judges to constitute a chamber as something to be "determined by the Court with the approval of the parties," Article 26 (1) of the 1972 rules of court requires the president of the court, far more broadly, to consult with the parties regarding the "composition of the Chamber," this in addition to the requirement in Article 26 (2) of the 1972 rules of court to determine the "number" of judges with the approval of the parties. Article 17 (2) of the present rules of court, which were adopted in 1978 to replace the 1972 revised rules, is a restatement of the requirement in Article 26 (1) of the 1972 rules, and perhaps just a little stronger verbally in the role it gives to the views of the parties in the final composition of the court.

While Article 26 (1) of the 1972 revised rules requires the president of the court to "consult the agents of the parties regarding the composition of the Chamber, and [to] report to the Court accordingly," Article 17 (2) of the present, 1978 rules stipulates that "When the parties have agreed, the President shall ascertain their views regarding the composition of the Chamber, and shall report to the Court accordingly." Is the intention here, in the interests of increasing the International Court's working jurisdiction, to edge toward court acceptance of the parties' complete freedom-as in the constitution of a special arbitral tribunal - to choose their own panel of judges by mutual agreement and bargaining? If so, it would be a departure from the normal conception of a court as something independent of and above the actual parties, and the necessary and useful classical institutional distinction between court of law and panel of arbitrators, with different legal values and legal processes and even different legal objectives as to dispute settlement, would tend to disappear.

Judge Lachs seems to have envisaged the utilization of the special chamber system of the court as being directed toward certain specific subject matters and thus encouraging some mobilizing of specialist expertise within an increasingly "generalist," non specialist tribunal. The specialization by chamber would be of a functional character, one panel suggested by Judge Lachs to be devoted to the subject of protection of the environment, particularly as to pollution of rivers and lakes on borders between states; the other panel suggested by Judge Lachs to be devoted to the Law of the Sea. One is reminded of the lesson of the Sibylline Books and of the merits of acting in timely fashion, especially as to the adoption of proposals for institutional reform.

If Judge Lachs's suggestion for a specialist Law of the Sea chamber of the International Court had been acted upon even a decade earlier, it might have successfully headed off or controlled what by the end of the 1970s had become the burgeoning pressures not simply to create a plurality of special chambers within the one International Court but to duplicate that court by creating a plurality of tribunals specialized by function, with a specialist Law of the Sea tribunal heading the list. The movement for creation of such functionally specialized international tribunals has gained strength from the Third World's image of the International Court of Justice as a highly conservative, traditional tribunal mired in the legal procedures and values of the past and hence committed inevitably to the legal status quo.

It is no doubt helped also by the tendency, common enough in United Nations circles, to proliferate institutions even where this means overlap or duplication, or to proliferate numbers of personnel within existing institutions, as a somewhat roundabout way of increasing opportunities for professional placement for nations of the 150-odd Member States. Judge Lachs is right to point to the disadvantages of competing jurisdiction and jurisprudence involved in the creation of such additional specialist tribunals, and the challenge to the organic unity of international law.

On the other hand, specialist final tribunals, just as much as special senates or chambers within the one final court, are very much part of continental European civil law experience, even if they tend to be foreign to the Anglo Saxon common law systems, and on the basis of such continental European civil law experience should be capable of being lived with if they do in fact develop. Some of the political as well as legal problems inherent in the special chamber system, particularly as applied under the International Court of Justice's statute and rules of court, are demonstrated in the experience of the constitution of the first such chamber of the International Court, in regard to Delimitation of the Maritime Boundary in the Gulf of Maine Area (Canada/United States of America), as the International Court's order of January 20, 1982, Constitution of Chamber, strikingly indicates.

The two state parties had concluded a special agreement in March 1979, entering into force in November 1981, by which they agreed to submit to a chamber of the court a question as to the course of the maritime boundary dividing the continental shelf and the fisheries zones of the two parties in the Gulf of Maine area. The special agreement provided for the submission of the dispute to a five-member chamber, to be constituted in accord with Article 26 and Article 31 of the court statute. The original understanding of the two parties was that the five-member panel be constituted without any national from either party; there was a certain obvious common sense in this arrangement, as a five-member tribunal with one national judge and one (necessarily) ad hoc national judge would reduce immediately, in effective terms, to a three-member tribunal.

The original understanding had been reached with the then president of the International Court, Sir Humphrey Waldock, but his sudden death before the expiration of his term, and before the court had completed formation of the special chamber, upset the whole process; and matters were further complicated when the United States government insisted that its own national judge sit on the case, which meant, of course, that an ad hoc judge must be appointed for Canada to balance the American judge. Even more complicated was the insistence by the lame-duck plenum of the International Court, one-third of whose membership would automatically be replaced on February 5, 1982 (by the five judges elected or reelected by the General Assembly and

Security Council in the autumn of 1981), on deciding immediately on the composition of the special chamber-apparently with the concurrence of the two parties.

This was done by the court order of January 20, 1982, rendered only two weeks before the expiration of the retiring judges' term and thus also of their eligibility to be included in the special chamber. In fact, one of the judges so selected was Judge Gros, whose membership in the International Court of Justice automatically expired two weeks later. The objection here, if objection there be, is notional only, rather than substantial. The major criticisms of the court order of January 20, 1982, would be addressed first of all to the haste with which it was rushed through in the dying hours of the particular fifteen-member plenum of the court making the decision. In a tribunal whose personnel and philosophy of law are subject to change, and properly so, through the operation of the legal processes of selection of judges at the regular triennial elections, the judges already elected and waiting to take their seats were denied the opportunity of ruling on a matter which by no stretch of the imagination could be represented as requiring an urgent, immediate decision.

The remaining criticisms address the fact that it was the two parties who in fact determined the choice of the five members of the special chamber, with the full court of fifteen apparently merely rubber-stamping their choice in the court order of January 20, 1982. This would seem to go well beyond the letter of the relevant provisions of the court statute, and even, it may be suggested, beyond the spirit of the more facultative provisions of the court's revised rules of court. In the result, the two parties chose a five-member tribunal which, apart from the two national judges from English-speaking North America, was wholly Western European in composition.

We thus have a tribunal which, in its membership and composition, reflects that "classical" Western, Eurocentrist character which has been the Third World's main ground of complaint against the old Permanent Court's jurisprudence, and also that of the new International Court since its foundation in 1946. Add to that the fact that, by reason of the bilateral consensus required to achieve the parties' own special agreement as to the constitution of the chamber, one of them apparently objected to selection of that member of the full court with the greatest acquired expertise in the subject matter of the suit, the Law of the Sea- Judge Oda of Japan. What can and should be the status, qua court jurisprudence, of the eventual decision of the five- member special chamber, with its own special "regional" composition, granted the insistence by the Third World states and other regional groupings in the world community that the Law of the Sea today cannot be reduced to the "classical" international law conception of logical, analytical construction divorced from policy, but must be considered instead in the light of the "new" international law-equity, the general principles of law recognized by nations-and as a constituent element in the New International Economic Order?

It may be, in fact, that the eventual judgment of the special chamber, because of the special political factors in the chamber's composition and organization, will come down to a decision *inter partes* - like that of the arbitral panel it was supposed to avoid - and thus not be ranked as general international law jurisprudence and part of the progressive development of international law. The declaration appended by Judge Oda to the court's order of January 20, 1982, and also the two dissenting opinions of Judge Morozov and Judge El-Khani indicate very clearly the objections, philosophical and practical, going to the character and integrity of the special chamber qua court, attaching to the plenum of the court's apparent conceding of carte blanche to the parties as to the choice of the actual members of the chamber.

Judge, later President, Jiménez de Aréchaga, in his discussion in early 1973 of the court's 1972 revised rules of court, had suggested that the main change effected thereby was to give the parties decisive influence in the composition of ad hoc Chambers.... Recourse to ad hoc Chambers would prove more attractive to potential litigants if the election of their members were to be based on a consensus between the Court and the parties. This may or may not be so, but it would hardly be a justification in itself for making a change, *praeter legem*, going beyond the clear language of the court statute, to which, of course, the rules of court are and must remain subordinate, and which requires the court to act "with the approval of the parties" only as to the "number" of judges. Judge Jiménez de Aréchaga further suggests that from a practical point of view, it is difficult to conceive that in normal circumstances those Members who have been suggested by the parties would not be elected. For that it would be necessary for a majority of the Members of the Court to decide to disregard the expressed wishes of the parties. This would be highly unlikely since it would simply result in compelling the parties to resort to an outside arbitral tribunal or even to abandon their intention to seek a judicial settlement of the dispute.

To all of which it might be asked, should that matter? If the parties wish to have the extra political prestige and legal authority of a court judgment, as provided in Article 27 of the court statute, then they would seem morally obligated to accept, in good faith and with good cheer, the normal principle that they practice in their own internal, municipal, national law of the independence of the judiciary and the legal incapability of the parties to dictate or control the composition of a court qua court. From the court's own viewpoint it would seem at the least undignified - even if the court is indeed short of cases for its roster - to surrender on such a fundamental point of the integrity of courts and the judicial process simply to attract or retain otherwise unwilling parties.

Judge Oda, in his declaration attached to the court order of January 20, 1982, on Gulf of Maine Area, contented himself with the tart comment:

> While I voted in favour of the Order, it should in my view have been made known that the Court, for reasons best known to itself, has approved the composition of the Chamber entirely in accordance with the latest wishes of the parties as ascertained pursuant to Article 26, paragraph 2, of the Statute and Article 17, paragraph 2, of the Rules of Court.

Judge Morozov, in his dissenting opinion, was more caustic. Not merely did he consider that the full court's choice of the special chamber's members should have been postponed for the two weeks necessary to enable the full court as newly reconstituted after the autumn 1981 judicial elections to make the choices involved, but he also castigated the majority order as taking as point of departure the erroneous presumption that, contrary to Article 26, paragraph 2, of the Statute, the Parties...may not merely choose what should be the number of the members of the Chamber, but also formally decide and propose the names of the judges who should be elected by secret ballot, and even present these proposals to the Court in the form of some kind of "ultimatum."

In rejecting the "incorrect presumption of the Parties that they may dictate to the Court who should be elected," Judge Morozov insisted on the "sovereign right of the Court to carry out the election independently of the wishes of the Parties, by secret ballot in accordance with the provisions of the Statute and Rules of Court." Judge El-Khani, in his dissenting opinion, was equally hostile to the court majority's acceptance of the parties' dictate as to the composition and membership of the special chamber:

> I find that the imposition of an unduly close time-limit for the Chamber's formation and of a particular composition renders the Court no longer master of its own acts, deprives it of its freedom of choice and is an obstacle to the proper administration of justice. Furthermore it diminishes the prestige of the Court and is harmful to its dignity as the principal judicial organ of the United Nations. It results in its regionalisation by depriving it of its basic and essential characteristic of universality.... On these grounds I find that this ought not to constitute a precedent, as it would be a dangerous course to follow in the future.

THE FUTURE OF JUDICIAL SETTLEMENT

If the special chamber system within the court, at least as interpreted by the court majority in Gulf of Maine Area in 1982, as involving the court's acceptance of the dictate of the parties as to membership of the chamber, appears very much like a reform manqué and, in any case, one ventured on too late and only after the political pressures for creation of specialist tribunals functionally specialized by subject matter and separate and distinct from the International Court had gathered strength, there still remains reason for optimism as to the future of judicial settlement notwithstanding all the bitter political criticisms of the International Court following on its South West Africa, Second Phase decision of 1966. First, the new political sophistication in the General Assembly-Security Council processes of election of judges to the International Court, and the possibilities thereby of creating - with only some modest patience in view of the staggered triennial system of election of judges - a liberal-activist majority on the court genuinely committed to the progressive development of international law, should do a great deal to remove the earlier marked suspicion and distrust of Third World countries in regard to the court, and their reluctance to see their great political-legal causes célèbres transferred before it.

As early as 1971, one of the politically most dispassionate and intellectually open Western students of the court, Leo Gross, was able to suggest persuasively that even by that time the "new" countries might be considered as having achieved "equitable representation" on the court, and this perhaps at the cost of full "equitable representation" on the part of the "traditional clients of the Court." If it be too much to expect the "new" countries-after the negative example of the United States' own self-defining "domestic jurisdiction" exception to its acceptance of the court's compulsory jurisdiction, -themselves to opt for unreserved acceptance of the court's compulsory jurisdiction, at least in regard to conflicts between themselves and the West, or for that matter the Soviet bloc, there is absolutely no reason why they should not resort to the court in purely "regional" intra-Third World conflicts, as, for example, the Tunisian-Libyan dispute over their respective continental shelves.

The major hope, however, for fruitful extension of the court's work load and its role, in consequence, in international law making in an era of transition, would appear to be in the advisory opinion jurisdiction. The charter provisions as to recourse to such jurisdiction are broadly framed and are facultative in outlook. In terms of Charter Article 96, not merely the General Assembly and the Security Council may each request an advisory opinion from the court, but also other United Nations organs and specialized agencies at any time so authorized by the General Assembly may make a similar request, and the list of such additional institutions and agencies is already extensive and not closed to future names. Some of the International Court's most impressive and intellectually imaginative and courageous work has, in fact, been achieved in the form of advisory opinions: Judge Lachs cites as examples Reparations for Injuries Suffered in the Service of the United Nations of 1949; and Namibia (South West Africa) of 1971, which, following on earlier General Assembly action in the immediate aftermath of the judgment in South West Africa (Second Phase).

West Africa (Second Phase) of 1966, and designed to "correct" that judgment by declaring the Republic of South Africa's old League of Nations mandate over South West Africa to be terminated forthwith, set in motion a train of political events toward national self-determination and independence for Namibia. We should certainly add to that list Western Sahara, 1975, with its openings to the "new" international law as to sovereignty and title to territory. The surprise, indeed, is that the General Assembly has not been tempted to approach the court more often and more systematically, as a supplement to its own action, as in Namibia, 1971; or as an alternative thereto when its own internal political processes become clogged or bogged down in proceduralisms, or when its coordinate parliamentary organ, the Security Council, finds its actions legally frustrated by a permanent member's veto. To fill the gaps in the United Nations effective peace-keeping powers in the case of such Big Power veto arbitrarily applied in the Security Council, the legal remedies are not only General Assembly action on the precedent of the Uniting for Peace Resolution of 1950, but also recourse to the court for advisory opinion, or a prudent and staged combination of both.

Suggestion that there exists a malaise within the court that can be cured only by increase in its membership or by more special chambers should be looked at coolly. There is no firm evidence as yet that an increase in members would increase the court's efficiency, and it hardly seems necessary as yet to correct its "representativeness," for which other, political-electoral remedies are available under the Charter. As for the special chamber system, the evidence suggests that the reform of 1972 was not fully thought through, and that it would be sensible to reinforce or restore the court's own sovereignty and absolute control over choice of members of such panels; within this premise, there is scope for adoption of Judge Lachs's suggestion of functionally specialized chambers having jurisdiction over such matters as environmental protection and the Law of the Sea.

The main challenge to the International Court today, however, would appear to be to use, and to use to the full, the very ample facilities and processes already existing under the Charter, the court statute, and the revised rules of court. The court itself could help, even without any change in its existing rules of court, by moving to "demystify" its own internal processes, particularly those concerning the preparation of the written brief or memorial, and the character and conduct of oral argument. A notion exists that somehow or other the preparation and presentation of a case before the court is an esoteric art, with its own elaborate folkways enjoined by the judges, ending up suspiciously like the forms of appellate advocacy (particularly oral advocacy) practiced and applied in one or two Western countries only.

So far from these being ideal types or models for all the rest of the world community, comparative legal science today teaches us that there are very many different roads to Rome in terms of legal argumentation and advocacy addressed to a court, and that no one system, common law or civil law, Western or non-Western, has any monopoly on truth in this regard. The court, taking note of the potentially intimidatory (and no doubt designedly intimidatory) effect upon litigant states from the poorer areas of the Third World created by the batteries of expensive, and often quite unnecessary, counsel maintained by the wealthier states who regularly appear before the court, has already done something to allow itself to limit and control any such excesses.

Beyond that, however, the court could recognize that form should sensibly yield to substance, even in the realm of procedure. The court could both clamp down on unnecessarily prolonged or gratuitously mannered oral argumentation and also liberate the parties from any special obligation of deference to past stereotypes of written pleadings. Such a liberating intellectual-legal approach on the part of the judges might allow a break-out from the small "club" of predominantly Western lawyers who seem to monpolize the court's practice today, and also encourage more and more non-Western states to approach the court with their own national teams of jurists.

Bibliography

Alfred M. de Zayas, *The Follow-Up Procedure of the UN Human Rights Committee*, 1991 *Int'l. Commission Jurists Rev.* 28 (1991).

Amnesty International USA, *The Universal Declaration of Human Rights, 1948-1988: Human Rights,* The United Nations, and Amnesty International, New York: Amnesty International USA, 1988.

Ann Marie Clark, *Strong Principles, Strengthening Practices: Amnesty International and Three Cases of Change in International Human Rights Standards*, 1995 (unpublished Ph.D. thesis, University of Minnesota).

Asbjorn Eide, *Pocket Guide to the Development of Human Rights Institutions and Mechanisms*, Strasbourg: Council of Europe, 1989.

Conference on Security and Cooperation in Europe: An Overview of the CSCE Process, Recent Meetings and Institutional Development, Washington, D.C.: Commission on Security and Cooperation in Europe, 1992.

Diana Vincent-Daviss, *Human Rights Law: A Research Guide to the Literature—Part I: International Law and the United Nations*, 14 N.Y.U.J. *Int'l L. & Pol.* 209-319 (1981).

Diana Vincent-Daviss, *Human Rights Law: A Research Guide to the Literature—Part II: International Protection of Refugees and Humanitarian Law,* 14 N.Y.U.J. *Int'l L. & Pol.* 487-573 (1982).

Dominic McGoldrick, *The Human Rights Committee*, Oxford: Clarendon; New York: Oxford University Press, 1991.

Economic, Social, and Cultural Rights: A Textbook, Dordrecht; Boston: Martinus Nijhoff Pub., 1995.

Glenn A. Mower, *International Cooperation for Social Justice: Global and Regional Protection of Economic/Social Rights*, Westport, Conn: Greenwood Pr., 1985.

Gregory J. Walters, Human Rights in Theory and Practice: A Selected and Annotated Bibliography, Metuchen, NJ: The Scarecrow Press, 1995.

Ian Martin, *The New World Order: Opportunity or Threat for Human Rights*, Cambridge, MA: Harvard Law School Human Rights Program, 1993.

Jack Tobin and Jennifer Green, *Guide to Human Rights Research*, Cambridge, MA: Human Rights Program, Harvard Law School, 1994.

Louis B. Sohn, *The Human Rights Movement: From Roosevelt's Four Freedoms to the interdependence of Peace, Development and Human Rights*, Cambridge, MA: Harvard Law School Human Rights Program, 1995.

Matthew C.R. Craven, *The International Covenant on Economic, Social, and Cultural Rights: A Perspective on its Development*, Oxford: Clarendon Press; NY: Oxford University Press, 1995.

Nadine Strossen, *United States Ratification of the International Bill of Rights: A Fitting Celebration of the Bicentennial of the U.S. Bill of Rights*, 24 U. *Tol. L. Rev.* 203 (1992).

Philip Alston, *Making and Breaking Human Rights: the UN's Specialized Agencies and Implementation of the International Covenant on Economic, Social and Cultural Rights*, London: Anti-Slavery Society; La Crosse, Wis: National Association of Interdisciplinary Ethnic Studies, (1979).

Rosalyn Higgins, *Admissibility Under the Optional Protocol to the International Covenant on Civil and Political Rights*, 1991 *Can. Hum. Rts. Y.B.* 57 (1991).

Scott Davidson, *The Inter-American Court of Human Rights*, Aldershot, England; Brookfield, VT: Dartmouth Pub. Co. Ltd., 1992.

Scott Leckie, *Towards an International Convention on Housing Rights: Options at Habitat II,* Washington, DC: American Society of International Law, 1994.

Scott Leckie, *When Push Comes to Shove: Forced Evictions and Human Rights*, Mexico; Utrecht, Netherlands: Habitat International Coalition, 1995.

Thomas Buergenthal & Harold G. Maier, *Public International Law in a Nutshell*, St. Paul, MN: West Publishing Co., 1990.

Thomas Buergenthal, *International Human Rights in a Nutshell*, St. Paul, MN: West Publishing Co., 1995.

Thomas D. Young, *International Human Rights: A Selected Bibliography*, Los Angeles, CA: Center for the Study of Armament & Disarmament, California State University Los Angeles, 1978.

Torkel Opsahl, *The Coexistence Between Geneva and Strasbourg Inter-Relationship of the International Covenant on Civil and Political Rights and the European Convention on Human Rights and Their Respective Organs of Implementation,* 1991 *Can. Hum. Rts. Y.B.* 151 (1991).

Ved P. Nanda, *The United States Reservation to the Ban on the Death Penalty for Juvenile Offenders: An Appraisal Under the International Covenant on Civil and Political Rights* (Symposium: The Ratification of the International Covenant on Civil and Political Rights), 42 DePaul L. Rev. 1311 (1993).

Walter S. Tarnolpolsky, *The Canadian Experience with the International Covenant on Civil and Political Rights Seen from the Perspective of a Former Member of the Human Rights Committee,* 20 *Akron L. Rev.* 611 (1987).

Index

Index